EARTH AND WATER

Earth and Water

ENCOUNTERS

IN

VIET NAM

Edith Shillue

Foreword by Kevin Bowen

University of Massachusetts Press

AMHERST

This book is published with the support and cooperation
of the University of Massachusetts, Boston.

Copyright © 1997 by
Edith Shillue
Printed in the United States of America
LC 97-17136
ISBN 1-55849-128-7 (cloth); 129-5 (pbk.)
Designed by Jack Harrison
Set in Electra by Keystone Typesetting, Inc.
Printed and bound by Thomson-Shore, Inc.
Library of Congress Cataloging-in-Publication Data
Shillue, Edith, 1963–
Earth and water: encounters in Viet Nam / Edith Shillue ;
foreword by Kevin Bowen.
p.   cm.
ISBN 1-55849-128-7 (alk. paper).
— ISBN 1-55849-129-5 (pbk. : alk. paper)
1. Vietnam—Description and travel.
2. Shillue, Edith, 1963–
I. Title.
DS556.39.S55   1997
959.704'4—dc21   97-17136
CIP

British Library Cataloguing in Publication data are available.

For Brian P. Shillue

Each time I took a trip overseas—and I have taken my share—my father scolded me before departure and told me not to go. When I returned home from Viet Nam I came across the bundles of letters I'd written him over the years, and discovered the envelopes were worn thin from handling. Even more surprising, when I walked around town I found that my stories had spread through Father's boasting. So this book is for him. He died before I could finish it.

Contents

Foreword

ANOTHER VIET NAM

Like most who served in Viet Nam, I have images of that country indelibly etched in mind. Some days the images are there so close to the surface, even the slightest gesture, the slightest prodding, will bring them back. Often the first images are the strongest: a plane landing in the night; first steps out onto tarmac; a shimmering, hot summer night; mountains in the distance, a stream of red fire falling into them; a school bus twisting through sandbags to a replacement station; my first sight of the Vietnamese, women bent over scrubbing pans behind a mess tent. From there, images weave back and forth: images of sandbags and barbed wire, planes and helicopters, roads crowded with trucks and convoys, tanks and quad fours. There are images of ordnance, of riding in a chopper above deep blue paddy fields at the foot of mist-shrouded mountains, of landing in and out of small fire bases along the DMZ, and later, of the Cambodian border. There are images of friends— some dead now, some still living—who remain twenty years old in my mind. There are images that like old photographs litter my bed at night and some-times even my waking hours.

These images will never go away. They are images complicated by later return trips to Viet Nam, visits to hospitals for the disabled, visits to or-phanages and to the poorest part of the countryside where ordnance still explodes. They are images complicated by the sight of a twenty-two-year-old farmer just blinded and maimed by an old M79 round he struck in his field; complicated by the sight of a mountain that seems so much smaller after twenty years; complicated by nights waking to strange movements in my room, by late night conversations with Vietnamese veterans who tell of brothers disappeared in the war, by memories of a woman singing in a garden in Song Be and of Cheo performers moving in intricate motions in the cold white mist of Thai Binh; complicated by the presence of a statue of the Buddha that appears in the yard of a house in Dorchester, Massachusetts, now a temple that I pass on my way to work.

It is difficult to rid oneself of these images, and I would not want to be rid of these essential parts of myself. They are my reminders of the vicissitudes of war and peace; they are my images of the troubled history of America and Viet Nam. They are my images of a country and a people caught between extremes. But do they adequately represent America or Viet Nam in a different time and context? Where would one look to find appropriate images of America and Viet Nam today? How would one go about finding them? It is almost twenty-five years now since the Paris Peace Accords were signed, and an entire generation who has no memory or consciousness of that war which once divided us has come of age in both countries. What do young Vietnamese now think of America? What do young Americans now think of Viet Nam?

Edie Shillue's first memory of Viet Nam—an oblique encounter—dates from when she was thirteen: the memory of an awkward moment one Memorial Day in the classroom, the students lowering their heads and shuffling their feet as the name of a classmate's brother killed in the war is read off. Who was this young boy, and how did what happened to him set his sister off from her friends? Edie Shillue finds no answers to these questions in her world; just as there are no answers to the question What is Viet Nam? Fifteen-odd years later, Edie Shillue searches through the shelves of a university library and finds title after title about the war, but few titles, a handful only, written about the history or culture of the country of Viet Nam. "Discard" is stamped on one volume of Vietnamese poetry her friend finds for her at a local library yard sale. Silence, amnesia, an awkward shuffling of the feet are all that seem to await inquiry.

In *Earth and Water*, Shillue details her own encounters with a world where these questions remain unanswered; with a world where young Americans and young Vietnamese meet each other, not quite for the first time, like distant cousins at a family gathering. The view she offers is sometimes disconcerting, sometimes frustrating: so much we don't know about them, so much they don't know about us. *Earth and Water* is the story of this second-generation encounter, of attempts to live without the burden of the past, prejudice, presuppositions, false expectations, or traces of war. Not easy things to do. One of the great virtues of this book is the way Edie Shillue is willing always to cast a cool eye upon herself, to gauge and assess her own reactions and measure the motives of her Vietnamese acquaintances. She is always honest, and we learn as she learns. Though she refuses at first to study the language, she can't help being taught by the people she meets; and, in page after page she is insistently at work teaching us: teaching us that beautiful language, the lush smell of the market after rain, the feel of red dirt at our feet, the legends and folktales of Viet Nam.

In *Earth and Water*, we see Americans and Vietnamese looking across at each other again, not across the distance of rice paddies, jungles, and sandbags, but across the distance of the classroom, that very place where so many of us should have been sitting when instead we were fighting the war. Yes, Viet Nam is beautiful, just as we always knew it was. And so are its children. But it is no idyll. In the last days of the twentieth century, here, as in so many places, life for everyone, for Vietnamese and Americans alike, has often become diminished to a simple equation of ambition. Everyone getting on and up. And is that right or wrong? And what do we as Americans have to offer? And what have we still to learn from the Vietnamese?

Earth and Water poses these questions, poses them beautifully and lyrically. For this we must thank Edie Shillue, thank her for this book where, in page after page, the love for language, for teaching and learning, for a people and a country, come burning through.

Kevin Bowen
William Joiner Center
February 1997

Preface

I think the single most interesting aspect of any culture is its language. In my attempt to convey the beauty of the Vietnamese language, I have recorded many interactions verbatim, in an italicized mix of English and Vietnamese. Names and dialogue are written with Vietnamese diacritics. To guide the reader, I have given simple sound descriptions and pronunciation comparisons. Also, I have quoted Vietnamese poetry based on a mix of written text and oral tradition. In learning about this literature, I have relied on the guidance and patience of many Vietnamese friends and informants. However, any and all mistakes in either spelling or definition are entirely my own.

It should be noted by the reader that the city known as Saigon was renamed "Ho Chi Minh City" after 1975. Because the Vietnamese use the names interchangeably I have also taken this liberty. By doing so I make no political comment.

Acknowledgments

With great appreciation I would like to acknowledge the following: Neal Bruss and Kevin Bowen of the University of Massachusetts, Boston, helped get the work off the ground while it was still a very rough draft. I appreciate their faith and encouragement. I am indebted to Paul Wright of the University of Massachusetts Press for agreeing to look at the manuscript early on and continuing his support through its development.

Patrick Hanan and Ed Baker of the Harvard-Yenching Institute encouraged me to go to Viet Nam in 1993 and introduced me to David Vikner and Pat Magdamo of the United Board for Christian Higher Education in Asia. The board was responsible for funding my trip and placing me as a lecturer at Ho Chi Minh City (HCMC) University. In Viet Nam, the English faculty and students of HCMC University were consistently inspiring and encouraging to me in my teaching and learning. Ms. Nguyen Thi Kim Thu deserves special attention for her gracious guidance on cultural matters, excellent translation skills, and true friendship.

Charlie Miller, director of the Catdang Basket Project, helped arrange my time in northern Viet Nam and I'm grateful to both him and the wonderful people of Catdang for their generosity.

In the United States many others encouraged me, even when I felt I was not up to the task of completing the book. For sheer enthusiasm I am indebted to Trish Ward, who cheered me on from Viet Nam, India, France, and Australia; Susan Karaczkowski, who spoke with certainty about my skills; and Elizabeth Welch who listened closely and often prompted stories with the casual phrase "Tell me about the time. . . ." Vivian Zamel of the

University of Massachusetts, Boston, was equally encouraging and interested. Many others read excerpts at various stages of development, and I appreciate their time and effort, including: Larry Heineman, Esther Iwanaga, Barbara Tran, Dawn Tyson, Margaret Bodner, Joan Schoellner, and, last but not least, my mother, Edith Shillue.

All folk tale excerpts are from *Vietnamese Legends*, adapted from the Vietnamese by George F. Schultz (Rutland, Vt.: Charles E. Tuttle, 1968). All Vietnamese poetry is excerpted from *A Thousand Years of Vietnamese Poetry*, trans. Nguyen Ngoc Binh, with Burton Raffel and W. S. Merwin (New York: Alfred A. Knopf, 1975); excerpts from *The Tale of Kiêu* by Nguyen Du, are translated by Huynh Sanh Thong (New York: Vintage Books, 1973).

EARTH AND WATER

Chapter One

Of the thousands of worlds, numerous as grains of sand,
  Which is not home?
      from, "Home" by Thu'ơng Chiêu (Ly Dynasty)

I have no early memory of Vietnam. But I have an image, preserved like an old photograph, that comes into my head each time the country is mentioned. In a classroom in a small American suburb a frail, dark-haired girl is standing beside her desk. It is Memorial Day and we all stand as our junior high school principal reads the names of the community members who served and died in the U.S. military. This is a group of strangers to most of us, but we wait, with an anticipation none will admit to, for the one name we will recognize. Occasionally we look at the floor, and the dark-haired girl stands, like the rest of us, staring at nothing while the names echo in the empty hallways. As nervous teenage girls do, she adjusts her glasses, moves her foot in a strange twisting motion. She runs her hand along her desk.

It's almost June in a New England beach town; we're all anxious to put the cold behind us and stand in the heat of the sun. But grief holds our attention—inexplicable, sudden. *Sssshhhh*. As if he too were holding his breath in anticipation, the principal pauses before he says, "Lance Corporal John F. Lazarovich Jr." No one looks at the girl who has lost a brother in Vietnam. Later we will gossip as they do in small towns, say someone heard something from someone: "I heard she burst out crying." "Did she?" "I heard he was MIA." "What's MIA?" We will look at the girl and listen to the gossip with sympathy and curiosity, trying to prompt a response to this exposure of family loss. But she will register little. The curiosity passes and it seems to me that this death of a stranger in an unimaginable place is not so important. It's only gossip.

If you ask me about the '6os and '7os I will tell you stories like these:

When I was thirteen my brother was a blur on the edge of my consciousness. In a family of ten he was the one away at college doing crazy things with loads of lighthearted and handsome friends. When Brian came home for weekends and holidays, we'd joke and laugh.

"Edie, you're my favorite sister," he'd say, coyly.

"I just heard you say that to Beth, what do you want?" I answered.

The occasional girlfriend came to the house and sat nervously in the kitchen, surrounded by my sisters and me. When I was fourteen Brian took a year off from college and worked at a construction site in Boston. I packed a lunch for him each night, making a sandwich filled with meat and vegetables, cheese, salt, pepper, and mayonnaise. Then early the next morning, before sunrise, I heard him carry it to his car and drive away.

Then, at fourteen, I did not know the landscape of Vietnam—a landscape that made such a significant mark in the social consciousness of the United States.

Fifteen years later I know Vietnam only as the homeland of so many of my students, and I know it as I knew China before I traveled there: *as an entirely different planet.* From the United States the Orient looks like an insane combination of extreme delicacy and intensive labor: roads built completely by hand; palaces and monasteries laid, painted, lacquered, assembled by hand; an ancient stone tribute to the Buddha that is the size of a building; ceramics so fine that they are transparent; needlework and dyeing so complex that workers must be blinded by concentration; jade and jewels dug from the ground by peasants. I'm romanticizing in the way of the colonialists—Asia is silk, warm weather, fine food, and thousands of people who will work very hard for you.

Shaped like an 'S' on the map, Viet Nam is on the south side of China, and east of Kampuchea.

So begins my first experience of Viet Nam. Sentences like this have become a standard opening for Vietnamese students in the English composition courses I teach in community colleges in Boston. The compositions begin with perfectly structured introductions; then, as if tripping on stones, the writers tumble into run-on sentences that repeat over and over again, "In my country . . . in my country . . ." I ask for stories from home and I hear about *Tet* (the New Year holiday), family weddings, and village life. For a time these students are my only avenue into this culture, and their voices are compelling.

I've read all the newspaper stories—the one about the successful Vietnamese businessman, formerly a penniless boat person, and the story about the family that worked and scrimped to bring over the children or grandparents they left behind. And I've heard about the impenetrable nature of refugee society, loneliness and loss behind incomprehensible language and customs, isolated and isolating communities.

"These people don't do things like us!"

"What are they doing here? Why don't they learn English?"

I often hear about the academic excellence of American-born Vietnamese children, the growing economic prosperity of the Vietnamese immigrants, and the strength of the Vietnamese family unit. People point to a hundred untouchable things to describe the discipline of "the model minority." In newspaper articles and student essays, children and grandchildren reach forward, using words like "strength" and "prosperity"; parents and grandparents reach back, using words like "custom" and "family." I write in my diary: "Underneath history, struggle, opportunity, and loss most relocated Vietnamese live with something missing, something that is gone or something that eludes them." My students are filled as much with pride as with longing and grief. They come from the "S," the "two rice baskets at the end of a pole."

I'm not a historian. I'm a teacher and a writer. It is the summer before I go to Viet Nam and I insist on not studying history books. I am adamant about not going in with preconceived notions. *Viet Nam is . . . The Vietnamese are . . .*

Neither am I like my older friends, who stare, mouths agape, when I tell them I am going to Viet Nam; this place is no wound inside my memory. I'm not like the generation after me either, with movie images of Thailand doubling as Viet Nam, and journalist historians telling me about lost causes and cabals.

It's June 1993, I'm thirty-one years old and I know all the joys and burdens of having an older brother. Every summer I laugh with Brian and his friends at parties created by a batch of clams and a case of beer. I also have terrible arguments with him that alternate between screaming matches and tense silence. When Brian and his wife Sue need me to, I babysit their son; and when I need to get to the airport I throw my luggage into the back of his truck and we go. I think of all the years that have passed since 1975 and of how wherever I go, I gather stories and share them with Brian when I return. I'm leaving for Viet Nam and the one thing I know for sure about her modern history is the size of a small town girl's loss.

And I know this: I have met hundreds of people with the family name

Nguyễn, or Ngo, or Quoc. When I meet them I cannot say their names. I cannot pronounce them correctly; I stumble and stutter.

"It's OK," they say. "Never mind, it's not important." They reach out to soothe my embarrassment and comfort me in my clumsiness. They hold compositions with stories of a holiday called *Tet* and descriptions of large houses and warm places. They want to help me imagine something called dragonfruit, or tell me what a fresh pineapple tastes like; they want me to see a wedding parade. Their hands are full . . . with a gesture they say: *My name is not important. Look at me.*

*   *   *

In August, foggy-headed and tired I walked slowly through the Arrivals door of Than San Nhut Airport and looked around. Out on the sidewalk, behind an iron railing, hundreds of Vietnamese pressed anxiously forward, their heads bobbing softly to see who walked next through customs. To my left I heard a suitcase drop and then two women began the hysterical screaming and crying that goes with reunions too long in the making; I stood absent-mindedly and watched. A young boy reached to pick up the visitor's suitcase. I looked to my right and saw a fellow passenger I recognized; he blushed at the drama. I smiled.

"Long time comin', right?" I said.

"Yeah," he said, a little wistfully.

Hoàng, my new friend, was an overseas Vietnamese (*Viet Kieu*). I met him on the flight from Hong Kong. He was round-faced and handsome, with short black hair and glasses. He looked like the young entrepreneur he was, wearing a royal blue polo shirt and khakis rather than a suit. Our conversation began as countless others would:

"Is this your first time in Viet Nam?"

I told him that I'm a teacher, and I would be living in Saigon for a year. He looked startled, then said, "I hope you can stand the heat."

After I swung through the large doors onto the sidewalk I found him waiting for me with a worried look on his face. The press of Vietnamese seemed daunting. Paper signs floated above heads like flags, names were shouted in a mixture of shock, surprise, and relief. Among the loud voices I heard taxi drivers yelling out for fares.

"Would you like me to get you a taxi?" Hoàng asked.

"No, thanks. I'll be OK," I replied.

"I can get you a taxi. It would be safer," he repeated.

"No, no, I'll be OK," I reassured him.

He shifted around nervously. "Keep an eye on your bag," he warned, pointing to my small backpack. His attention struck me as silly, until I realized that he was returning to a place from which he had probably escaped.

"Escuse me," a young man said.

I turned, ready to refuse a taxi driver's plea. A young man in dark khakis and a pink oxford shirt smiled at me.

"Are you Miss Sillue?"

"Shillue," I corrected with a smile.

"Miss E-E-Edith," he stuttered.

"Yes, that's me."

"I am Nguyễn Ngọc Thảo."

I leaned forward and turned my ear toward him to gesture that I didn't catch his name.

"You can call me Thảo. I am from the university to w-w-welcome you."

Hoàng was reassured. He wrote down his telephone number on a slip of paper and handed it to me.

"Maybe we can get a beer or something this week."

A young woman stood awkwardly behind Thảo with a bouquet of orchids. She stepped forward to catch my eye, laughed nervously, then smiled. Her eyes were brown, with long lashes. Her long hair was pulled back in a ponytail and, as her narrow face broke into a smile, I was struck by how pretty she was.

"I am Mỹ Ngọc," she said, in what sounded like a whisper.

"Mmh?" I turned my head to listen again.

"Ngọc."

I looked at her again, with my face betraying my confusion.

"Never mind," she said politely.

As we drove to the university guesthouse I spent much of the time leaning forward as Ngọc uttered sentence after sentence in her hushed, polite tone. The cab had pulled slowly out of the airport, but was moving aggressively through the motorcycle-filled streets. I nodded occasionally as Ngọc spoke, and watched the city with interest.

"Miss Edie," Thảo said as he was carrying my bags upstairs at the guesthouse, "I would like to show you my friends' house. They have a room they would like to rent you."

"OK."

"How about tomorrow morning?" he asked.

"Fine," I said, lifting the suitcase onto my bed.

"OK, fine," he repeated, as he walked out the door. "See you, then." I smiled and waved goodbye. Outside the guesthouse the motorbike traffic increased, and I could feel my blood quicken.

*   *   *

"I think the herbs are not q-quite g-g-good for you, Miss Edie," Thảo said at breakfast. He pointed to the fresh greens that lay on the table next to our bowls. His stutter was marked now, and I knew it was not nervousness. He blinked.

"Oh," I said, "OK, Thank you."

We were sitting in a noodle shop on Vo Thi Sau Street. In the front a large wood counter dominated the doorway, so that customers had to turn sideways to enter. Next to the counter was a large noodle pot that let out a cloud of steam every time the lid was lifted. A thick-armed woman with a jade bracelet banged a cleaver against the counter and then pulled the leg off a chicken. She began to cut and pick the meat off the bone.

We were sitting in folding chairs at a rather unsteady table. Thảo took a piece of paper and folded it into a small square, then bent over quickly and steadied one of the legs by inserting the paper under it. Outside it began raining heavily.

"*Phở* is the tr-tra-traditional soup of Viet Nam," he told me, pointing to our bowls.

"Yes, I've had it in the U.S.," I said, picking up my chopsticks with one hand and a spoon with the other.

"It's quite d-d-delicious," he added.

"Yes," I agreed.

With her left hand, the woman at the counter picked up a handful of chopped spring onion and sprinkled it over the noodles in two bowls on the counter. With her right hand she poured a ladleful of broth.

"My friends work at the biochemical lab of Ho Chi Minh City," Thảo said, referring to my future landlord and his wife.

"Mmh, hmh," I mumbled, chewing noodles.

"They have a thirteen-year-old son."

"Mmh," I nodded. Thảo used his chopsticks to wrap a piece of meat around some noodles and then put them in his mouth. We ate in silence for a few minutes.

"I have known Thảo since I was a child. He is like my second father," he said.

"Who is he?" I asked. "I mean, what is his name?"

"Mr. Thảo," he repeated. "His name is Thảo—like me—his wife's name is Bình."

I shoveled another tangle of noodles into my mouth. "Mmmh," I said, trying to look knowing. I still couldn't make out the names, but I trusted Thảo already, in his Oxford shirt and combed hair. I slurped some broth. "It's near here?" I asked.

"Yes!" he answered, like a salesman closing in, "it's very convenient to the university," he said, then blinked again. "They are well educated," he continued, "and speak English very well." I could tell these facts meant a great deal to Thảo, so I smiled my reassurance.

I fiddled with the long onion floating in my broth. Thảo poured more tea into my cup.

"Thank you," I said, "it all sounds very nice."

"Iss very near here," he indicated, pointing over my shoulder into the street. I fell quiet, considering both the opportunity and the best bowl of soup I had ever eaten.

The woman's cleaver scraped against the counter as she pushed aside a pile of onion. Thảo lifted a mint sprig from the broth at the bottom of his bowl. I spooned up peppery remains of my soup. He put his spoon down; I laid my chopsticks across my bowl. He raised his eyebrows in question.

"All set?" he asked.

"Yeah," I answered.

I said goodbye loudly to the woman behind the counter, "Thank you."

"Thank you," she replied, smiling. She fingered a pile of meat on the counter, then shoveled it into a large bowl.

The house, only a block from the shop, was at the dead end of an alley. The entry area for the last three houses was gated, and the heavy door dragged across the pavement as we opened it. Thảo called in through the housegate, and a dog started barking.

"Nục (nook)," he said through the metal latticework.

A man in a pair of beige pajamas walked out. He and Thảo talked as he unlocked the door; then he smiled at me and said, "Please come in."

Thảo introduced us as we sat down on the Chinese-style bench: "Miss Edie, this is Mr. Thảo."

"Hello," I said as we shook hands, then stuttered, "Mr . . . umh."

"Hello," he responded, with an understanding smile. "You may call me Thảo." His skin was darkened a bit, as though he had been working on a farm. I smiled again and wondered how I was going to manage pronouncing Vietnamese names for an entire year.

"I'll get Bình," he said, after I sat down.

I felt a cool breeze blow in softly across the tile floor. The room was high-ceilinged, long and spacious. Overhead a fan was turning softly. The dog circled once around the coffee table in front of us, then ran to the back room, following Mr. Thảo. In the back of the room, underneath a staircase, a young boy was playing on a computer ("Thanh" young Thảo explained with a gesture. He didn't want to disturb him. "He is very clever."). A television set was nestled in the corner, and a fishtank bubbled softly by the door.

Thảo and "Mr. Thảo" took me upstairs where I wandered through two large, square whitewashed rooms. Each had its own bath, and one—mine if I wanted it, they said—had a large bed. Immediately taken by the breeziness and size of the house, I decided to move in.

When we returned downstairs, the woman looked at me expectantly. Clearly there would be no small talk; I liked that. We were negotiating right away.

"I can pay five dollars a day."

Mr. Thảo smiled softly and shifted in his seat.

"Ahem," Bình said, "that would be fine. Or seven dollars, if you like. It's up to you."

The comment was a fabulously polite invitation to bargain. I looked at her. She had black hair, neatly combed, cut above her shoulder and trimmed in a straight fringe across her brow. Her thin lips spread into a soft smile, and she batted her brown eyes. "Seven," I murmured, then looked out the door. Fuchsia bougainvillea tumbled down the wall outside the gate. Seven dollars a day, in 1993 Saigon, is a bargain. Most cheap guesthouses begin at twice that amount, while here I would have my own room, bath, and phone as well as some privacy.

"Seven," I repeated slowly.

Bình cleared her throat. I admire good bargainers, and it was clear to me that she was one of them. Though my budget called for only five dollars in rent, I knew I could afford the extra. I accepted. To find something that quickly was a real stroke of luck and I was grateful for my good fortune.

"It is a prestigious neighborhood," young Thảo said softly as he was leaving.

The street, formerly Duong Duy Tan, was lined with towering trees and filled with French colonial architecture. Although it was on a main street, the house was set back in an alley away from the noise. I wrote a postcard home: "I live with two lab scientists and their computer hacker son. They have a dog named Nục Nịch (it means 'Fatso,' but he's not)." It was all so regular—working people, their son, a dog, and a fish tank in the living room. Since I am both romantic and superstitious, I noticed the colorful blossoms in front of my door, as well as the white alley cat with one blue eye and one green. A Viet Kieu returned from France lived to the right, a jeweler to the left, and further down an old woman who had a running feud with Nục Nịch. There was an eighteen-year-old girl being courted every day by her male classmates, and a four-year-old who called into our house every morning on her way to school.

Bình, Thảo, Thanh, and I agreed easily on our rental arrangement.

"We will go to dinner tonight, OK?" Thảo asked. They have a friend who owns a restaurant downtown, he explained. Bình smiled and leaned toward me, her eyes aglow.

"He's a millionaire!"

It's a great tale. Their friend is a Saigon success story, country boy makes it big.

"He wanted to go overseas," some said.

"No, no, he wanted to start his own business. . . ."

"He quit his job ten years ago. . . ."

"During the war he was a dockworker in Danang," Bình told me as she drove me on the back of her motorbike to his restaurant. "He was *very* poor."

The restaurant was all bright lights and city slickers. Dinner began with a small bird and ended with a large fish. I was mesmerized by the entertainment—a series of singers, a magician, and a fire-eater.

"This song is for Miss Edie," a male singer in a lime green suit announced before he began "My Way." Phương, the owner, lifted his Coke can and smiled at me. I smiled back, saluting him with the piece of fish tail that hung from the end of my fork. I popped it into my mouth and smiled again.

Outside the door, at the Chinese style fountain, families posed their children for photos, and newly engaged couples tried to look romantic for the camera. The front door swung open in a continuous stream of guests, waiters, hosts, and people wanting to schmooze with Phương. Though not tall, he was a big man, with a large belly and a voice to match his reputation as the rich guy on the block.

Later, as we were finishing the chilled dragonfruit dessert, a song floated out of the mouth of the young woman singing under the blinking lights. With its quick beat, it bounced out the door and into the streets of the city.

Saigon đẹp lam, Saigon Oi, Saigon Oi!

Oh Saigon, beautiful Saigon. It is an old song and was received with great enthusiasm by a table full of drunk men on the other side of the room. Singing it, I think, is a semipolitical act that makes people feel both sentimental and brave. It was played always and everywhere in the city, and I began to feel it was a mantra for the coming century.

Saigon đẹp lam, Saigon Ơi, Saigon Ơi

At the end of the evening I went home laughing. I thought about Asian millionaires and what they're made of, and I wondered what road brought a poor country boy south and turned him into a hot shot. Whether truth or gossip, stories record the elements of culture better than historical text. Stories are the texture of lives, they mark place in our memory, and they lend form to the imagination of those who were not there.

They never told me, but I knew that Bình and Thảo had a story behind the impressive house they lived in; it was spacious and airy, modern and high-income in a high-income district. The ground floor was a long living room; in the back were a kitchen and a bath. Upstairs were the two bedrooms, one fronting the house, the other overlooking the kitchen. I had the back room, which was cool during the day and hot at night. Bình, Thảo, and Thanh occupied the front, which was cool at night and hot during the day.

In a place as crowded as Saigon, it wasn't exactly close quarters, but we were living together and that made it intimate. Even if the living room was empty, one of us would somehow manage to get in the way of the other; then there were "ahem"s, "oh"s, and "excuse me"s that brought on blushes and soft laughs. Thanh sat in front of the computer for hours on end tapping the keys furiously, engaged in some pirated computer game. Nục, a short-haired brown-black mutt with pointed ears and a thin nose, sniffed around the kitchen until Bình shooed him out, when he would sidle over to the doorway and paw like a horse, revving himself up for a run through the house. His nails tapped out a trot, then a gallop; by the time he reached the fish tank he would slide, hips under, across the tile floor. His front legs akimbo, he went out the door into the courtyard, where he would spring up and hit the metal gate with all fours. BAM! He had to do it three times before Bình yelled out to Thanh:

"Thanh, ơi Thanh—let the dog out."

Thảo leaned back in his chair and watched the evening news every night until 7:00. From my room I could hear Bình preparing dinner, the dog panting and puffing, slipping and sliding, and Thanh playing computer games with his persistent flick of the wrist. The television would announce the hour, a government public service announcement would remind children to brush their teeth after meals, and then—like a song, or a game, or a dream—I would hear my name sung out: "Edie, ơi! Ăn đi!" It was time to eat.

Thanh was quiet and shy. Thảo was quiet and reflective, but Bình was never still. From morning to night she never sat down unless she was study-ing English, and even that she did with astonishing energy, leaning into the table and concentrating so hard that I was afraid that some time, somehow, her will would force her head to pop off. I always told her to rest, that studying too late each night produced sloppy work, but she ignored me and kept at it, as if she had entered the race late and needed to catch up. She hadn't, she was always ahead of the game, but she had plans for herself and her family. Like so many, Bình knew that Viet Nam was really opening and that it was time to seize the day.

It was Thảo who gave the house serenity; I admired him immediately. He was an intelligent man who had studied for years in Russia and Europe, as well as the United States. Thảo listened well and waited until his thoughts were clear before he expressed himself. His presence was less timid than serene. Tall and handsome, he had a sincere smile with beautiful teeth and dark skin. He worked in biochemistry and was the head of the government lab in Saigon responsible for helping strengthen the farming production technology in Viet Nam.

"I try to help Vietnamese farmers," he explained when we met.

He was sitting in a Chinese-style mahogany chair that was part of their living room furniture, his elbows propped on the armrests, fingers inter-twined. He looked straight at me when he said this, and his brown eyes dissolved my initial distrust of the statement. Thảo brought farm coopera-tives together with fruit and vegetable export/import firms; everyone seemed to profit financially from the venture except for him.

"No," he told me one day, "I introduce the businessmen to help the farmers. I don't charge them."

"You don't charge the foreigners? You don't charge anyone?" I asked.

"No," he told me.

"Be careful," I warned him. "Things are happening very quickly in Viet Nam. There will be a lot of investment. You should be paid for your work."

Nục jumped onto the chair next to him.

"Chairman of the Board!" I said to the dog. Thảo started laughing.

"Yes," he said, "he is very clever."

He ran his hand slowly down the dog's back, and Nục wagged his tail. This interchange became a habit the two of them displayed in business meetings. Thảo would sit across the coffee table from his guests; then, at some time during the conversation, the dog would wander in from outside, or leave the kitchen and its garlic and fish sauce odors behind, hop up on the chair, and wait patiently for his rubdown. He'd perk his ears, tilt his head, and stare at the clients during their discussion. New clients often shifted a little in their seats, unsure how to respond; this uneasiness made Thảo smile.

"But the Americans like it," he said to me with a wink one evening.

Later he showed me pictures of the farms where his lab raised banana plants and orchids. In the photos he stood smiling softly behind the knee-high plants and I tried to imagine having the strength to bear the burden of encouraging plants to grow, first in the petri dishes of his lab, and then in the soil of postwar Viet Nam.

He had a solitary nature, and in it I could see a desire to avoid the discomforts that arise in human interactions and to stay in the clarity of science. A laboratory is a trouble-free environment, full of challenges that don't entail the complicated web of human emotions, expectations, and disappointments. It was a pleasure to attend social events with him because I discovered that his tolerance level was the same as mine. I knew that before things became unbearable, the conversation too trite and fawning, the stories inflated, he would take a breath and say kindly but firmly, "OK"; and our goodbyes would begin. It wasn't that he was not ambitious; on the contrary, his reputation was hard earned and well maintained, but his priorities were clearly in order, a very traditional order. He didn't mess around with vanity and its petty games. He had more important things to consider.

Thanh, with his neatly cut hair, looked very much like his father.

"He's so handsome," I told Bình one day.

"Oh yes!" she agreed, abandoning traditional modesty.

But he was unbearably shy, seldom looked at me, and always talked to me at dinner through Bình. When I made jokes to try and coax a giggle, his response was silent or soft. As if the laughter found another outlet, his eyes lit up; and then, unable to suppress it, he smiled and released a soft "ha" before he turned away. He was in the eighth grade and, according to Bình, "even doesn't talk to Vietnamese!" When I heard him speaking to her his tones were highly exaggerated, the risings rising high, the falling dropping down suddenly, and the broken tones cracking abruptly. I liked listening to him, until one evening lying in bed I laughed at my failure to connect his age and his voice.

"Bình," I whispered the next afternoon in the kitchen, "Thanh's Vietnamese pronunciation . . ." I wanted to put it delicately, "his tones are very strange, they are not like yours. Is it his voice?"

She laughed at me, then leaned across the glass-topped table and said proudly, "Yes. Thanh is growing up."

Most nights after dinner Thanh rode his bike to basketball practice. I would come out of the kitchen to find him sitting on the stoop tying his Nikes, his legs stretching on to forever from his white shorts. He would stand up, straighten his polo shirt, and climb onto his maroon Flying Pigeon bike. As I watched him ride through the alley gate on to the street, sitting up tall and thin and semiconfident, I worried about him maneuvering around the motorbikes and cars in the shadowy light of the early evening.

It is likely that Saigon, like Shanghai, got its nickname "Paris of the Orient" because of its atmosphere, not its environment. Site of a million dramas, large and small, Ho Chi Minh City is a fast-moving, energetic place, a magnet for the ambitious. It has all the political intrigue, excitement, and romance of Southern cities worldwide—broad boulevards, warm weather, and palm trees. It has a "worldly" population, all the latest fashions, and the most fashionable entertainment. Its politics are incomprehensible, but they make a good read; and for every five Vietnamese northerners who look down their noses at the city's population, four will move to Saigon anyway. It is full of showy millionaires, socialist cadres, beggars, philanthropists, artists, and actresses. Every other person you meet will tell you, "I am going to start a business."

Hoàng, whom I met at the airport, returned to my thoughts after I settled in; I called him and suggested dinner.

"I know a place," he said, as we pulled away from the alley on his motorbike. "My cousin said it's not bad."

The large, open style of Vietnamese restaurants means their doors are virtually movie screens for the well-seated diner. To the left of the bar I watched the street scene: small herds of children migrated from place to place asking for tin cans.

"No," I said to a boy standing next to our table, thinking he was begging. He stayed and pointed to my beer can.

"They collect cans," Hoàng explained, "and sell them."

A car was stopped out in the street. An old woman in a beige shirt and black pants walked in front of it, as if it weren't there. I looked over Hoàng's shoulder in alarm. Four young men were knocking on the hood. As it inched forward, two of the men gestured toward the restaurant.

"Hell of an incentive to eat," I said, laughing.

Behind me a pan sizzled, and at the bar a young woman lifted a weight and banged it against a block of ice. The car pulled away and the men swarmed around two slowed motorbikes. The barmaid dropped chunks of ice into glasses and poured beer over them. A child beggar approached again and began to whine. Our waitress snapped at him and he left.

I shook the ice in my beer, stared at it for a moment, took a sip, then put down the glass and looked at Hoàng.

"When d'ya leave?" I asked.

"Seventy-Five," he said, too matter-of-factly.

"When?" I pushed.

"April 30th," he said, with a soft laugh.

"How?"

"It was right over there." He gestured over his shoulder to a nearby statue.

"I was only seventeen," he added.

I smiled and shook my head.

"We got on a ship that took us to the Philippines. It was strange. We almost didn't come, my cousin and me. We just woke up that morning and thought, 'Let's try.' It was a madhouse." He stopped there.

"Saigon is getting wild once again," I said.

"I'm thinking of moving here to do business for three to five years," he said, "but there's not a chance in hell I'll bring my family. Not to this." He gestured to the street.

"You mean this chaos is a bad thing?" I joked. "I myself have a fondness for chaos."

"I'm told," he continued, referring to local sources, "people were murdered." Intrigue is inevitable in Saigon.

"What?" I asked, suppressing a giggle.

"Assassinated. Party leaders. In order to get the city to only this point. To see what you're seeing today. Believe me, it wasn't like this two years ago."

A young woman strutted by in jeans and high-heeled shoes; another woman sent her four-year-old to our table to sell us gum.

We had a dinner of fish and soup, conversation and conjecture. Why *should* he come back to Viet Nam, we wondered. Why not? *When?* That was the lingering question.

"I'm tired," I said at eleven.

As we ended the evening, the streets were a blur once again. We ran red lights, and cut through alleys, we shook off restaurant brokers and pushed away children. Underneath it all, under the sound of the traffic, the cries of the hawkers, the hiss and steam of the kitchen, I heard the sing-song voices of the Vietnamese talking and talking into the late hours of the night.

We drove to my apartment and made tentative plans to go out during the next few days.

"But I have to visit my father-in-law's grave," Hoàng added, "so I may not be able to. We'll try," he said.

"Visit his father-in-law's grave?" I muttered as I wandered back into the house. It seemed an odd excuse.

*   *   *

"You Americans like to wander," a woman said to me some months later. "We Vietnamese cannot travel far. We are like one big family." But Ho Chi Minh City contains hundreds of Vietnamese wanderers. They come from the countryside looking for money; they come from Melbourne or Seattle or Paris, looking for business. They live in the street or in shacks; they stay in fancy hotels or family homes. I imagined Hoàng, the prodigal son returned home to his family's native village. I could see him, the successful Canadian businessman, making his way through the streets of the city out to the countryside.

Eighty percent of Viet Nam's population lives in the countryside, and every streetwise city dweller you meet will tell you about his home town in some rural province. The Vietnamese farmer has a mythic stature; the Vietnamese countryside, second only to heaven in beauty, is his beginning and end. If part of America's myth is the poor man rising to power from nothing, Viet Nam's greatest story is the claim people make to land; it is the endurance of that claim through centuries of struggle and deprivation; it is the glorification of that claim in success and prosperity. It is, in the twentieth century, their biggest boast.

In 1968, during the American War, a fable circulated around Viet Nam and its telling reflects the emotional identification Vietnamese make in their lives; land, family and, within these two, self:

> During that year's fighting a unit of the South Vietnam Army went to a village in Quang Nam province to evacuate the area to make way for a free-fire zone. During the evacuation an old man ran from the soldiers and yelled that he would never leave his home; he explained that this land was all that he had left. The "land" was a small garden that he wanted to look after for his grandchildren. "If I leave, the graves of my ancestors, too, will become forest. How can I have the heart to leave?" This link broke the soldiers' resolve, and the old man was left behind.

Later, I would remember this story as I rode down the Mekong Delta and saw white tombs settled neatly in rice fields everywhere. Families, my Vietnamese friends told me, return their ancestors to the land they worked all their lives.

In another war story American writer Tim O'Brien recorded a simple incident in a line of shocking, sweet, and true-false tales: A platoon of American soldiers in a rural village was confronted with the task of crossing a series of mine fields. Out of fear of their clumsiness an old man volunteered to act as guide. For five days the soldiers literally walked in the footsteps of the old man to safety.

> He had a tightrope walker's feel for the land beneath him—its surface tension, the give and take of things. Each morning we'd form up in a long column, the old poppa-san out front, and for the whole day we'd troop along after him, tracing his footsteps, playing an exact and ruthless game of follow the leader. Rat Kiley made up a rhyme that caught on, and we'd all be chanting it together: *Step out of line, hit a mine; follow the dink, you're in the pink.* All around us, the place was littered with Bouncing Betties and Toe Poppers and booby-trapped artillery rounds, but in those five days on the Batangan Peninsula nobody got hurt.

I found the anecdote in an unclaimed copy of O'Brien's *The Things They Carried* that I had found on a bookshelf at the university. After reading it I put down the book and looked at my map for the Batangan Peninsula. I imagined, on a thin jut of land, the heavy, immature steps of boys following a man so familiar with the land around him that he can walk safely in a mine field. In Viet Nam, where my heart is aware of all the American myths, lies, and truths about the war, and my body and brain are awakened to the nation, I am most taken with this little anecdote, and everything else O'Brien wrote fades.

Viet Nam is a dreamlike environment for me. It is pure atmosphere. I admire all the details of Saigon, its fast pace, its ambitious hum. I love the light of early evening and the withdrawal and quiet of the dinner hour. I don't see soot and pollution; it is a romantic haze. I am not unnerved by the crowds or traffic; this is "Eternal Asia." Elderly peasants in conical hats lend innocence to market scenes. I love the color of the orchids against walls mildewed and crumbling with age. I like the presence of cafes everywhere, filling the sidewalks of all corners of the city with chairs, stools, and tables. I hear the city moving into the late hours of the night, and wake at 7:00 already a step behind.

I am an unattached American. My feet are not planted anywhere in this world. I have been raised to move confidently from place to place. I grew up imitating my mother who would walk, even into a grocery store, with her head up and shoulders back. Like many Americans before me I move with strong steps in a place where treading lightly is considered a virtue. On September nights I close my eyes and can see myself moving through sound and color with a face so curious that it may border on foolish, but I cannot resist. Each night I climb under my mosquito net to sleep and the fan makes a light breeze; the net flows softly, like water rippling under wind. One draft brings with it a sweet smell. I open my eyes; it fades. A moment later it enters again. It reminds me of honeysuckle, with a richness that borders on excess, then disappears. I sigh my way into sleep.

I feel fatigued just watching Viet Nam. Each night I fall asleep to the hum of Saigon, my head spinning with impressions. I am in bed, my belly warm with fish and rice, and I hear the sounds people make trying to speak English, the songs that float out onto the street from restaurants, the musical sounds of the Vietnamese language. In the heat and humidity I lie under my mosquito net, waiting for a breeze, intoxicated by the smell of the evening flower— Queen of the Night.

Chapter Two

Bình wanted to know if the fish was too big.

"Không lớn" (No), the vendor replied. She took the fish out of the bucket by the tail and held it in order to press the sale. Bình paused. The vendor was a country woman who squatted on a piece of wood all day selling and skinning fish; I wondered whether her knees didn't ache. The fish flopped around on the board.

"I'll take it," Bình said.

The woman lifted the piece of wood and thumped the head. It made a clapping sound and the fish stopped wiggling. It jerked briefly and she slapped it again—flat across the top. She scraped the skin with a large knife and made a pile of brittle, silver dust; she turned the body slowly while she scraped, like spinning a bottle, and the scales crackled, split, and fell onto the pavement. Next, she took a cleaver, raised it briefly, and chopped off the fins. Then, putting her hand into the fish's mouth, she scraped off the skin outside the gills, opening the slit and forming a bloody fan. She cut around the mouth and face, pulling out the bone and gut. She left the red pile of innards on the ground, then placed the fish in a plastic bag, the gray-brown eyes staring out through a smeared pink haze.

*   *   *

I am always enchanted by "place" and all its elements. I wrote to a friend that I was recording as much of Saigon as I could before its novelty faded, before it all becomes so ordinary. In letters home I tried to describe the contradictory presence of the cute and the cut-throat. Children with acid tongues live on the streets; elderly vendors smile softly while changing black market currency; women wear hair ribbons, grown men giggle, and half of them do business as pirates and smugglers.

Saigon is a magnet city. For the Vietnamese, it is a metropolis, a desirable symbol of the modern world. Wide boulevards divided by long island gardens meet at roundabouts and markets, where they become an island of quiet from which to view everyday life. Nguyen Hue Street begins at the former Hotel DeVille—a matronly overseer, conservative, but with a certain Old World charm. Le Loi Street starts at the city music hall and runs down, past department stores, T-shirt vendors, fancy hotels, and photo kiosks, until it reaches Chợ Bến Thành, the biggest of the city markets, which looms broad and round over a long-distance bus station where buses load and unload a human cargo bound for new opportunities. Passengers arrive from the countryside with bundles of clothing, food, and paraphernalia and stand in the exhaust and soot of the intersection looking for what everyone is talking about.

I filled out bundles of postcards to mail home: "I've moved in. I'm here. I live in a two-story home at the end of an alley in downtown Saigon." I wanted to shout it across the oceans: I LIVE IN VIET NAM! In Chinatown's all over the United States I had caught a glimpse of the romantic alleys of Asia. In Viet Nam they are full of voices, music, odors, darkness and light. They both drew me and repelled me. My alley was spacious, clean, and quiet; it provided a haven from what seemed an endless amount of everyday din elsewhere in the city. In the morning the songs of vendors woke me, the bread seller, the tinker, the trashpicker.

Ve chai bán hông . . .

"What is that?" I inquired one morning, at breakfast.

"What?" Bình replied.

It was soft and beautiful. "Ve chai bán hông . . ." a woman's voice sang.

"That!" I said, excited, "did you hear it?"

"Ve chai bán hông . . ."

"That?" Bình asked, laughing.

"Ve chai bán hông . . ."

"Yes," I said, "yes, what is it?"

But the song is not translatable. Bình continued laughing.

"She is only wanting trash! Plastic, paper!"

This was the moment when the Vietnamese language began to lure me. It was such an intimate part of my landscape. I didn't know what any of it meant, but I could see so much of it, could already feel it.

"Ve chai bán hông . . ." is the sound of a beautiful young woman in a bamboo hat tied by a ribbon. She carries that most romantic of oriental elements, the shoulder pole (a bamboo basket), and it swings softly from side to side as she makes her way out of the alley. Outside my door people wandered up and down to do business, selling bread or corn from a basket strapped to a bike, or pots of hot breakfast porridge wrapped in cloth. Later in the morning came feather dusters and brooms, sleeping mats and machine repairmen. Some of the calls started deep and low, rising at the end for emphasis. The trashpicker sang softly and rhythmically, as if she were bringing us cool water at noon. One day she caught my eye as I was sitting in the front of the house. Silenced for a moment, she stared. She didn't expect a stranger here at the end of the alley.

"Cô . . ."

The sound hung in the air like a musical note.

"Tôi không biết nói tiếng Việt."

She laughed at me, as if to say, "Of course not, of course you don't speak Vietnamese." Her voice was part of daily life; her call, like a lullaby, rose up over the hundreds of other elements that made up the world of our alley. There was the splashing water of the woman shooing Nục, his barking reply, and the humming motorbikes that pulled in from Pham Ngoc Tac street and stopped with a sputter outside Thúy's house. The sad strains of Dexter Gordon ballads rose up out of my tape player, and the gate that cordoned off our cul-de-sac dragged against the pavement.

"Ve chai bán hông . . ."

What was interesting about the trashpicker's voice is that it was so soft for such a gritty business. Her voice should have grumbled the *chai*; it should have crackled and folded like the plastic packing she collects, but it didn't. It flowed as surely and sweetly as honey off a spoon, and I was tempted by its beauty.

*   *   *

"Will you study Vietnamese?" Bình asked at breakfast one morning.

"Oh, I don't know," I said evasively, "maybe." She seemed puzzled by this response. It was a little insulting.

"It's not very practical," Thảo commented politely.

"It's not very easy," I mumbled.

The winter before I left the United States for Viet Nam I had tried to study Vietnamese. I knew a teacher at Harvard who invited me to attend his class. In addition, I spent time with a Vietnamese librarian who taught me to recite verbs and sentence patterns. Initially I told myself that these lessons would help me avoid the pitfalls of my Chinese language learning. Since I had learned Chinese by talking to people in the streets, I said things wrong for a year, and the Chinese were all polite enough not to correct my errors. When I returned home I had to relearn all the sounds I loved. I would not learn Vietnamese that way. I thought I would get Vietnamese right from the start. I enrolled in a class.

Thầy Bình, my teacher, was an accomplished linguist, fluent in English and Russian. He had attended university in Hanoi, taught in Russia for many years and now lives, with his Russian-Vietnamese-English pronunciation in Cambridge, Massachusetts. He spoke slowly, and I could see thoughts moving across his brow before they turned into words, rolled softly around his mouth, and came out. I was charmed by this. It seemed to me he had been teaching Vietnamese to foreigners forever.

I did not know about "Hanoi intellectuals" at that time. I did not know that Hanoi is a proud, ancient intellectual center in Viet Nam. But I was aware of Beijing *Ren*, Bostonians and Connecticut Yankees, who know that "zhou" is not "zou" and "aunt" is not "ant." Street-learned and self-educated, I sneered at them, called them "pronunciation snobs." I was sure, before I entered Thầy Bình's class, that he was not like that; he, like me, simply loved language.

It was a traditional "listen and repeat" classroom. Students read sentence patterns, an exercise I came to love only *after* two years of studying Chinese. In this kind of classroom the students listen to the slow and clear pronunciation of the teacher, then read text trying to imitate him.

"Đi dâu?" (Where are you going?)

"Tôi đi—"

"Tôi," Thầy Bình interrupts.

"Toy"

"Tôi đi bưu điện" (I'm going to the post office), Thầy Bình said.

"boo dian," the student repeated.

"bưu diện," Thầy Bình drilled.

"boo dian."

"No," Thầy Bình said, "bưu điện."

He kept repeating it. *"Bbuuuu"* goes out very far, then *"dien"* comes back in and hides in your nose. Eventually the word began to haunt me.

"Boo Dee-en." I said aloud one night, staring at another inane dialogue from a 1973 Vietnamese textbook. "Toy dee boo dien." I slammed the book shut in disgust. "I don't have to learn every language in the world!" I stated aloud to my wall. I was fighting with the exercises.

"I'm not gonna learn Vietnamese!" I declared, packing the book away. "I had headaches for three years straight studying Chinese. I don't need that."

I confess that I cringe at "ant," "can't," and "hahba." It is, an unidentifiable voice tells me, "aunt," "cahn't" and "harbor." In China people did not line up to hear me speak what one writer called "the language of heaven," but they are suitably impressed with my pronunciation. I am proud of this, because the Chinese are not easily impressed with Western speakers. In the end, yes, I am a bit of a pronunciation snob; but in the Vietnamese lesson Thầy Bình was a perfectionist and a pronunciation snob, and I was a beginner; as a language teacher I believe that with beginners, snobs are too stifling. In Cambridge, in February, I was not keen to learn Vietnamese. I quit.

Language is a universe, however, and in Saigon I could not resist the urge to eavesdrop on the lives of the Vietnamese. Words wove like music in and out of the still surreal landscape. Downtown, young boys—orphans, runaways, dropouts—walk the streets tapping bamboo pipes and calling out to get work as errand runners. The traffic and the conversation are all backed by this percussion that beats quick and clear, like a set of spoons, through the day and night. The boys sell take-out for local restaurants or handle routine tasks for shopowners. People call down from second-floor apartments, asking for spring rolls with lettuce and bean sprouts, or a plate with rice and meat and greens. Only while I was still new could I be charmed by the Felliniesque presence of a businesswoman in a black silk suit riding through traffic on a Honda Dream next to a young kid with a tray of food balanced on his shoulder. They were both waiting for the light to change at the rotary on Le Duan Boulevard. My mind flashed back to the sound of the pipes and I tried to imagine his voice.

*   *   *

"You are from rich country," Bình said to me one afternoon as we sat in the kitchen, "look, I peel very thin." With a look of disapproval she pointed to my thick apple skins lying on the tabletop. I had just arrived in the household of my Vietnamese friends, and my every move felt awkward. We laughed about the way I peeled fruit. I would go into the kitchen to help with dinner, drop things, bump into Bình, cut the vegetables the wrong way; I had trouble cracking the ice. Like the barmaids I saw in restaurants all over the city, I had to grab hold of a small block and hit it with a silver weight until the chunks and shards fell through my fingers into a bowl. I'd hit and watch the block crack, then hit again, only to have the crack thicken but not open, and the ice would slip out of my hand.

Household work in Viet Nam is labor intensive; they have few machines. Instead, they use straw brooms and rag mops, hoses and wash-boards. There is a lot of lugging things around. In general I worked poorly and felt clumsy and incompetent. My lack of the basic household skills meant that I was what Bình called "Princess not laborer." In the classroom this is a compliment. Inside the house it is a socialist insult. I swerved and swayed as I carried in buckets of water from outside. My wrist bent back as I tried to lift iron cooking pots. For a while all our interactions were slow and laden with misunderstanding. Eventually this jerkiness turned into an idiot's rhythm. The family would work and talk while I occupied myself with reading and writing, then came down from my room and floated among them deaf to the meaning of their words. I came when I was called and ate quietly; English conversation was more simple and explanatory than interactive.

In the street it was the same—I floated around shops and markets a little dazed and shy, trying, without success, not to look like a fool. Told that I was overly polite, I laughed because I was trying to respond in kind. I didn't yet know the rules of personal interaction and was attempting to operate on instinct. I was "too nice" a friend told me. But I felt too large, too tall, too clumsy, too stupid.

"Would you like to come with me to the shops?" Bình asked one day.

Often when she spoke she leaned in close and her face took on an absurd eagerness. She spoke with a Russian accent, gained from six years' working as an engineer in Kiev. Her hair, cut in a bob, circled her face, her brown eyes grew large, and her smile, so wide as to be immodest, made it appear as if she were about to burst into laughter. Speaking loudly and pressing herself onto me, she made simple, sweet, and silly comments.

"Thanh is verrry shy."

"We make ferteelizer at the lav."

"Nục is verrry clever."

"I am good cook."

"Come," she said to me that day, "we will go to the shops." So we rode, very early in the morning, around the corner, past the park on Hai Ba Trung Street to the old market. It was a large, long stone building surrounded by a crowd of people on bikes or Hondas, or vendors milling around with shoulder poles. Two young female fabric sellers, setting up shop, folded and refolded hundreds of colors and prints. One girl hung bright-colored cotton cloth on the back wall, red silk over a display stand. The other, finished and ready for business, lifted, placed, and replaced her measuring stick. At the front door was a swarm of people. A man in a red polo shirt parked his Honda and walked inside, while a flower vendor in a bamboo hat stepped back out of his way. An old woman walked past a sidewalk liquor vendor and spat betel into the gutter. A businesswoman in a pale green jacket came out of the crowd with a bag of oranges, walked toward me, turned left, and stepped, ever so lightly, over the garbage that had collected on the curb.

"Stay here," Bình yelled over her shoulder.

I waited on the Honda while she ran into the crowd the same way I run into a convenience store, grabbed what she wanted, bargained with the vendor, and came out with a bag of bananas and oranges. I ran through the Vietnamese numbers I had learned back in Boston. "Một, hai, ba, bốn." Waiting and watching, I decided I would work my way up to buying something in the market.

It's not as if the market were any single place, however. It was every street corner with space to spread a plastic mat or fit a stool and basket. If I wanted to, I could get everything I needed by wheeling around the alleys near the market building, talking to folks, and having my groceries handed over to me on my bike. While I was waiting, I sat watching a woman at a nearby food stall. She raised her arms, gestured, and said "Cái này" (That). I mimed; my lips moved ("Gaiy naiy").

The next afternoon, craving some Lipton tea, I walked into a nearby shop selling imported foods and tried to look as though I knew what I was doing. Behind the front counter the boxes of tea piled high on shelves looked like red and yellow flags bordering each end of the wall. I tried to remember the sound of the woman's voice in the Hai Ba Trung market. My arms went up casually and I stuttered "Gay nay," pointing clumsily to the teas. I blushed as I handed the money over to the young woman, who didn't look at me, then I whispered, "Cám ơn nhiều" (Thanks very much). In September, October, and November the only language that was easy for me was what passed between the Vietnamese and me in these foreign shops. I bought imported goods at Western prices because I could not speak in the market. In the shops we all smiled a lot. Relieved.

"Xin lỗi (Excuse me) . . ." "Cám ơn nhiều (Thank you) . . ."

"I will tell you," Bình said, "you know," her index finger went up for emphasis, "in Viet Nam, you must bargain. I will show you the shops to bargain and the shops where you cannot bargain. They are government shops."

We walked into a fabric store.

"Chào Chị" (Hello, Miss), Bình said, as the young woman working behind the counter leaned forward eagerly.

"Hello, Madame," she said, when she saw me.

"Hello," I replied with a smile.

Large bolts of raw silk were on display, and I fingered a dark red fabric; another young woman began to hover nearby. I smiled at her and wandered over to where Bình was standing. She had silk chemise in her hand and was negotiating a price with the clerk. She ran her hand over the fabric and looked at the woman in inquiry.

"Một mét bao nhiêu?" (How much is one meter?), she asked.

The clerk replied in a soft, nervous voice.

"Mắc quá" (Expensive), Bình said, and put down the fabric.

She walked away from the counter, and the young woman looked over her shoulder at the shop owner. The older woman came forward and told Bình the silk was from Hong Kong. Bình approached the counter again, picked up the silk, and examined it closely.

"Edie, what do you think?" she asked, "Do you like?"

I leaned on the counter and looked at the fabric. It was a sheer, white chemise and felt like a rayon/poly mix, not silk. I didn't particularly like it; it reminded me of the shirts sold in cheap clothing catalogs.

"I don't really, no," I said plainly.

The young clerk giggled nervously. Bình pushed her bottom lip out decisively, put the silk down, and said, "OK."

We left the shop. Bình leaned on my arm as we walked and said, conspiratorially, "I go back when the owner is not there, eeh-hee!"

"Very clever!" I replied, with a smile.

Shopping is a colorful but serious business. Migrant vendors, shopowners, even black marketers, hustle for their daily bread. It's a hand-to-mouth existence for most, and underneath its tradition and color the bargain, and the barter, is about coping and surviving, not reaching the top of the pile. All this haggling led me, early on, to the conclusion that Saigon is a city with an edge to it. An American friend Dave, a young investor living in the city looking for business, decided he probably wouldn't stay long.

"This place makes me nervous," he said. "Does it make you nervous?"

"I suppose," I replied, thinking about it for the first time.

It is the headiness the Saigonese have these days that makes the place exciting. There are a million entrepreneurs who have been nurturing ideas in silence for twenty years, and now all that creativity and ambition is on the loose. The city did make me nervous, but I enjoyed it; I was challenged by it, so I was happy to be there. Another American friend called the atmosphere "greedy." I'm not sure that any more greed existed in Ho Chi Minh City than elsewhere, or who the greed came from—only that it seemed closer to the surface. These contradictions and puzzles were things that I wrote home about and shared with my foreign friends in Viet Nam. But it was the intimacy of daily life that made me fall in love with Asia; it lives in a spiritual memory with these small sights and sounds that will forever remain part of my mental and emotional landscape. Early on I knew that this would be my lifestyle for the next year. Inquiry balanced by wonder and study. Work, I knew, would be peripatetic. As a "foreign teacher" you have an oblique role that falls somewhere between that of diplomat and tourist.

"Come here, see this!" the Vietnamese seem to say to the foreign resident. Come see my daughter, my son. Go see my hometown. Visit many beautiful places. "Miss, you are welcome."

*   *   *

I met the head of academic affairs for the university English department. She was a quiet, observant woman with a clipped British accent.

"My name is Kim Thư," she introduced herself one morning as we rode in a car taking me to the department's administrative offices. I couldn't understand her name, so I asked her to repeat it.

"I'm sorry, what is it again?"

"Kim Thư."

"Um, Kim?" I said awkwardly.

"Kim Thư," she said.

Rather than continue stumbling, I decided it was Kim-something. With a conservative look and short black hair, she struck me as very proper. She wore glasses and had a serious look in her eyes, but her cheeks were round and plump; if she were a little girl you'd want to pinch them. As I was trying to work out how I would refer to her, I realized she had been speaking for a minute or two. "It's probably something I need to know," I thought, but I was too embarrassed to ask her to repeat. "Better to change the subject," I advised myself.

"Excuse me," I said, "your English. Did you study with British tapes? You have a British accent."

"Oh really?" she replied.

"It's very nice," I told her, hoping she hadn't been telling me something important. "It's much nicer than an American accent."

"Oh?" she said, tilting her head, puzzled by my frankness. The car pulled up to the gate of the university and, by now overcome with embarrassment that I couldn't catch her name, becoming slowly convinced I would never be able to say anyone's name in the entire country, I dashed from the car. I didn't get far before I realized I didn't know where I was going; I stopped and waited for Kim. She approached slowly, then took me by the elbow through the gate.

Housed at the site of a former French prison, Ho Chi Minh City University is the established star of southern Viet Nam's academic community. The main campus consists of one large stone building three stories high, and three smaller, single-story buildings used for classrooms. The buildings are laid out in a horseshoe design, creating a large lot in the center, which is primarily used for parking. The main building housed classrooms, department offices, a library, a video center, and the newly created English Resource Center. The ERC was a small room at the end of the second floor with three sets of shelves full of textbooks donated by the British Council and British Petroleum. The texts were largely technical, including a few sets of teaching reference books from Cambridge University Press, a complete set of Headway Intermediate (a popular English instruction text), some radical history and politics texts (including a collection of lectures by Noam Chomsky), and three college-level books on basic accounting published in the early eighties. Except for the Chomsky lectures, there was little that caught my eye, and I had no idea what the Vietnamese were able to make of the material. Students and young faculty flocked to the room when it was open, however, and the books were looked at, notes dutifully made and—so it seemed—papers written, and lessons planned, from the information gathered. Undeniably, the room was used.

Like most buildings in the city, the classrooms were built in the very center of the structure and had wooden jalousies or steel bars in place of glass windows. There are no hallways, only one large balcony that wraps around the building. With the open space, sun streams through the window frames casting shadows and creating a heavy heat. Because it is located in the center of the city, street traffic outside the gate left a blanket of soot on desks and frequently drowned out lectures. It is not an ideal working environment for either students or teachers. But during my year, it was a busy, humming campus, open from 7 a.m. until 10 p.m., and, like the polytechnic university and the pedagogical college on the other side of town, it was bursting at the seams with ambitious students.

When I walked into the English department the dean was talking on the telephone and gestured politely for us to sit on the couch next to the door. A fan turned slowly overhead. The office was painted a light turquoise-green, but looked a bit ragged, with overcrowded bookshelves full of texts suffering under the humidity of the tropics and a thick layer of soot that spread across everything with a mysterious kind of creep.

Ms. Nguyễn, a thin, forty-something woman was the department dean. She wore her hair in a fifties-style bob and made up her face with reddish lipstick, blusher, and mascara. She had a habit of smiling like a Cheshire cat while she spoke, which altered her pronunciation and made talking with her a strange and confusing experience. The young woman who picked me up at the airport, Mỹ Ngọc, came over and sat down next to me while Ms. Nguyễn made another phone call.

"Do you have brothers and sisters?" she asked politely.

"Yes, I have seven," I told her, using my slow "foreigner English." Her eyes widened, her jaw dropped.

"I have four sisters and three brothers. I am the youngest."

She began giggling, and then said something else with a knowing smile. Cultural modesty requires that she place her hand over her mouth when laughing, so I couldn't hear what she said. I leaned forward.

"I'm sorry, what did you say?"

"You are *ut*. In Vietnamese we call the youngest *ut*. They are very precious."

"Is that anything like imp?" I teased. "My father used to call me imp."

She giggled, and I winked at her. She laughed again and turned away as if she knew a secret. For a time there was much of this attitude of preciousness. I was the American teacher, and though I replaced a woman who was very popular ("You are American?" they said when we met, "Do you know Rosemary?"), the level of warmth, mixed with eagerness, made me feel special.

"When will the term begin?" I asked Mỹ Ngọc.

She smiled uncomfortably and said, "We don't know, yet."

"Oh," I said, "well, you know, um . . . soon, right?"

"Yes, Miss." She laughed nervously.

"Do you know the times I'll teach?" I continued.

"Well," she said, blushing, "I will take your American Studies class. I am in class 3B."

I smiled, surprised to learn I would be teaching American Studies (which I am completely unqualified to teach). "Class 3B is third year?" I asked.

"Yes," she said with another smile. "We want to study at 10:30 on Tuesdays and Thursdays."

I started laughing. "Well, I'll see what I can do!"

"Tell Miss Kim Thư," she whispered.

"Kim who?" Ngọc pointed to my round-faced friend talking to the department dean. "What's her name, again?" I asked.

"Kim Thư," she replied softly.

"Kim Ter," I repeated.

Eventually Miss Kim Thư did work out a schedule for me. There would be no rush-hour rushing to class; I taught only late morning and early afternoon.

"How nice of you," I commented, when she told me.

"Well," she replied politely, "Americans enjoy late evenings and like to sleep in the mornings."

"Yeah," I said, smiling. I was still new in town, but already it was apparent to me that sleeping "late" in the morning was anathema to the lifestyle around me. The streets were full by 7 a.m. and my 8-o'clock rise from bed was a sign of either sickness or laziness.

It was only the beginning of the term, Ms. Nguyễn said, but I had already been assigned: Composition, American Studies, and something called "American Culture." That was the maximum amount of time required in my contract. However, in a long, awkward conversation I was praised, welcomed, and asked whether I would be willing to participate in occasional special programs and to teach short-term special courses. These requests were phrased with the necessary politeness and formality; they were handed to me like an invitation. It was all very pleasant, but I knew full well the scarcity of foreign teachers and the prestige attached to courses taught by native speakers. I had been in this situation before: In China university administrators asked, "Can you teach a conversation class?" I said, "Sure" and ended up with sixty students. Under such circumstances no one learns anything and I become disagreeable. In Saigon, I could see this coming, I smiled and looked around the room, as if I would find an excuse hidden somewhere. "We'll see," I told Ms. Nguyễn.

"Enjoy some fresh oranges?" She gestured to a plate in front of me.

The phone rang and she went to her desk. A few minutes later she began talking with the woman I was mentally referring to as "Kim-something," but she didn't use "Kim." I recognized the more polite workplace reference, "Chị." They talked for a bit and then Ms. Nguyễn turned to me and began to speak. I stood up and walked a little closer to hear her.

"I'm sorry?" I said.

She said it again. Still not understanding, I looked at Kim-something.

"Em," she said politely, "I will have to go to the other campus to do some work for the international office, will that be OK?"

I was puzzled by this politeness until I realized they were trying to tell me that the driver who brought me here was also leaving.

"Oh!" I said, "yeah, sure. I'll just take a cyclo home."

Ngọc looked startled and spoke up.

"I'll take you home."

"Well," I said, "I need to run an errand anyway." I wanted to mail my postcards. I stepped back politely and sat again on the couch. A young woman had come in during the meeting, and now the teachers called her over to negotiate a way to get me home without embarrassing me by making me go alone. To hop into a cyclo, or to walk the five blocks to my house, was the most natural thing in the world for me; but for the Vietnamese, making me do so was tantamount to neglect. "Certainly!" they said, they would drive me home. Ngọc walked over to me on the couch and leaned down to talk.

"Miss Edie, Thúy Kiều will drive you home."

"Oh! it's OK!" I protested (an instinctive but useless response). "I can make my way home."

Thúy Kiều walked over bashfully, holding her hands in front of her and looking down at the ground. Mỹ Ngọc explained that she was a part-time faculty member, she had a free moment before lunch, and she would be happy to take me on my errand, and then home. Thúy Kiều was timid to the point of skittishness; and after smiling for a rather awkward period of time, she asked me where I wanted to go. I broke into a wide smile, pleased that I recognized my opportunity to use the one sentence I knew in Vietnamese.

"Tôi đi bưu điện" (I'm going to the post office).

Kiều's face lit up: "Oh! Your Vietnamese is very gooooood!" She patted my shoulder with the exaggerated encouragement of a kindergarten teacher, and I laughed softly at her courtesy.

We got on her motorbike and rode down Le Duan Boulevard to the post office. Though by 1993 Viet Nam had had an open-door policy for a few years, my presence was still unusual enough to cause double-takes in traffic. Kiều, wearing a wide-brimmed sunhat, provided only the smallest space for me to hide.

"They are wondering who thee beautiful foweigner is," she said over her shoulder.

"They are, are they?" I said, playing along.

We pulled around a rotary and Kiều stopped at the post office. As I climbed off the motorbike, a group of children ran toward me.

"Buy postcard," they called.

"Don't buy anything!" Kiều said with slight alarm.

"Don't worry," I said, wading through the kids.

Kiều waited for me as I went into the building. A few minutes later I returned and saw her standing beside her motorbike, hands behind her back, just as she was when I had left her. I stopped in my tracks, puzzled by her stillness. She continued looking at me. I walked to her side.

"All set," I said, brightly.

"All set," she repeated.

She turned the bike around and I sat on the back. As we pulled away, I got another look at the billboard that loomed over the intersection. It was a portrait of Ho Chi Minh holding a child and, I assumed, a large propaganda message.

"Miss Kiều," I said, as she drove, "what does that mean, the words *Đất Nước Viet Nam?*"

"What?" she asked.

"Dat Nuoc Viet Nam," I repeated, "what does it mean?"

"Viet Nam?" she said, slowly.

"No," I said, I tapped her shoulder, "could you stop for a minute?"

She stopped. I pointed across the intersection to the billboard.

"*Đất Nước Viet Nam.*"

"Oh! *Đất Nước*" she said, correcting my pronunciation. "It means Viet Nam."

"Oh," I murmured, a little disappointed, as she pulled away from the curb.

"But what is the definition of the words?" I pestered her.

"The defeenition?" she asked over her shoulder.

"The definition," I repeated.

"Em, it means the country, or nation, of Viet Nam," she explained.

"Oh, *Đất nước* means country," I said.

"Well, no," Kiều said, then she stopped talking and thought. We slowed to cross an intersection near my gate.

"It's up there," I pointed over her shoulder, "on the right."

She edged through the traffic.

"Well," I continued, as we slowed and pulled into the alley, "what does *đất* mean and what does *nước* mean?"

"Oohh," Kiều said, understanding. She came to a stop outside the gate. "*Đất Nước* is earth and water."

"Can I say, *Đất Nước Mỹ?*" I asked.

"Well, we say *Là người Mỹ* to wefer to America."

"Sooo," I said, drawing out my conclusion, "*Đất Nước* is Viet Nam."

"That's right," said Kiều, again touching my shoulder like an elementary school teacher. I walked into the house overcome with childish wonder. Earth and Water is Viet Nam.

*   *   *

I began meditating soon after I arrived so that I could keep calm in an environment that seemed hectic twenty-four hours a day. The hours became days, the days weeks, and everything around me seemed a blur of vision and sound. I meditated to get myself acclimated, to fight off the headaches that plagued me, and to retain all the images that I saw each day. I meditated to dissolve loneliness and to sleep comfortably; I meditated so that I could handle my culture clashes and match my expectations as a teacher to the reality of my students' world. During all my hours of meditation, images and impressions rose and fell with my breathing. I recorded much of my experience in Viet Nam in this way. Snapshots and illusions appeared before me while my breath moved in and out. Some of the pictures were comforting, some disturbing.

For a week I had been suffering head and face pain that I couldn't shake. Originally I called it jet lag, then I told myself it was a result of changing seasons; for a while it was the full moon, then it was the sugar in my coffee. I practiced yoga in the afternoon to try to work the tension out, but only the sitting still and breathing seemed to ease the pain. When my anxiety arose in meditation I had nightmarish visions. I imagined giant bugs invading my room as I slept. I saw clearly the bodies of the beggars pushed to the margins of my vision during the day. I pictured myself caught in the fast-moving street traffic, people coming at me from all directions. I saw myself in shops, stupid, clumsy, and unable to communicate.

One evening, after sweating through beggars and bugs, after wishing I could hear a familiar voice speaking English, after being afraid, I saw a line of children standing by the side of the road laughing and flying white kites. This image gave me a lift, and I finished my meditation thinking perhaps I would no longer be burdened by exaggerated visions. I rubbed my ankles and knees, stretched out my legs, and sighed, ready for sleep.

I slept on a large wooden, double bed placed in the corner of my room. Right after I arrived Bình had given me an old mosquito net. It was bright pink and made of polyester cloth, the four corners adorned with white shoelaces that were tied together and then secured each night to loosely placed wall hooks. To hang it, I had to stand on my desk chair to reach the first hook by the door, then climb onto my bookshelf to reach the second hook. When I was finished with the operation each night the bed resembled a collapsing cabana. I climbed inside and lay prostrate on the mat, wishing the fan could produce enough breeze to cool me. In the kitchen a gecko wandered among the glasses, making them clink together softly. Nục circled around the patio, pounded on the gate, and barked. Thanh rolled over and sighed, then called softly from his half-sleep.

"Ttt. Nucooii." His voice cracked, and I giggled.

Then, like a midnight serenade, a bicycle entered the alley. The rider pedaled slowly. The chain brushed occasionally against its guard and, as his foot pressed down, a soft creak was released. It was very much like my own recently acquired bicycle; the creak came out on a three-count beat, and the man sang softly.

"Bắp nấu đây" (Fresh, hot corn).

Country people in Viet Nam do whatever they must to bring home money. Like countless others, this man wrapped dozens of ears of hot corn in foil, placed them in bamboo baskets, kept them warm with piles of checked cloth, then rode around the city trying to sell them. I rolled over to my side and smiled.

"Bắp nấu đây."

The sound came out soft, but quick and clear, like kernels falling off cobs. After the dog's barking faded, after his nails clipped around the pavement in the circle he drew before he settled, I heard the man turn, and he left. I fell asleep hearing his voice echo through alley after alley after alley.

"Bắp nấu đây . . . bắp nấu đây . . . bắp nấu đây."

Chapter Three

We were sitting in the kitchen, having breakfast.

"Look!" Bình said, "we can make Nục walk!"

She held a piece of bread over the dog's head and he rose on his hind legs. As Bình backed away, Nục moved, like a circus dog, on his two legs to the other side of the small kitchen.

Thảo smiled and gestured toward the dog with a mingled look of pride and embarrassment.

"Oh, he is very smart," he said.

Bình gave the bread to Nục, snapped her fingers, and pointed to the door. "Đi!" she said, "go!"

The dog ran with his prize to the front courtyard.

"He woke me up yesterday morning," I told them.

Thảo tilted his head in question.

"I mean he came into my room. I was half asleep, and I thought it was a mosquito or something."

"Nục likes you very much," remarked Thảo approvingly.

"He surprised me," I continued, "then I yelled at him and he came running down here."

The dog isn't allowed upstairs, but on occasion he sneaked up and sniffed around. When I opened my eyes that morning he began wagging his tail and tried to lick my foot through the mosquito net.

"Hey!" I snapped. Nục jumped back, posed like a runner in a race, then bolted out the door. "Ơi," I mumbled and rolled over. He trotted around downstairs, ran into the courtyard, jumped against the gate, and let out a bark. Up in my room I sighed contentedly, then looked at the clock. It was after eight. I sat up and decided to get out of bed. The house was empty. Thảo, Bình, and Thanh left nearly every day by 7 a.m., pushing the gate latch closed with a heavy scrape and then dropping the handle with a clang. I would go down then and make my coffee in the quiet.

The roof over the kitchen was thick, corrugated plastic, with a sliding piece in the middle that could be opened to let the sun shine in. I pulled the rope on the attached pulley to open it while I waited for the coffee to drip through the silver French filter into my glass. The sun rose in the morning over the kitchen and then worked its way to the front of the house. I padded softly across the dark front room to open the door fully so that the dog could more easily run in and out. It was only recently that Thảo and Bình had started leaving the door ajar when they left. Nục was just passing out of his shoe-chewing phase.

"Nục, ơi, Nục," I called softly. He was chasing something under the furniture.

"Nục Nịch," I called again. He scrambled out backward, turned, and ran outside with his prize. He settled into his corner; as I approached for a closer look, he glanced up only briefly, then resumed tearing it apart. It was a wall gecko he had chased and caught. I backed away as the reptile convulsed in death. It is always unsettling to discover our pets are animals.

In the kitchen I sighed in boredom. My late mornings were losing their novelty, and I thought it was time to follow up on Bình's recent suggestion that I volunteer to teach at Thanh's middle school. It would get me out of bed each day and be fun. Each week since my arrival it seemed that someone new was pestering Bình and Thảo for an introduction, and the suggestion that I could be their private tutor. Bình often posed these ideas politely. She folded her hair back over her ear, cleared her throat, smiled slightly, and said that it was so wonderful that I was an English teacher, and everyone wanted to meet me, and wouldn't I like to work more often than I was at the university? Didn't I want to keep busy? Stop reading books all day, Edie!

"I like reading books," I said with a smile.

"You know, Edie, you can teach at Thanh's school!" she said one morning. "They will pay you!"

I nodded as graciously as I could, worn down by the repeated requests. "We'll see," I replied. I brought it up again a few days later, at dinner.

"Bình, I think you are right," I began, "I think I should spend less time reading. I will be happy to meet the director of Thanh's school and talk with him about teaching."

"Great!" she answered, with a laugh. "You know, we will go tomorrow!"

The next morning, when Bình introduced us, the school director didn't quite believe me. He was a small man, with graying hair and a gracious smile. He introduced himself, and I awkwardly tried to repeat his name.

"You can just say, Anh (Sir)," Bình whispered. I found relief in this advice, and made a mental note to surrender to Viet Nam's courtesy and simply call all men Anh rather than tongue-tie myself with their names. His family name was Nguyễn, which made me comfortable since it was so familiar. Anh Nguyễn smiled again after the introductions and then sat down across from us at his desk. He worked at a cluttered wooden desk, with book shelves pressing in on him from behind, and a small oscillating table fan providing intermittent breezes. Bình told him that I was interested in teaching at his school, and he nodded happily in understanding. But after a pause he cleared his throat and put his hands together in front of him, as if he were about to break bad news to me. Perhaps between their original talk and today he had realized that Bình's offer would create a strain on the school's resources. Perhaps he looked around and realized that he didn't really have a place for me. The look on his face looked serious enough for me to wonder if I had made a mistake. The breeze from the fan blew across some papers. He lifted a paperweight and placed it atop them, then laughed slightly.

"We can't pay much," he said. Bình shifted uncomfortably in her seat. I sighed in relief. Was that all? I replied that I didn't mind the local salary. I said I would teach every morning that I was free. He kept repeating that I could work "according to your pleasure, one, two days—whatever you please."

I said I was free five days per week. He made me repeat myself.

"Five days?" he asked again.

"Five days," I answered.

"At local salary?"

"At local salary."

He was looking for the catch, but there was none. Vietnamese people didn't understand why I would volunteer to take the lowest paid job in a poor country. They were taken aback by this idea; it was so impractical. In Viet Nam of the 1990s, after war, hunger, and failed revolutions, ambition is not just how you get ahead, it is how you keep up. Today's schools, quickly being consolidated and privatized, bear the same burden as businesses; therefore, what a boon I was for this little private school.

My introduction to classes was arranged for the following week. Again, Bình drove me on the back of the Honda, explaining that we would visit the school's two campuses (one for grades six through nine, one for ten through twelve). If Americans try to be off-hand about many formal occasions, the Vietnamese, on the contrary, work hard to make even an introduction an event. But reality often intercedes in its usual comic fashion. Though we had an appointment to meet that day, Anh Nguyễn was disconcerted by my arrival—surprised again, as if I was an apparition—and called on one of his supervisors to find a class for me to meet. I sat in his office and drank tea while the teaching supervisors ran from room to room, looking for a class to interrupt. In soft and sure voices they negotiated the scene and I was escorted to meet a sixth grade class. In my plain beige skirt, Birkenstock sandals, and flowered top I stood in the front of the classroom next to a female Viet-namese teacher wearing a beautiful red *áo dài* (an elegant mandarin-style top over billowy, white trousers).

"Hello!" I said, increasingly aware of the awkwardness.

"Hello!" the students responded after the teacher's prompting.

The school principal spoke to the class in Vietnamese, explaining that I was the new foreign teacher from the United States.

"Oooooh," the kids said, and they all began clapping.

I smiled some more and looked over toward Bình standing in the doorway. A seemingly endless pause ensued; but just as I thought I would never live through it, the teacher floated over to my side, said "Thank you," and asked the class to say goodbye to the new teacher.

At the second campus the students were well prepared for my arrival. The teachers, however, were surprised. As I walked down the hallway (the build-ing was horseshoe style, like the university, with no hallways, only balconies, and jalousied windows), young people whispered to one another in strange but knowing tones. I wondered if one of the janitors or parking attendants at the other campus had said something, then spread it through the bamboo grapevine and it had somehow eluded all the faculty. After pauses reflecting their shock the young teachers muttered something that must have trans-lated as: "Why didn't anyone tell *me?*" There was no collective "Hello" from the tenth graders, but the class monitor presented me with a small bouquet of limp roses (they had been waiting for my arrival since the first period, it was now the fifth); and while the class teacher stepped aside gracious but uninformed, the students asked me questions.

"Miss, what part of America are you from?"

"Boston, Massachusetts," I said.

"Oooh," they mumbled and, running through memories and letters, they tried to place my home on their mental maps.

"Do you know where Massachusetts is?" I asked the group.

"In America," someone replied boldly.

I laughed out loud, then, talking to myself, said, "Well, Edith, ask a stupid question . . ." I turned around and walked to the chalkboard.

"That's right!" I announced. "Now, where? That's another question." I picked up a piece of chalk, wrote "USA" on the board, and tried to sketch a map. The students laughed.

"I can't draw very well," I said sheepishly.

"Does that look like a cow to you?" I asked. There was a pause. "A cow?" I repeated, loudly. They laughed again.

"Well," I said, accepting my embarrassment, "anyway, here's Massachusetts." I drew a dot, then added a curl for Cape Cod. The cow was then wearing false eyelashes.

"Massachusetts." I said, standing with my hands together in front of the class.

"Do you know Texas?" someone asked.

"I know Texas," I replied, "but I have never been there. Do you know people in Texas?"

"My cousin lives in Texas."

"Do you like Viet Nam?" one student asked.

"I love Viet Nam," I replied. "I think Saigon is very beautiful."

"Oh no . . ." My opinion was summarily dismissed and laughed at; they shook their heads, unbelieving, as if to show that now they knew the foreign teacher was being too polite.

"You don't think so?!" I replied.

From the corner of my eye I could see the school director edging forward to end the session. Perhaps he had appointments of his own to keep, or perhaps the teacher had reminded him of the unfinished lesson in the textbook. He spoke softly to the class in Vietnamese and I knew it was time to say goodbye.

"Goodbye now," I said, waving from behind my flowers like some contestant in a silly beauty pageant. The bell rang to end the class period and chaos came running out of all the rooms. In a gesture of great discomfort the principal hurried me from the school. As we left, I realized it was because he didn't want me to get caught in the crowded stairwell. Perhaps he thought that schools in the United States have some sort of orderly change of classes, "well behaved" students, and all that. Down in the parking lot Bình explained to everyone that since it was later in the morning, she had to bring me back to the university.

"We are very happy you are here," Anh Nguyễn said. "Thank you so much for teaching at our school."

Over in a corner of the courtyard teachers rinsed their dusty hands under a tap and wiped cloths across their dry irritated eyes. This casual gesture, reflecting one of a hundred small elements of poverty and development, caught my eye. I turned my head away, as we were pulling away on the Honda, and I looked up to see most of the tenth grade standing on the balcony, watching the princess-teacher being carried away, kicking up dust in the parking lot, and leaving limp rose petals in her wake.

Bình's phone rang for the next few days with calls from parents of students at the school.

"They are all very happy to have a native English speaker for their children!" she said. "And the students think you are pretty! And the director is happy you are young! And the kids will love your class!" I smiled, wondering if Bình was practicing her use of "and."

The involvement and demands of parents meant that I became the school's floating teacher; instead of working with only one grade level, I saw each class in grades five through twelve once or twice a month to help with pronunciation. This arrangement was not one I agreed to with enthusiasm, but I acquiesced because I knew how eager everyone was to have as many young students as possible exposed to a foreign teacher.

"Don't worry to prepare," Anh Nguyễn, explained. "Just read textbook."

My work was overseen by Mr. Lam, who doubled as the school electrician. A country boy moved to the city, Lam usually wore black cotton sneakers and jeans. He was thin with long hair, cut in a bowl style, and had freckles and a flat, wide nose. His hands were calloused and he walked with a slouch, a condition that I thought came from carrying large television sets every day from room to room for teachers. He bounced around offices, teachers, and children like a rubber ball thrown too hard, while people shot everyday questions at him and children ran circles around him. Mr. Lam is a Vietnamese Everyman, with the nebulous title "Supervisor." ("What's my job?" he answered me one day. "I am supervisor"—an answer that, in Viet Nam made everything perfectly clear.) He possessed a reliability that must have felt like a burden. When he said something was his duty, he meant it; and his gestures demonstrated such sincerity and trust that a con artist would stop a swindle mid-stride from a guilty conscience. Mr. Lam studied English from textbooks he bought in bookstores, listened to the tapes that went with them, and tried, with unfailing energy, to recreate the dialogues he found there.

"Hello, Miss Edie!" he'd say.

"Hi, Mr. Lam," I'd reply.

"How are you today?"

"I'm fine thanks, and you?"

"I'm fine, thanks!"

Then we would hang there in the empty silence that follows such structured interactions, smiling and smiling and smiling.

As the weeks passed into months I realized that the whole city was full of an eagerness to get going with the new tools of the twenty-first century. Everyone wanted to imbibe the secrets of the so-called "developed" countries. They wanted to learn the English, get the job, collect the cash. On the way home from the university one afternoon I sat at a stoplight on Dien Bien Phu Street looking straight ahead and waiting for the light to change. An older man was openly staring at me. I don't think being stared at is unusual, but it can feel a little strange. He spoke:

"Hello. Where you from?"

"Hello. I'm from the United States."

"Oh, America. Very nice. I speak English a little. I want to learn English. Do you teach English? Can you teach me English?"

Well, not there at the stoplight, no, though I think the Vietnamese would take the lesson (and take it seriously) if I offered it. And I can't teach while I'm trying to steer through traffic, sitting in a restaurant eating lunch, or buying a newspaper on the street. Over the course of the year people stopped me everywhere—at the post office, in the street, in the alley outside my house. A stream of business people pestered Thảo to convince me to teach them English; a group of translators at the university wanted my "expertise"; some local artists asked me to teach a Saturday morning conversation class; Phương, the restaurant owner I met on my first night in town, wanted me to coach his twelfth-grade daughter. It seemed that my prospects were wonderful for opening our gate and setting up the business of teaching. It was all sincere, but relentless, and I discovered early on I didn't have an interest in getting rich by teaching English.

But for reasons I never quite understood I seemed to make the administrators at the middle school very nervous. They were always asking when I would be leaving, or whether I would stay on, since the children loved me so much. Although the school had no money, it did have the hearts and voices of about one hundred sixth graders who sang a song to me every time I entered the classroom, who told me that they loved me and that I was beautiful, and who were, in every possible way, endearing and entertaining.

This was the hook; and though it became immediately apparent to me that my presence was no help whatsoever to their language study, I stayed because the image of these children floated through my mind every day, and I didn't have the heart to leave them.

✻   ✻   ✻

Viet Nam lies in the middle of monsoon country; it has two seasons, wet and dry. My Saigonese friends hated the rainy season, which was messy and created endless problems of flooding and dirt. Like so many things in Southeast Asia, it was overly abundant. September and October were full of days with humid mornings and high air pressure that broke with afternoon showers. I loved the showers. The drops were heavy and hard. They fell like hail on thirsty sidewalks and quickly became running streams on crowded streets. If it rained after lunch, a quiet descended over the city, as people in rooms and houses everywhere lay taking a siesta and listening to the rain fall on tin and plastic roofs. The showers never lasted over an hour, and at the end I liked to ride my bike around the moist streets and listen to the city reawaken. The air smelled clean and was heavy with the sweetness of tropical flowers. People moved quietly. Just woken from slumber, they peered out from doorways and from under the plastic of rain ponchos; then they moved on to the rest of the day. The quiet faded with the increasing hum of wet tires. Stores opened, workers returned to offices, students returned to school, and the sun began to dry the seats and tables in sidewalk cafes. The smell of damp earth and pavement mingled as I rolled around the streets.

"Hey lady, wanna buy stamps?" a girl's voice said.

I was standing outside the post office, holding a handful of letters home. It was a little girl, maybe six or seven, who was part of a group I saw every day. She wasn't a beautiful child. She had the hardened look that poor street children have, but none of the quick-witted appeal. Her hair was mousy and hung in strings on her shoulders. Her teeth were crooked and yellowed. She didn't sparkle in that stereotypical way; she was no Dickensian waif. Although I had seen her before, I had never looked at her face. Something about her appearance bothered me. She had freckles on top of dark skin and a big nose.

"No thanks, kid," I said, as I walked away. On the steps it occurred to me that she looked like a street fighter. I entered the shade of the post office, then stopped suddenly and sighed.

"Oh, no. It's been broken," I said out loud.

It wasn't the girl's clothes that upset me, the dirt on her skin, or the raggy look of her hair. It was the odd shape of her nose and the dull look in her eye. She had been beaten.

On that same afternoon I saw the other little girl. Sitting on my bike at a stop light behind St. Mary's Cathedral, I saw an old woman with a mis-shapen body lying on a board with wheels by the side of the road. A lot of beggars like this come to the tourist section; their legs are either missing or stunted, and they get around by pushing themselves along with their hands. This old woman, her head and face covered with a scarf, took up three-quarters of the board and shared the rest with a five-year-old who held out a cup. Just as the light changed I saw a man reach down and hand the girl a 500 dong note. She tilted her head to the right and smiled, holding the note out for the old lady to see. Although they couldn't even buy bread with 500 dong, the girl was pleased. She had a child's missing-tooth smile—all gaps, giggles, and charm. Her hair was short and stuck out over her ear, and the sunlight hit the right side of her face through the veiled panel of her sunhat, I thought, "My God, she's lovely." And it was true—she was absolutely lovely. She thought, for only that moment, that 500 dong was a treasure. She was pleased, and she sat in the exhaust and dirt still smiling as I rode away.

"Who does she look like?" I wondered aloud.

I was riding along, listening to the hum of my bike tires on wet pavement, staring at the ground in front of me and talking to myself. She reminded me of someone, but I couldn't say whom. Thinking perhaps it was some charac-ter in a movie, I ran through my memory bank. Nothing. A student? No. It slipped away.

After an hour I finished circling the downtown area. I had looked into shop doorways (she seemed to be sitting in the back), peered at the signs for photo booths (was that her in the sample pictures?), I had wandered down an alley or two, and stared down into the glass cases in the souvenir shops in the tourist section. I rode my bike along the waterfront, past the Floating Hotel ("Saigon's only five-star Hotel!"), hooked around the statue of the warrior Tran Hung Dao, and headed up Hai Ba Trung Street to my house. I saw the girl at least once every week; and when I didn't see her, even when there were no other children around to jog my memory, her face rose in front of me and still I couldn't place her.

Like the sixth graders and the street children, the entire country seemed to be tugging at me in some way—pulling my heart strings, grabbing my senses, asking for my attention. My life quickly became, and stayed, peripatetic. The middle school wanted me to float around, the university didn't quite have a place for me, only the oblique title "Foreign Teacher," and on a daily basis someone tugged at my sleeve on the street and invited me to catch a glimpse of their life. The days stayed a blur of images broken up by encounters both subtle and blunt.

Teachers are overly empathetic attention banks. If we don't have answers, we have energy, empathy, and attention, and we give them freely. At the end of every day our alertness quotient is exhausted. My host family with their independent ways and busy schedules created a blissfully serene environment for me without even trying. Questions about English were handled with good humor, conversations held, movies shared, but most of the time it was quiet. It was marvelously quiet.

That night in meditation I saw the faces of my sixth grade students. They all had warm, white lights shining from their foreheads, and they called my name, craving my attention, excited and eager to please me. I saw a group of Vietnamese beggars, covered with flies, gathered outside my gate. I saw the tilting head of the young girl by the streetlight near the cathedral; I saw it again and again and I didn't know why. I saw the form of Shakyamuni sitting in meditation. I saw the giggling faces of eighth grade girls as they brought bundles of dried marigolds home to their mothers. I saw the fields that unfolded before me as my plane landed at Than San Nhut. I saw Nục sneak up the stairs from the kitchen and heard the anxious blare of motorbike horns as Saigon drivers tried to hurry forward.

Chapter Four

Our state of Dai Viet (Greater Vietnam) is indeed a country wherein culture and institutions have flourished.

—Le Lôi, fifteenth century

Bình called to me as I opened the gate, "Edie Ơi, I'm in the chicken!"

The dog went racing down the alley and stopped to pee in front of a neighbor's door. Seizing the moment, the old woman came forward quickly on the balcony overhead and swung a bucket through the air. "Ttss!" she hissed. Water slapped hard against the alley wall and Nục scrambled back to our courtyard. I couldn't quite believe what was happening, and for weeks I persisted in letting Nục out until he would simply stand at our gate and bark at the empty alley. Like some vision in a Latin American novel, the woman's head floated around on the porch of her house, her body hidden by the high wall. She sat in a wicker chair. I assumed she was just waiting. I watched the feud, not knowing who was stupider, a dog who wouldn't learn or a woman who held a grudge against a dog. I walked into the kitchen.

"You're in the kitchen, Bình? or in the chicken?"

She started laughing. "Ơi, Eeeeeeeenglish." A thought suddenly occurred to her and she shook her head. Her eyes lit up. "Edie! Can we say *at* the lav, or do we say *in* the lav?"

"In the lab," I said. "B. ba. You can say both."

"Mmmm hmmmh," she murmured dramatically, her hunch confirmed.

Of all my students, Bình, who wasn't my student at all, was the best. She was persistent and picky, never letting a new word pass her by without using it at least twice during the day.

"And then!" she said to me dramatically one day.

I tilted my head. I didn't understand what she was doing.

"We went to the market," she continued, "*and then*, I went to work, *and then*, I took a break for lunch, *and then*, we went to the field!"

She was imitating the grammar I had used the day before when giving her instruction on how to do a yoga exercise.

"It's called 'Salute to the Sun,'" I explained. "You stretch up to touch the sky," I said, "and then reach forward to touch the ground." I placed my leg back behind me. "And then you stretch one leg back, and then the other," I stretched my spine up like a cat. "And then," I said in an exhale. "And then," we muttered together as I lay myself on the ground. "And then," I wheezed a bit and pulled myself up again.

For days Bình walked around the house, raising her hands to the sky and saying, in a long drawn out voice, "and then. . . ." Like her ambition, Bình's readiness to experiment with English was refreshing. She had no problem speaking up, in any language. When I taught, one of the greatest cultural difficulties I encountered was voice. In my lessons volume, confidence, and pronunciation all come together to create "voice." It is something akin to "presence" in theater acting. At the middle school I was a teacher of pronunciation and a painfully precise listener. I forced students to isolate sounds and words *ad nauseam* and stood over them listening to their every breath. From the first day, as I moved up and down the aisles, leaning on desks, turning my head and listening for swallowed *p*'s or stray *f*'s, it became clear that in my class parroting sounds was not enough. I was not like anyone these students had ever seen. I did not float and sway like the Vietnamese female teachers in their *ao dai*. I had white skin, huge round eyes, short hair, and a funny, turned-up nose. I was an encroaching presence, with demands that sent consonants skipping back down the throats of students. Although I never intended the practice to be bullish, my face and ear were an unavoidable part of the vocal culture clash between East and West.

Vietnamese, with its rounded corners and swallowed ends, is a language so unlike English that it surprises me our two countries can speak to each other at all. The beauty of Vietnamese lies in its softness. Consonants are rarely hard, and vowels rise and fall six different ways, with a curviness that the broad, flat sounds of American English never duplicate. "Can," we say with a hard sound, like a "*k*." "Cảm," the Vietnamese say, with a soft sound, like a "*g*." American English does not have the lilt and appeal of British English, with its "ken" or "wot." We have *a*'s that are wide and nasal and *e*'s that seem to extend just a little too far. Each day I would attempt to teach this broadness to my students, and each day I realized how very strange it must sound. I couldn't understand them, and they couldn't understand me.

These young students swallowed words in English, their vowels rolled like pebbles pushed and pulled by waves.

Where, I wondered, do these mistakes come from? And what are those sounds they make? *"oc . . . anh . . . th . . . ang . . . ong . . . u . . . uo, . . . ua."* I listened. I heard not *th*, but *d*, not *c* but *g*, and the tones, of which there are six, all seem to rise out of their mouths gracefully and surely, like balloons to the sky.

"Cô! Cô, ơi! Cô!"
(Teacher!)

As a teacher, I wanted to prevent the continued mispronunciation of common sounds—*th* as *t*, *p* as *f*, and *s* in place of aspiration. To do this I made every student speak individually. Speak. Repeat. Combine. Repeat. In general, these kids were incessant talkers. Loud and vigorous, they babbled endlessly all through my lesson—all through every lesson from what I could see. They were "average kids." But the difference between their loud group chatter, their endless sociability and playing, and their silence when asked questions was spectacular.

On occasion I would have students stand in order to use them as examples, to show the meaning of the words, like "hair ribbon" or "red," or to ask them to read a word or sentence. After a month of work, I noticed that students who misbehaved in class were ordered to stand against the wall of the main passageway, removed from their peer groups and forced to stand out. In my pronunciation classes I consistently asked students to stand alone and speak. In a way my exercise was awakening a sense of shame among them. On occasion I drove them into stony silence. For me the silence was a sign of disrespect, and often, despite my best efforts, an edge entered my voice that only sealed the students' resolve. Those that tried to respond spoke softly. I edged in closer to listen. They spoke still more softly. It was a classic case of East meets West, and I continued this chase day in, day out, knowing no other way to recognize and break debilitating pronunciation habits. But I was failing somehow, and that left me frustrated.

"Grade six," a colleague said to me one day in the teachers' room, "grade six will make you feel good. They are so innocent and beautiful. I enjoy teaching them."

Middle school classes in Viet Nam are broken down into groups A, B, C, and so on, depending on student exam results. Class 6A was considered the smartest ("the most clever," my colleague said) of the students in grade six. Although, they were a bit quicker in class than the other groups, I couldn't say that they retained lessons any better than 6E, which was the lowest class. I was on a rotating schedule and 6A became a welcome break from the teeth pulling I endured on the second campus. The 6A students were not a well-behaved group, but they had endless charm and energy; they openly adored me and giggled and screeched whenever I taught them. They talked every minute of my class, playing with the sounds I made, laughing at each other's pronunciation, and imitating me at every possible opportunity.

It sounds like chaos—it was—but I have a fondness for chaos. Class 6A had all that, plus a handful of endearing elements that tickled me every time I saw them. A young boy seated in the front row laughed constantly, baring a gap between his front teeth. His hair was always cut close to his head, so that his ears stuck out, and his eyes had the indescribable light that lives in people of high energy. When I entered the classroom I often found Huy under his desk. Since one of my own favorite haunts as a child was the space under our dining room table, he immediately became a favorite. On the other side of the room was the class Casanova. Already handsome at ten, Nam was too cool to own a pencil box as the other students did. He floated around the school with his hands in his pockets and a self-satisfied grin. During recess he sat on a bench, wearing sunglasses and reading a newspaper; clearly he had big plans for himself. I liked his confidence.

Each time I was assigned 6A I would enter the classroom and my front row pal Huy was performing some feat of furniture gymnastics, crossing his eyes, then breaking into laughter. He caught sight of me, stopped and called out.

"Cô!" The room erupted. "Cô!" A student in the back stood on his chair and yelled, "Cô!" They began my class as they did every English class, by singing and screeching a rewrite of Frères Jacques.

Hello teacher, hello teacher, how are you? how are you? . . .

Another half-minute of giddiness ensued and then, in the following quiet, a strategically placed:

"Cô đẹp lắm" (Teacher is very beautiful).

I looked over to the window.

"You're pretty smooth, kid," I said to Nam.

He already knew it.

Just as in the United States, gadgetry for schoolchildren in Viet Nam is plentiful. My young students all carried book bags and elaborate pencil boxes that meant a great deal to them. It was as if with a spacecraft pencil box they could all become astronauts, with a bookbag that looked like a computer they would become geniuses in the next century. Starting class each day was a complicated ritual:

"Please take out your notebook and pen," I announced.

Snap. Flap. Click. Slap.

Rocket launchers holding pencils rose in readiness; bundles of colored pens were fumbled through; the mathematics paraphernalia was examined, played with, admired, and then returned to the box. No slide rule today, no compass or triangle ruler in Miss Edie's class, how sad. While I wrote sentences on the board, with my back turned, 6A gabbed and fidgeted. Students drew geometric figures and looked at Japanese comics.

In general they talked about any number of vital issues:

"Where did Thảo get that sports shirt?"

"Who has the latest issue of Doerman?"

"Girls can't use computers!"

I found this chatter very amusing because, according to my Vietnamese colleagues, my students were awestruck by me. They were puzzled by my strange left-handedness (children there are still raised exclusively right-handed) and my white skin (as ten-year-olds, they've rarely seen a white woman outside of films).

"They are so quiet," the teachers told me again and again, "they are so shy."

It seemed that in pronunciation exercises I frightened them. When I talked I leaned close, and when they spoke I looked directly at them. Oh, but when my back was turned. . . .

For these ten- and eleven-year-olds, English from the American "Cô" was fun; and as they wrote, staring hard at their notebooks, changing to colored pens to underline, circle, or emphasize, they showed an eagerness that was often missing in my older students. As I worked with individuals, I would praise them with "Very good!" and frequently heard a Vietnamese replica of my voice nearby, "Ooohh, vverly goood!" They weren't mocking me. They were pleased they understood. Group exercises became comical.

I would point to a word on the board and pronounce it: "Short."

"Short," they repeated.

"What does 'short' mean?" I asked.

"What does short mean?" they echoed.

"No, no . . ." I waved my hand.

"No, no . . ." they waved their hands.

The correct way to teach is to say, "Please repeat," as the tape does, then to provide an illustration of "short" and "tall." But it was early in the morning, and early in the term. "What does *x* mean?" I kept asking. (It's a tough habit for a teacher to break.)

The students eventually understood that I wanted a definition. They all looked up at me, brought both hands up beside their heads and began turning them left and right. (This is Vietnamese body language for "I don't know.") They also had a look, though, that told me I was silly. In the traditional classroom, a teacher doesn't ask questions to which she hasn't already given students the answers.

We mimed new vocabulary words, and the children squirmed around with discovery.

"Short!"

"Skirt!"

"Sky!"

"Shoe!"

"Fish!"

By the end of class I felt as though I was on a roll. I turned my back and wrote on the board: "Dish." Dirt, exhaust, and soot are everywhere in Saigon, and the windowless classroom is no exception. I could feel a sneeze coming—I turned to the class with my hand lightly touching my itchy nose.

"Dish!" I said, with my crinkling nose.

A collective "ah" rose from the group. Pairs turned to each other, enlightened, and began rubbing their noses.

"Dish."

I couldn't suppress my laughter. Mercifully, the bell rang and class ended.

"Are you going home, Miss Edie?" a woman asked in the teachers' room.

"Yes," I replied, unfolding the red scarf I always carried with me. It was a red cotton square that I rolled up and wrapped around my neck. It hung like a necklace over the loose collar of my sport shirts. I snapped it in the air and refolded it into a triangle. Lan, my colleague, looked puzzled.

"Oh," I explained, "I often wear this across my face, because of the exhaust."

Her eyes widened a bit. "Oh! The pollution, yes, I see," she said.

"And," I lowered my voice, "when I have it on people won't talk to me while I'm in traffic. They can't tell I'm a foreigner."

"Very clever!" she said brightly.

"I'll see you tomorrow, Lan," I said.

"Good-bye Miss Edie. See you tomorrow."

My ingenious plan only half worked. I certainly didn't suffer from the motorbike and truck exhaust, but my scarf was bright red and undeniably American. Riding home at the end of the morning, I was approached at a stoplight by a cap salesman. His "shop" was a line of colored baseball caps strung between two trees outside the brewery on Dien Bien Phu Street.

"Chị la người gì?" (Where are you from, Miss?)

The smell of the brewery, a sticky mixture of beer, cigarette ash, and sewage, rose in the late morning heat. I pulled off the cloth and looked at him with a grimace on my face.

"Chị biết nói tiếng Việt không?" (Do you speak Vietnamese?)

"Không," I said, using the only word I knew for "no."

The light changed and I rode on.

*   *   *

Later, in the afternoon, I went to the university and bumped into an American colleague. He was talking with Mỹ Ngọc in Vietnamese. After he finished, he asked me whether I was studying Vietnamese.

"No, no," I replied, "I'm not studying anything. I want to work on my writing. Lessons take up too much time and energy."

Nevertheless, I remembered the sound of my young students' voices that morning. "It's an awfully pretty language, though, isn't it?" I said, wandering away.

In fact, I wanted to avoid a classroom with a Vietnamese teacher in it. My eyes glazed over with the idea of all the "listen and repeat" drills they would force on me. In the classrooms set aside for Vietnamese language instruction for foreign students, I could see endless charts and drawings describing the pronunciation of Vietnamese consonants, vowels, and tones. There were often students hanging around the university cafe between their morning and afternoon classes. A French man frequented the shop in the afternoons. He spoke in French with the old woman who ran the place and leaned casually against the wall in what I took to be ennui. On Tuesday and Thursdays I saw a German woman with auburn hair. She ate two containers of yogurt, and scraped her spoon against the bottom of the plastic container like she was hypnotized. Every day four chain-smoking Korean men sat on the small stools in the crowded shop, puffed on their cigarettes, spoke English with each other, and looked strained. "They're trying to stay awake," I thought dramatically. "You won't get me in there."

My Vietnamese students had learned English in similar classrooms, however, and they were pretty good with words. My "call and response" classroom at the middle school was a continuation of language learning in Viet Nam that went back well before the twentieth century.

*   *   *

In the United States my Vietnamese students had taught me that Viet Nam measures its history in centuries, not decades. There are thousands of years of culture and adaptation in the Vietnamese universe. Some historical context is necessary for the Western teacher (and student) to maintain her sanity.

In the United States, if we think of the history of education, we think of one-room schoolhouses in small towns. We remember movie and literature images of the naive young teacher going to the rural heartland to enlighten eager minds. In Asia education is the end of a long road that leads out of the countryside into the Imperial Court. It is to move from peasantry to status, from farmer's son to Emperor's Advisor. The history of Vietnamese education is interwoven with the rise and fall of the country's imperial system and full of foreigners trying to impose new ideas. The Vietnamese came under Chinese rule in the third century. The Han brought with them much of their own empire—military, might, government administration, education, and language. Up until the seventeenth century spoken language in Viet Nam was Vietnamese, but written, "educated" language was Chinese. As political power changed through the centuries, so did the dominant language.

The imperial examination system that China imposed on the Vietnamese involved strict adherence to Confucian tradition, memorization of a canon composed of "The Classics," declaration of utmost loyalty to the emperor, and a patrilineal hierarchy. It also entailed physical migration to the North (called, even today, the seat of Vietnamese culture) and commitment to rote and ritual. It was full of things that taxed the heart and brain in unimaginable ways. Memorization was painfully extensive because students had to continue the traditions of their ancestors. The practice is written in *The Annals* of the Vietnamese Nguyễn dynasty:

> Each village chooses a virtuous scholar, who is exempted from military service to instruct the children of the village. From the age of eight, children receive primary instruction and study the *Book of Filial Piety* and *Book of Loyalty*; from the age of twelve, they study first the *Analects* of Confucius, the *Book of Maxims*, the *Invariable Middle*, and the *Great Learning*; from the age of fifteen they study first the *Book of Odes* and the *Book of History*, the *Book of Rites*, the *Book of Changes*, and the *Spring and Autumn Classics*, the schools and their commentaries.

This endless series of memorized documents reflected the Chinese empire's standard of intellectual vigor.

The eighteenth century, however, brought with it the overthrow of the Chinese. One of the tools of that effort was *Chu Nom*—a written language based on Chinese characters that reflected the sounds of spoken Vietnamese. A political tool and a source of debate, Chu Nom was used by

Vietnamese literati and politicians alike. Emperor Gia Long, seeking to consolidate his power, used Nom to gain the support of the peasantry. Although intellectual elites disdained its use in favor of classical Chinese, the more politically minded sought to develop and expand the use of Nom as part of the nation's independence. Poets and writers, while remaining traditional in other areas, loved Nom as a medium of artistic expression. By the end of the century the language reached its artistic apogee with the publication of *The Tale of Kiều* by Nguyễn Du—a written epic poem utilizing a complicated six-eight verse structure that makes it musical in recitation. The story, a drama of the life of a woman named Thúy Kiều, is canonized as the greatest work of Vietnamese literature.

On the political front, Chu Nom was not only a well-spring of creativity; it also helped the members of this movement draw strength and energy from their enemy to defeat him. I love it because the Vietnamese made a new language; they took a written language they did not ask for and used it to further their own ends.

Twentieth-century thinking, with its focus on change and modernization, assumes that these ancient models would have faded in favor of newer and more "developed" practices. The French imposition of lycees and law schools in the nineteenth and twentieth centuries was meant to abolish the Chinese-inspired Confucian education system. The French arrived and fell in love with the ritual and beauty of Asia, but grabbed hold of the population, put them in stone schoolhouses, sent them to Catholic churches, and changed the content of curriculums. I imagine those teachers, in singsong voices across the country, telling students to memorize French verbs in all their different tenses.

By the 1950s, the Vietnamese had seen numerous foreigners come and go—the Chinese, the French, and, during World War II, the Japanese military. Imagine, then, the appearance of the American advisors, so big, a student told me, "that they scared me when they walked down the street." They came not to observe, as academics and researchers do today, but to teach. What, we still cannot say. Then, in the 1960s, American soldiers arrived and taught slang to country people who adored and despised them— wild they were, but fascinating. "Hey lady, how ya doin?" rings out today all along the southern coast and the Mekong Delta, the eyes of the speaker sincere, pronunciation clear as a bell.

By the year 2000 Viet Nam will have seen its share of instructors. In all this time, mixed in with all this history, there may have been talk, among the educated, of daring to abandon old ideas and rituals, but it has never been done. As they like to brag, the Vietnamese are able to acquire elements of other cultures and adapt them. They are Chinese-influenced, French-influenced, American-influenced. They smile and agree "to try"; they memorize and learn. When I looked closely, however, I saw this: they express, write, paint, sing, and perform distinctly as Vietnamese.

In Asia, time has testified to the correctness of the Classics and the ideas they conveyed, and so students do not question them. Academic excellence is not about change; it is about celebrating and upholding tradition. While these are not practices I embrace as an instructor, I have come to respect them, partially as a result of embarrassing and frustrating encounters. Raised to appreciate pluralism, I was teaching in an environment that valued unanimity. Forced to teach using a traditional approach, I came to respect my students' stamina and energy.

*   *   *

In October, weeks after the term started, I met my university students for their course in "American Studies." On the first day, to get the curiosity factor out of the way, I chatted with them. The first few minutes were full of awkward exchanges and questions. Students were eager to know whether I owned a car, and knew how to drive. They giggled and asked whether I had a boyfriend.

"Yes, yes, no," I said bluntly.

I don't have much patience for these questions, asked of me everywhere I go in Asia. A beautiful young woman in the front raised her hand.

"Do you like Michael Bolton?" she asked.

"Michael Bolton?" I repeated.

She had dark eyes and beautiful, fine hair. She didn't wear make-up, but her eyelashes seemed so long as to be false. There was a small mole by her lip, round and perfectly placed.

"Or Mariah Carey?" she continued. "They're blues singers." She pushed her hair back off her shoulder.

"Oh. Um, well, actually, no, they're not blues singers, they're pop singers."

She pressed her lips together lightly while I talked, and stared openly at me, looking at my clothes and watching the way I held myself.

"Can you tell me the difference between blues and jazz?" she replied.

She was asking me questions, but ignoring my answers. Her classmates watched silently as our pseudo-conversation continued.

"Actually," I said with a laugh, "I can't explain the difference. But I know they were both created in African-American culture."

"Do you like Michael Jackson?" She began to play with her hair.

I smiled. I liked her quizzing and showing off. The other students looked quietly at their hands. Some listened carefully, equally curious. Ngọc, who had to work with me in the department office and in the classroom, stared at her hands, overcome with shame at her classmate's brash behavior. Her darker, thicker hair, was pulled back and lay neatly between her shoulders.

"No," I answered the student, dismissively. Then I looked up at the class. "I can't teach you about popular American culture. I don't really know about it."

This announcement was very calculated on my part. Saigon is full of pirated movies and magazines from the United States. These students probably knew more about those topics than I did.

"What else would you like to study?" I opened my arms and gestured the question to the whole group.

"American history," someone said.

A soft wave of agreement ran quickly through the class, and it was decided. I would teach U.S. history.

This would not be an easy task. I had brought no history teaching materials, and the only resources available in the English Department were moldy texts left behind from the U.S. State Department. Of course, they wanted to know about popular culture, but I wondered what they had been taught. I discovered they knew about the American Revolution, and they had read the Declaration of Independence. With previous teachers from the United States they had read contemporary American plays. In bookstores in the city I noticed that Emily Dickinson had been translated into Vietnamese, as had Walt Whitman. This was how I discovered Vietnamese educators had included the culture of the United States in their curriculums.

I wanted to know what most of my students were thinking. I thought many of them would have friends or relatives who lived in the United States. Most of them were exposed to news, rumors and stories about American life. What did they think the place was like? Where did they think it came from? What series of events shaped it?

"Everyone take out a notebook and pen," I said. "Here is your assignment. You have to write about the United States. Begin your writing with this phrase, 'If I close my eyes and imagine America, this is what I see.'"

They tilted their heads. I repeated the assignment. Imagine America.

"Start with ten minutes of writing right now."

We all sat down to write. I opened my notebook. For a moment I tried to place myself in their shoes, then I adapted the assignment: "If I closed my eyes and imagined Viet Nam . . ."

Since I arrived, I had been learning bit by bit about the earth that my students came from, and the ideas, passions, discipline, and hunger that helped them grow; but I couldn't do this assignment. The realization came to me quickly. I stared at my paper, looked at my class of students writing, then out the door to the yard of the university. Silver gray leaves in a shape I had never seen were falling in late morning mist. Voices were floating across nearby rooms, and bicycles made a gritty sound as they were being wheeled through gravel to the parking lot.

During the summer before I left home, I had gone to a Harvard University library to find some reading materials on Viet Nam that would not be about the American War. I went into the stacks, not really sure what I was looking for. For classification purposes Viet Nam as a subject is mixed in with both the Asia and Southeast Asia materials.

I looked up and down the stacks. These books were not handled often, and they had none of the sloppiness that comes with perpetual picking up and replacing. I tapped the spines and whispered the titles.

"Viet Nam . . . War in . . . Siege at . . . Tet . . . Peasant Politics . . ."

I curled my lip. "Is that it? Geez, did these things happen in a vacuum?"

Further down the shelf, the books referred to as cultural materials were the ones with ill-fitting covers and poor type. The publication dates were embarrassingly erratic—1968, 1973, 1985—and the books were written in stiff government voices and poorly edited prose. They were located on the bottom shelf of a set of tall stacks, and I had to sit on the floor to read them. The spines had stiffened in leaning postures, and they stood like kinked sleepers, awoken and in need of a slow, gentle stretch. Most were published by small presses, a few by the authors themselves (all Vietnamese). I cringed over the disrespect heaped on them by American readers. It wasn't that they were damaged; it was that they were ignored.

A Vietnamese man who started his own publishing house had written a book on traditional culture in flowery, immature English. A 1956 U.S. State Department official wrote a *very* long report in extraordinarily dull language on Vietnamese history. The translations of poetry and prose were awkward, to me a terrible sign of disrespect. I felt uninspired and disheartened. My Vietnamese students were so lovely and interesting; surely they came from a place that was as beautiful and intriguing as their personalities?

Not too long afterwards, I told a friend about my search.

"Oh, I have something on my bookshelf. Come by the office and have a look," he offered.

He gave me a collection of Vietnamese poetry in translation that was published by Alfred A. Knopf in 1975. It covered one thousand years and was, the translator noted, "a modest introduction." I looked inside the cover. On the first page, DISCARD was stamped in big black type by the previous owner, a small town library; my friend had bought it at a yard sale for a quarter.

Sitting in Viet Nam and realizing the historical breach that lay between me and my students shocked me into a harsh and sudden anger. Before I left the United States I had given up learning about Viet Nam. I rationalized this decision by saying I wanted "no preconceived notions." In a way, that was my determination. But how much *could* I have known before then?

I got up from my desk to walk outside. I leaned against the wall and tried to calm down by counting my breaths. Hundreds of contradictory voices ran through my head. There was one that told me I made a conscious choice; another said I had only news photographs and school curriculums to lead me; a third pointed out that I lived in the most privileged but isolated country in the world. There was a voice that claimed that this vacuum I lived in was created by the CIA; there was one that said I couldn't have known. ("You can't know everything," it reassured me.) Still another voice said I should have known, after all I live in the United States, where access to information is, by law, a right.

All the voices on paper of the Vietnamese students I had taught at home were haunting me as well.

"We have fought invaders for thousands of years," they wrote.

"We have long history," they said. "There are many beautiful folk tales and folk songs from my country." They told me about houses and weddings and Tet, but most of the time I only saw broken English.

I heard another voice that cried in grief over the holes in my life. I wished I could have been a teenager who looked at pictures of women and men in traditional Vietnamese dress, or who ran her hands over the weaving of montagnard tribes. I wished someone had told me that Vietnamese is a pretty language, that it is ancient and musical, or that this is a culture that traces its origin to a myth of the meeting of two gods.

History had determined that I had no mental map with which to imagine this country. I grew from adolescence to adulthood in the 1970s, when we "just didn't talk about" Viet Nam. Americans shrug over this national amnesia when I bring it up.

"Yeah, so?" they say.

In contrast, my tenth grade students in Viet Nam were studying English books with poems by Langston Hughes. Two Australian women I had recently met were teaching a middle school English curriculum that covered major Western authors. My university students were fluent in my native language before the age of twenty. I thought the absurd ideas running through my head meant everything and nothing at the same time. I wanted to dismiss them, but I couldn't. The affront was overwhelming. If there wasn't a destructive, complicit silence in American society about Viet Nam, why did I burn with such frustration and shame?

Standing in the doorway, I didn't know who didn't tell me what when. I didn't know when I wasn't listening or when people wouldn't allow me to ask questions about this place. In such a short time blood had rushed up to my head in fury, voices spun around inside me and my hands shook with something undefinable. I don't know who I was angry at.

Ten minutes had passed; I had to calm down. It was late in the morning and I looked up at the sky and made another mental note to write home about Saigon. "During the rainy season the air gets thick all through the morning until, just after lunch, the sky bursts open and it pours for an hour or two. Until that rain the air smells strongly of pollen and flowers." I smiled as the sentences formed and reformed in my head. Leaning against the dusty classroom building, I watched silver gray leaves fall like coins to the ground. I remembered early winter snows in New England with their romance and mildness and wondered whether my students could imagine snow; I wanted to help them try. But the realization was still running through my mind, and I could feel a headache growing. Jaw tense, hands still shaking, I returned to my desk, riddled with a wordless anger. After a clumsy attempt at conversation, I collected the papers and ended the class.

That was a very fruitful lesson. The next afternoon I reviewed the essays in my room during the siesta. The house was quiet as the rain began. Thảo lay downstairs in his wooden lounge chair. I heard a click as he folded it back, then the sound of the dog walking over and settling next to him. Bình lay in the front room, gossiping with her sisters who had come over for lunch. My fan turned softly, spinning and respinning the smells of garlic, rice, and greens that rose up from the kitchen.

I read my students essays about skyscrapers and space in America. One described it as, "A country so large you cannot imagine"; another asked questions about Mariah Carey and Michael Bolton, and many of them wondered could I explain jazz and blues? Some thought it must be "like heaven" in the United States, but one student wrote about how proud she is to be Vietnamese and wasn't this fascination with things American irritating? "Anyway," she wrote, "I realize that America has an irresistible power on ourselves, after threatening us, it attracts many Vietnamese to rush into it—like mayflies to lights."

I am listening to the rain on the roof outside my window and realize my students know more about the United States than I do about Viet Nam. There are 4,000 years of history, music, literature, and language in this place; the realization fills me with contradictory feelings. I am happy, angry, hungry, and overwhelmed. I am awake.

Chapter Five

"You see," my colleague Phương Thiên said to me, after a morning of schmoozing with business people and officials, "you see how the Vietnamese must do things?"

She was referring to the circles we had just finished running in, the errands, the conversations, the cups of tea, the chitchat, and friendliness I sat through while she cultivated her good relations. There was no real business that could be referred to as "pressing," but I came to realize that this cultivation was vital if she wanted to get things done in the future.

"Anh, ơi!" she said to a man as we waited on her motorbike at a stoplight. I listened while they spoke rapidly; then she introduced us.

"Edie," she said, talking over her shoulder, "this is Hồng. He's a journalist."

"Hi," I said.

"Hi."

"Hồng is an investigator," explained Thiên. She laughed softly and added, "He ferrets out corrupt officials, you know?" she added, flirtatiously.

The light changed and we said goodbye.

"You know 'em on all sides, eh, Phương Thiên?" I teased her.

Thiên was one of the few Vietnamese women I could talk to in the same way I talked to my friends back home. Although she was vice-dean of the English department, I enjoyed talking fast and loose with her about Viet Nam and the United States, gossiping about the English department, and trading career boasts. She wore Western-style tailored suits, make-up, and large, showy earrings, and drove a Honda Dream (the high-end motorbike). She dropped names often and flirted mercilessly with men. The Vietnamese considered her too ambitious, and Western women I knew didn't trust her, but Western men often fell for her hook, line, and sinker.

"I'm sorry I had to make you wait at that office," she apologized, picking up the conversation again, "but he owns an import/export business, you know?"

"I understand completely," I said over her shoulder. "Listen, Phương Thiên, I need to go to the post office. Can you drop me off?"

"Sure, no problem," she said.

I laughed at her. She used American-English vernacular with excellent timing and intonation. She had a master's degree from a university in Great Britain, but there wasn't a trace of British accent in her voice. I tried to imagine how many hours she must have spent listening to the details of everyday English coming out of the mouths of Americans. We pulled up to the post office and I hopped off the back of the motorbike.

"Hey, lady—" the freckle-faced girl with stringy hair began.

"Sorry kid," I cut her off.

"See you, Phương Thiên," I said.

"See you," she said as she drove away.

A tourist van pulled up and the girl ran over to show her postcards as the group got out.

The Central Post Office of Saigon was located two blocks from my house. Sitting opposite St. Mary's Cathedral, it was an ornate relic from the days of French colonialism. The building saw a fair amount of traffic at any given hour—creating a mass of street children, cyclo drivers, and lottery ticket sellers in the front lot. The office was nearly always full, with operating hours from 7 A.M. unto 10 P.M. Entering through the front doorway, with its gracious glass canopy and tiled step, always brought an initial feeling of relief from the heat; but the bustle soon prevailed, and the place became as hot and irritating as a crowded market. Eight glass booths on each wall were available for making long distance calls. A large U-shaped marble counter took up most of the room and behind it sat postal workers who were, like workers everywhere, bored and overworked by turns. The room had a relatively sociable air about it, and was subject to a continuous stream of Vietnamese and foreigners sending faxes and telegrams, waiting for phone service, or sitting at tables addressing letters for posting.

In Viet Nam the prices for postage and communication are excessively high. This inflation adds to the atmosphere and amid the multilingual conversation could be heard the universal grumbling that comes with exorbitant prices. Without the slightest knowledge of French, German, or Vietnamese, you could easily find yourself nodding in pained agreement as you sealed and addressed your letters. Eventually I found the cost burdensome, and I began mailing postcards in lieu of letters.

On any given day there were crowds (not lines) of people at the various windows, buying stamps and sending faxes or telegrams. At one window two clerks handled domestic mail and two others international mail. There was a counter with four clerks for phone calls; and for faxes, a group of three or four women rotated shifts, taking your fax, faxing it to another post office ("central fax office," the clerk told me one day), where it was then faxed to its destination. For such a well-staffed place people were constantly in a hurry for service, and there never seemed to be enough to go around. Customers pushed, cut in front, and asked for help as though they were the hungry asking for food. This is a peculiar habit that I also found in China. The Vietnamese complain about this tendency, but there is no clear explanation for it in a society that considers polite behavior to be one of the cornerstones of morality. I think that it is desperate behavior based in poverty and isolation. It seems that the Vietnamese are hungry for news from the rest of the world.

A week after the American Thanksgiving holiday I was overcome with an urge to call home. I was spending close to eight dollars a week on letters and feeling little satisfaction. Thảo and Bình had a phone with which I could receive international calls, but not make them. I was told by a colleague that phone calls to the United States cost approximately five dollars a minute. For an entire week I debated and rationalized the expense. I didn't care about the shouting and gaps, and the awkward phrases that make up international calls. I simply wanted to hear a familiar voice.

"No," I told myself as I rode home from university, "that price is insane."

I sat at a stoplight and missed my family. My brother and his wife were having a second child and the baby was due any day. My father, who never wrote, would be looking down into another baby basket, teasing, humming, and talking to the baby as if it were an adult. My mother, who sometimes wrote, would send me pictures with cryptic notes like, "Another member of the tribe!"

"Call collect," I said to myself.

Call collect! I turned my bike around and pedaled hard back to the post office. It was a fabulous idea that turned into a surreal experience. The Quiet American strolls into the cool interior, walks up to the marble counter, smiles at the clerk and says:

"Hi! I would like to place a collect call to the United States."

"No," the woman in the yellow *áo dài* replied, "no collect calls."

It was a blunt response, born, perhaps, of her low level of English, perhaps of the pressure of crowds waiting to use only sixteen phones. Since this was my first time trying to do this, I was certain she misunderstood. I smiled and rephrased the request.

"No, you see, they will pay in America."

I had a smarmy tone of voice, as if I were introducing her to a new concept. It wasn't intentional, but something didn't make sense. She caught me off-guard. She ignored the aesthetics-of-grace rule I had become accustomed to. I assumed it was because we were in a government office.

"No. No collect calls for foreigners, Vietnamese only."

"You don't understand," I pressed, "they'll pay. In the United States. They'll pay."

"No," she said, stiffly.

A man pushed his way in front of me. I raised my voice to him because I was angry at her.

"Hey!" I exclaimed, as I elbowed past. "Let me get this straight!" I said loudly. "If I am a Vietnamese, I can make a collect call, but if I am a foreigner, I cannot?" I stretched my arms across the marble counter in demand of space.

"Yes," she answered curtly.

"Only Vietnamese can make a collect call?" I insisted.

"Yes."

The man elbowed past me again. By now I wanted someone to explain this to me. I wanted to say, "Explain this to me like I'm six years old." But the woman in the yellow *áo dài* was ignoring me by this point; and even if she weren't, she wouldn't tell me what she knows. It is that lack of explanation that pains the foreigner so much. She wasn't interested in saying, "Our phones don't work that way," "U.S. embargo," anything that would fill in the gaps in her cryptic reply. She continued to go about her business, ignoring me and the plea for help I tried to express with my face. I felt as though I was living a psychotic version of Lily Tomlin's AT&T operator. "We don't care, we don't have to. We're the phone company."

I left. Surely there was an explanation. I asked Bình to call the phone company and find out how to make a collect call. She called and asked.

"You just go to the post office and tell them you want to make a collect call," she told me, hanging up the phone.

In the afternoon I returned. I was certain I had come across a stubborn office hack who simply had to be shown the error of her ways.

"Hi. I'd like to make a collect call," I said with a smile, as if she wouldn't remember me, as if the morning were simply a crowded dream.

"No collect calls." There it was again, a steely voice in a silk outfit. I was jolted awake. With great determination I began my reply, "The operator said . . ."

"No collect calls," she cut me off.

Irritated, I took a breath and sighed heavily.

"Why?" I asked. (This is an infuriating question in a government office.)

"No collect calls for foreigners! For Vietnamese only!"

Her voice was high-pitched, like a screech. She looked mean. My lips were pursed. I was glaring. I decided to try being direct.

"The woman on the phone said," I began.

"No!"

I was pushing where I shouldn't push. I was close to looking her in the eye and telling her she's *wrong*. I raised my voice and banged the counter.

"BUT WHY?"

In response, she tightened her jaw.

One of us is being very rude.

She was right, of course. Bình hadn't received wrong information—it's just that she is Vietnamese. When she called, she asked the operator, "How do you make a collect call?" and the woman replied, "Just go and tell them you want to call collect!"

For any number of reasons there were two sets of rules for phone calls in Viet Nam in 1993. Only Vietnamese made collect calls because the phone company could track them down from the form they filled out before the call was placed. They showed their house card, identifying them as residents, and listed their address in case the phone call was not paid for overseas. The government could find them and present the bill if it went unpaid. On the other hand, as a foreigner I had no permanent address in Viet Nam, and if the call went unpaid for on the other end, then no one could collect from me. Certainly, the economic embargo imposed by my government had a heavy hand in the situation, but I didn't know, or care, how. The poverty of infrastructure in Viet Nam meant they just didn't have the technology to efficiently handle international phone lines. However, it felt like the tediousness of the process, the regulation, and the politics involved made the red tape have two sticky sides, and the more you tried to cut through it, the more entangled you got. All I really knew was that our governments made the process of simply talking to one another complicated, expensive, and difficult. If I had been able to make a phone call that day, I'm not sure I would have known what to say by the time it went through.

In Viet Nam this bureaucratic hassle is another daily obstacle for the local population. Almost all my Vietnamese colleagues had family in the United States. Many of them told me they couldn't afford the price of calls, and most couldn't place collect calls because of the cost incurred by family on the other end. Such small obstacles on a daily basis mount up and become an infinite amount of difficulties that yield an attitude of defeat. It is easy to be defeated by a faceless, complex maze, a "system." When letters, calls, communication in general becomes too much trouble, they simply stop. Whatever the technical reasons, my Vietnamese friends had little communication with their relatives abroad. It is one thing for us to lose touch with family because we forget, or are busy. It is another to not be able to call or afford postage. It is another thing entirely.

By the end of the day I hated everything. I hated the steely voiced woman in the colorful *áo dài*. I hated the men who stepped in front of me. I hated the marble counter and the forms required for placing a call. I hated the crowds sitting on benches waiting, the bang of the phone booth doors. I hated the way voices echoed from behind the glass doors of the booths, and the sound of the voice that spoke over the PA system to tell people their calls were going through. I hated missing my family, and I especially hated anything that prevented me from reaching them.

✳ ✳ ✳

The next morning I was assigned to teach class 8A at the middle school. In the front row a young boy was talking out of turn all through the lesson. He shouted out Vietnamese words and phrases when students were quiet.

"Chị, tôi không biết! Không biết tiếng Anh." (I don't know, Miss! I don't know English!)

In response, I ignored him. When this tactic failed, I tried calling on him. He became animated when we interacted, shaking his hand dramatically, shrugging and telling me he didn't know the answer. His friends adored him. I glared and came down heavy.

"Vocabulary," I said, "page 62. Park. Please repeat, 'Park.' "

"Puck."

"k, ark, park." I said to him.

"Puck."

"OK." I gave up.

I moved across the room to other students. The class began to murmur, as it always did when I worked with individual students. After a minute I heard a voice call out:

"PUCK! PUCK OOH!"

The class went silent. I turned to find the source. Everyone looked at their hands. It all seemed silly and stupid, then it dawned on me. *Puck ooh!* was the vulgar expression ("fuck") they heard in American movies. For a moment I cringed with shame, realizing what part of my culture the Vietnamese were importing. Genuinely irritated by the disruption, I wanted to be angry, but the moment passed and the sound was too funny for me to keep a straight face. I imagined them repeating it to each other on the playground. Here was a "p" they didn't swallow, but spat out with excitement. I could almost hear them whispering, "puck, puck, puck."

"It's *puck*," someone would say, the information verified by an older sibling.

"Puck iss!"

"Puck oss!" "Puck ooh!"

I put my hand to my mouth and walked to the chalkboard. With my back to the class I stood still, and after a breath began erasing the board.

"Close your books," I announced over my shoulder.

It was amusing, but also exhausting. I was tired, and my students were so terribly bothersome.

That afternoon Ngọc approached me with a slip of paper.

"Miss Edie, a package has arrived for you."

"Oh!" I said, "great, where is it?"

She handed me the paper. "You have to pick it up at the post office package office. It is on Hai Ba Trung Street, behind the central post office."

The package office at 119 Hai Ba Trung Street was a warehouse attached to the back of the post office, its gray drabness in marked contrast to the yellow and white of the post office itself. Just inside the door was a stone counter topped by iron railing with small windows for the clerks. Behind the counter was a long, wide room filled with tables manned by slow-moving personnel. The Vietnamese sat on rows of benches at the front waiting to have their ticket number called so that they could pick up their packages. Whoever's number was called would walk behind the counter and fill out two forms (which had to be paid for), approach another counter, receive the package, fill out another form detailing the contents, and then hand the package over to an inspector, who opened it, rifled through it, then asked for a tax on the goods.

I ignored the front line, walked behind the first counter, smiled at a young woman with short hair sitting at a desk, and approached another one behind a second counter. She had a round face and a small mouth, and she looked bored. I handed her my ticket.

She pointed at the first young woman.

I pointed also, "There?"

She nodded.

I gave her my ticket again "She told me to come here," I said.

She pointed to the table again. "Form," she said.

I walked over to the first woman, picked up a form, and walked away.

"Chị, ơi" (Miss).

I turned.

"Hai nghìn đong" she said, waiving a 2,000 đong bill in my face.

"I gotta pay for it?" I asked. "tsk." I handed her the money.

Walking and filling out the form, I approached the second counter again.

"I don't know vat is in the packej," a German woman said to the inspector, "tsk."

I smiled at the woman behind the counter.

"Hi," I said, in an excessively cheery voice, "I have to get a package!"

She took my ticket and form and walked into a back room.

For a moment I was thrilled. I had done it. I hadn't exactly stormed the office demanding my package, but I had managed to exploit my foreignness enough to get me past the initial wait outside the front counter. Since I was a foreigner, this strange behavior was expected of me in everyday situations. People either didn't notice or didn't care that I hadn't followed the correct procedure. I leaned across the table as the clerk came out of the back room, ready to receive my package as if it were a child. She put it in a pile. My head fell and I sighed.

She approached the table again, grabbed a form, and called out a number. I watched, leaning forward so that she would know I wouldn't go away. She ignored me. I gave in and stepped back. An old man came forward and gave her his ticket and form. She gave him a customs declaration to fill out, then lifted a suitcase onto the table, slid it across to the inspector, and called another number.

The old man was from the countryside. His hands were edged with white calluses and his eyes glassy. He wore a string for a belt, dusty sneakers, and a baseball cap that he quickly removed as the inspector opened the suitcase. A large white label was taped on the side with the address written out; the seams were sealed with thick gray electrical tape. It had been mailed from Texas. The inspector took a razor, cut the tape, and opened the suitcase.

"Oh my God," I mumbled, as the man stared at the ground.

It was only a package, but the man was being treated like it was search and seizure. Paper fell out onto the table. Inside, under tissue paper, cloth, and more tape, were countless household items and gifts—cups and glasses, shampoos and creams, a doll, and a set of glass figurines wrapped tightly in paper and tape. The inspector took out each piece one by one and cut off the paper.

"There's no reason for this," I mumbled to no one in particular.

The old man looked at the ceiling. After a minute the table was covered with the contents of his package, the floor around it littered with tissue paper. When the search was done he reached into his pocket for money to pay the duty. The inspector pushed the entire mess at him and told him to repackage it. My face flushed with anger.

The round-faced woman called my number. I walked over to her table and signed my name to a form. She slid the envelope across to the inspection table.

"It's a gift," I said, before the man could ask.

He cut open the package and pulled out a sweater. I started laughing.

"My mother doesn't know I live in the tropics," I said to him.

He pulled out an envelope.

"It's just a Christmas card, buddy," I snapped.

He handed it back to me unopened. I paid the duty, signed the form, threw the pen across the table at him, and turned to leave. He lit a cigarette.

As my patience was running out with the post office, I retreated down the alley to my house, then into my room. I laughed at myself as I saw an open book of Vietnamese poetry on my desk. The sixteenth-century poet Nguyễn Bình Khiêm advised me: "Come, come, not everyone is a Buddha! If you must deal with man: Patience. With yourself: Detachment, as a clear pool reflects the moon." It may be how Vietnamese cope with the struggles of daily life, but I don't know. For a time I tried to find the post office amusing. There are copious numbers of workers, a silly unnecessary seriousness about the tasks at hand, and there are always crowds of people waiting for service and talking. But during that week I mumbled the vague phrase, "the system," over and over. I found everything invasive and oppressive.

I sat at my desk, and ran my hand over the white sweater my mother had sent. I opened the card.

"We'll miss you . . . Shades of 1968 . . . Merry Christmas, Love, Mother."

A photo fell onto my lap. It was a picture of me in front of the Christmas tree.

I am five years old, holding a doll and smiling. My neck tilts back and I smile a holiday smile, my face full of delight. I'm missing teeth, my short hair is messy, my eyes sparkle with the idea of something new. . . . "My God, she's lovely." She was absolutely lovely. She thought, for only that moment, that 500 đong was a treasure. She was pleased, and she sat in the exhaust and dirt still smiling as I rode away.

It was the face on the girl outside the cathedral. It was naive and simple, undeveloped, unreal. I dropped the photo and started crying. Khiêm's refrain continued: "We are absurd petals in a puff of wind, drifting over a temporary and indifferent world."

All in all it was a terrible week. My eighth grade students were getting rebellious and my university students weren't showing up for class. It ended with this introduction to the package office. I was furious and humiliated when my Christmas gift was opened in front of a chain-smoking man who wouldn't look at me except to say, "Sign," and "Pay tax."

In short, it was time for a trip.

*   *   *

Being affiliated with organizations in Viet Nam means you do not simply work for them, but are a "foreign guest." This makes you someone they have to care for and entertain. Trips and excursions were a favorite form of entertainment. At the end of that terrible week in November the middle school invited me to chaperon an eighth grade excursion to Dalat, a vacation resort. It is a favorite travel destination among the Vietnamese. In general, I shied away from group excursions, unable to bear the mentality that they entailed—everyone traveled, played, and ate together. I enjoy too much wandering off alone or with a single friend, and I haven't got the patience necessary to follow along with a crowd.

"Should I go?" I wondered at breakfast.

"Dalat is beautiful!" Bình said, enthusiastically.

"Yes," Thảo said, definitively, "Dalat is very beautiful. There are many farms, and flowers."

And so, the trip was set for Thursday. I rolled out of bed early and walked over to the school to board the van.

"Miss Edie," the school director asked, through Lam, "do you have a sweater? The highlands are very cold."

"Yes," I said, smiling.

He nodded and told me I was very clever, then he put the sweater he brought with him back in his bag. The driver put Michael Jackson in the tape player, and we waved goodbye, rolled out of the city tapping our feet and weaving in and out of rush-hour traffic.

Leaving Saigon is a little like visiting another country. There is no place in Viet Nam as wealthy, fast-paced, or developed as Thành-phố Ho Chi Minh, so the countryside, beautiful as it is, is a shock after the abundance, the waste even, of much of the city. Viet Nam's poverty comes rushing at you, overwhelming the charm of its checkerboard hillsides and the richness of its flower gardens. It's slow pace, the tranquility of farming life, is viewed through the doorways of straw huts or wooden shacks. This picture is not one of total despair, but it is in sharp contrast to the fancy clothes and crowded shops that make up life in Saigon.

Mr. Lam was my translator for the weekend. He was the only English speaker among the supervisors attending and it was his duty to look after me. It was a good opportunity for him, he said, since he always wants to practice his English. Lam had the impressive and amusing skills of the self-taught, but his determination was strong and his efforts endearing. Most of the time I lived in an audiotape world with him, answering questions and reanswering them according to the pattern he studied. When he was around me he often had his hand to his chin in a look of fierce concentration then, eyes lighting up, he found the word or idea he was searching for and spoke. This was not something that happened only when he spoke English, but with English speakers he was especially nervous and the habit was pronounced. He anticipated your responses with eagerness and anything outside his expectations brought on chaos. We spoke only business each day and he liked the confines of those comments, but sometimes his face betrayed a crushing feeling of defeat as I failed to reply according to what he rehearsed. Each morning I was the recipient of any number of textbook inquiries or comments:

"The weather is quite fine today!"

"The students are very happy!"

"You look rather pale. Are you well?"

For two weeks I looked "rather pale." I began to worry that I was losing weight, until one day I discovered him staring at the *Ship or Sheep?* textbook trying to differentiate the sound of "pale" and "peel."

"You look rather pale, are you well?" the textbook said.

Whenever we finished our numerous two-sentence conversations, Mr. Lam would laugh, "Ah-ha-ha-ha," making that sound so exactly and so clearly that I thought someone must have told him once that that's what people do when they laugh and he rehearsed it until he got it right. He laughed out of nervousness, but it sounded like delight. It was as if he wanted to shout out, "I'm speaking English!"

"How are you, Mr. Lam?"

"I'm fine, thanks. Ah-ha-ha-ha."

I liked Mr. Lam. I liked his comical physique, his hysterical concern, and his country-boy mannerisms. He was not slick like so many men I met in Saigon; he appeared clumsy, simple-minded, and unnecessarily polite. My modern sensibility was amused by him. Ah-ha-ha-ha.

But look closer. Mr. Lam has his story: He came to the city to make a life for himself, and he worked hard. He taught himself and his children English, and he said he would continue to work at it until he got a job as a grade school teacher. It was easy to meet men like him in Viet Nam—his form was excellent but his meaning was not clear, so I was challenged, by both his language and his person, to look beyond the simple structures to find meaning and resonance.

Lam was the first person I met who talked to me about the war with the United States.

"Years ago, the war with USA, dropped many bombs here," he said, as we left the confines of the city. He put his hand to the window and pointed in the direction of Cu Chi.

Underneath its simplicity the gesture struck me as extraordinarily benevolent. I think he believed I didn't know this was our common ground. A moment later he told me, with equal warmth "We don't hate Americans, we hate war." But as he talked about it I could see the wheels spinning in his head, processing social change, "we drove them out, now we want them to come back." Ah-ha-ha-ha.

It's difficult to describe the range of incidents I had with Mr. Lam. At one point, I asked him for the time; he held up his wrist, stared at it, thought intently, and then said, with great seriousness: "I don't have a watch on." Another moment we were riding through a small town and passed a Catholic church; he again placed his index finger on the window:

"A Catholic church."

"I see," I replied.

"You are Catholic?"

I paused before replying. "Yes," I answered, with hesitation. (In a hierarchical culture it is easier to say yes than to explain why I would leave the religion my parents gave me.) Lam tilted his head and examined me. Catholicism isn't a novelty in Viet Nam, but I'm still not sure he'd ever met a Christian. He nodded his head, as if absorbing the information.

"Are you?" I asked him.

"No," he said, "I am *Bosom*."

"Buddhist?" I corrected.

"Buddhist. Buddhist! Ah-ha-ha-ha."

He tapped his forehead and made a mental note of the pronunciation. We drove another hour, passing, by turn, through towns with churches and temples and hillsides with statues of Jesus and Shakyamuni. We pulled into a truck stop and everyone poured out of the van, the children crowded together in a huddle that allowed them to easily shun beggars. I milled around among the supervisors. Mr. Lam came bouncing up a moment later.

"Miss Edie, would you like to wash . . . oorr (he drew out the 'or' in practice), to have something to eat?"

"Well, do they have any bread?" I asked.

"You want to use the lavatory?" (He was anticipating my reply again.)

"No, I just want some bread."

"I'm sorry?" he asked.

"I want some bread," I tried to clarify.

He took my hand and looked very serious.

"Oh," He scanned the truck stop anxiously, "you want to pray?" He was looking around for one of the giant Jesus shrines that dot the countryside. "You want to pray?"

"No, no. I . . ." I ended up following everyone to the lavatory and ordering whatever they ordered.

Viet Nam's southern highlands are made up of windy, narrow roads filled with the smoky, grassy smell of drying tobacco, coffee, and burning hay. The lives of country people close to the main roads, and Highway One, are now overwhelmed by two modern-day constants: bundles of crops, and trucks. Zooming through streets, our horn blaring ("Traffic safety," Lam explained), we weaved around families on bikes, on foot, on Hondas, and piled into motorized wagons, all moving their crops to market. Tobacco lay on bamboo trays drying in the sunlight and children stooped to gather rice on the side of the road. The peasant life of the Vietnamese farmer, under its romantic facade, does not lure me. I love its slow rhythms, but recognize too strongly the arduousness that prompted this poetic refrain:

> Ai ơi bưng bát com đầy,
> Dẻo thơm, một hột đắng cay muôn phần

"Whoever holds in his hands a bowl full of rice, I would like him to know how much pain and effort each one of those tender and odorous grains cost me."

But even in the harsh light of poverty there is a rhythm to this life, as if it were all dictated by an unseen metronome. Lifting and carrying was done with a soft, continuous bounce, and water, thrown by hand from buckets in quick, full spurts, fell over crops. *One and two and . . .*

A market economy means country life today is surrounded by the frantic rush of commerce, which sweeps into town and carries off fruit, tobacco, and coffee in a cloud of dirt. The trucks on Highway One—one of the few paved "highways" in the nation—run through towns at reckless speeds, stopping on occasion, buying and selling, picking up and dropping off. Thatched homes in rural towns have given way to rebuilt housing complexes, and television antennae rise in the sky like tin forests. In homes children gather together in front of computers to play video games and watch movies. But the swing and rhythm continue underneath all these less romantic elements—in the sloping shoulders working rice fields, in the bounce of an old woman carrying crops, or the slow, mysterious gait of a young woman with a cotton-covered bundle on her head.

I was amused by the response my students made to these rural scenes. These villages and towns, with farmers, and people from some of the sixty-odd hill tribes, were a different world from their city homes. For them, Dalat is a wealth of scenic spots and pretty things, but it was also full of people who are poor. The students walked to market carrying bundles of dried marigolds and boxes of strawberries, they used their Japanese cameras to picture themselves in mountainside rose gardens, and, like most of us, they fell to silence as the migrant poor, with their old clothes and callused hands, presented themselves in the middle of it all. Beggars called them "Miss" and "Sir," deferring to increasingly apparent class differences, and the kids' discomfort was so familiar to me, such a clash of cultures, that I ached for them in their city-bred ignorance.

*   *   *

But they spent most of the day in the lighthearted, carefree play of school-children on a field trip.

"Teacher! Miss!" The kids called to me at tourist sites. They waved cameras; I stood in front of flower gardens and Mickey Mouse statues posing for photos.

"Are you having fun?" I asked a young girl by a rosebush.

She shifted her weight from foot to foot, and began hyperventilating.

"Yes," she quivered.

"Good!" I replied.

"Good!" she said.

"Miss Edie!" I heard a boy's voice call; I turned around to find him.

Đường, from grade nine, was hanging from the bus window with his camera. I posed with a big smile; he snapped the picture, laughing.

"Would . . . you . . . like . . . some . . ." a student said, not finishing the sentence, but gesturing with a bag of sunflower seeds.

"No, thank you," I said.

"No, thank you," she repeated.

As the sun rose higher, my mouth began to hurt from smiling for pictures, and I was beginning to get a headache.

"Miss Edie," Mr. Lam called over a megaphone, "it is time for lunch."

We returned to the hostel to find hot soup waiting for us in the dining room.

"Oh, asparagus," I said with a smile, "and cauliflower. I like vegetables," I said, turning to Lam.

"Like vegetables, ah-ha-ha-ha."

The kids swarmed in around the tables, and began playing with the chopsticks and spoons. I rubbed my fatigued eyes; the day was only half over, but I was tired.

After I finished my soup and rice, and picked at the meat, I sat quietly watching everyone.

"Eat." Lam said, gesturing to the food.

"Oh. I only eat a little, I have a small appetite," I explained, "I'm OK."

"You look rather pale, are you well?" he said seriously.

"I feel fine," I said, with a soft laugh.

He nodded.

I became more and more intrigued by Mr. Lam as we encountered problems on the trip. On the second night of the stay he and the other supervisors decided that I would stay at the hotel next to the youth hostel because it was cleaner. The walls were thin in the hostel, the rooms cramped and dirty, and the children were loud. There are just some circumstances when chaos is a bit too pressing for me, and I was beginning to get irritable. Their offer was a polite gesture and I accepted, grabbing my bag and wading through the children, down the stairs to the kitchen and out through the front dining room full of kids pressing their faces up against the mirrored wall. In the lobby of the hotel a handful of men sat drinking beer and watching television. A European couple sashayed to their room. I saw Thúy, a young female teacher from the middle school, approach; she spoke a little English and had been accompanying me from place to place with gentleness, patience, and a burdensome desire to please me. She explained that the clerk needed to see my passport.

"My passport!?" I snapped, "I don't have my passport!"

"They cannot give you a room without your papers," she said sheepishly.

"That's ridiculous." I muttered. My arms gestured big, I raised my voice, "I don't know! I don't have my papers!"

Outside the door kids were running everywhere (some had followed me and were yelling the phrase "How are you?" in irritating, rhythmic repetition). I couldn't say what I was angry at. Was it me? Was it bureaucracy? Was it giddy, uncontrollable kids? (I mulled that question for a long time.) For a second, it was the stony face on the receptionist; for a second, it was my own stupidity (I've been through this before, I should know about "papers"); for a second, it was Thúy, who started to bear my anger like a smarting wound. She grimaced openly over my discomfort.

I took a breath, "No," I said, "it's not you, I . . ." She walked away quietly.

There was more noise, more banging of doors, the hotel seemed dirtier than before—people disappeared and reappeared. I sat on a nearby couch and began brooding. Thúy returned holding a photocopy of my passport and my letter of employment; these were my papers.

"Where'd you get those?" I asked, suspiciously.

"Mr. Lam had them."

Of course, he had them. I shook my head in wonder. He was my supervisor, I gave them to him when I started working. I went to my room, grateful for the quiet and grateful that, before we left, Mr. Lam had the foresight to handle all situations.

I poured a glass of hot water and opened my Lonely Planet travel book to the section on Dalat: "If, in 1934 France they had evacuated an entire provincial town and repopulated it with Vietnamese, they would have the old quarter of Dalat." Since I spent my mornings at tourist sites with the kids, I decided to spend my afternoons wandering the streets of the town. After a rest, I set out. But people alone here are odd, no matter what they look like . . .

Princess Teacher floats around waterfalls while ninth graders point cameras at her from 100 yards, she talks to local school children, who screech and giggle before they run away from her. She wanders off by herself, sneaks out the back way to walk through alleys and look into cafes, to stroll around the lake.

Again my discomfort over being stared at tired me out, so I retreated to the hotel.

The next morning, at the tourist site Cam Ly Falls the students poured off the bus like water overflowing a tub. Curiosity getting the better of me as it always does, I walked in the opposite direction. Not far away I met an elderly couple at a tea stand. The husband sat on a small stool and leaned back against the wall; the wife paced. She saw me and gestured politely—her hand down low, her palm turned in—"Come," she motioned, waving back and forth. Eight hours in the front seat of a van have given me a picture perfect view of the desired *simple life* that country people live. I romanticized as I approached and sat down. At a glance, the stand was simple. It had small tables with stools, a set of shelves holding nothing in particular, a thermos, faded plastic flowers, mismatched glasses. I was sitting and seeing it all so clearly—*wise old man, gracious matriarch.* She handed me a cup of green tea. It had a musty, gritty taste to it, but I was thirsty. Far away from the crowd, I could more clearly see Mr. Lam counting kids. The children ran like unearthed ants across the rocks and hills of the falls. Lam shook his head at one point, laughed—I could hear it "ah-ha-ha-ha"—and had to begin again.

I sipped the lukewarm water again. When your conversations consist entirely of smiles and nods it's easy to live in the illusion of "the pleasant peasant," and "the happy farmer." I was having just such a conversation. Smile. Nod. "No, I'm not French." I told the old man, with a shake of the head, "no *pháp.*"

The woman edged in closer to stare at me. She was not menacing, but I got the distinct impression she was sniffing me. "Mỹ!" I said, "American." She pressed forward. "Teacher," I added, "ơ thánh phô Hô Chi Minh." I cupped the warm glass between my palms and finished my tea. The bus was starting; I heard Mr. Lam's megaphone crackle.

"Miss Edie, Miss Edie, what-are-you-doing?" (with a lilt at the end, for a friendly question).

It was time for me to go. I gestured, 'How much for the tea?' The man nodded slightly, as if to tell me "never mind." Still, I opened my wallet, thinking in terms of ritual. *"Take it, I insist . . ."* *"Oh, no, I couldn't."* In spite of the man's politeness, the woman, who was standing close by, reached over my arm and with a quick, clean gesture, snatched a 2,000 đong note, folded it, and stuffed it in her pocket.

I looked at her, wanting to say: "Lady, you and I were doing just fine until this moment."

The money's nothing. But her betel-stained teeth became a hideous brown before my eyes, she suddenly sprouted moles and hairs on her chin. Her husband was sitting by the wall, frowning. He muttered a few words. I bowed and said, "Cám ơn, Bà" (Thank you, m'am). The husband became painfully thin, the woman looked meaner. Hungrier. They turned into The Bickersons, snapping at each other in curt phrases; the dust on the countertop turned to soot; the plank walls revealed holes. They were poor. They were terribly, terribly poor. And for a moment, the poverty of the entire country came crashing in on me. I felt primal and crabby. I wanted to sneer and snatch. I walked back to the bus, and cursed myself for feeling disillusioned. What did I expect? I was only passing through; they were in poverty for life.

Back on the bus Mr. Lam sighed with exhaustion.

"Oh, Miss Edie, I do not want to go anywhere anymore," he said dramatically, "Ah-ha-ha-ha."

*   *   *

A welcome break from the humidity of Saigon is the light wind, "the air" of Dalat. In December it is similar to a New England autumn. After the morning touring was finished and I had rested, I walked around the lake, through the market, up and down hills and streets. People stopped to talk to me, but I had my fill of conversation.

"Tối không biệt nói tiếng Anh" (I don't speak English), I said.

One man persisted, "Where are you from?" he asked.

"Tối la người Thụy Điện" (I'm Swedish), I said.

This sentence surprised most people and they didn't know how to respond. They backed up slowly, smiling. *Goodbye*, I murmur, *it was nice to meet you.* But this man smiled and continued. He knew I was lying, and his gentle demeanor forced a confession out of me. I looked down at the gravel path we were on and blushed over my transparency.

"I know," he said softly.

He was a pilot for the South Viet Nam Air Force and he told me he spent most of the past fifteen years in a reeducation camp, in a few months he would be getting a visa to the United States; he had excellent English. We continued talking and he wanted to know what I thought:

"Do you think someone like me will be able to find a job?" he asked.

I explained what kinds of jobs there are available for new immigrants. I told him that the United States may not be what he thinks it is, that it is a very difficult place, difficult in ways that Viet Nam is not.

The day was ending and some neighbors rode by on bicycles, wobbling along as they stared at me. My friend didn't care. The repercussions and the foggy prospects for life in the United States left him unruffled. He didn't care. When he came out of reeducation camp, he found all but one in his family were dead; he owned a farm where he grew orchids and lived in a house where he waited for news from the U.S. State Department.

"Miss Edie, would you like to have a cup of coffee?"

It was a simple request that required a bold gesture on his part. He would take me through the alleys of his neighborhood and down the center street of the town. His head moved nervously around, and his eyes darted about in tense observation. We walked a block and talked for an hour, and he became elated with the rebelliousness of it all.

I had no good news for him; I said that there are no overnight successes in the United States, that jobs with high salaries are hard to come by, and that most immigrants are relegated to work that U.S. citizens feel is below them. I don't do this out of meanness. I do it because I worry about the runaway glamorization of my country, and I remember the words of an older friend who emigrated to the States from Ireland when she was nineteen. She's eighty-four today, but she still remembers, as if it were yesterday, that she "really thought you could pick up money by the handful in the street!" There's too much grief and disillusionment when the dream of another place comes true. For years Molly suffered humiliation, and endured cold winters working Beacon Hill townhouses as a maid. I tried to imagine this man in the United States; he spent hours every night of his youth memorizing flight manuals, studying meteorology and mathematics—all in English— and then learned to handle a plane that flew at unimaginable speeds. It was hard to see a person with such extensive experience and such great dignity as a piece worker in some West Coast clothing factory. I cringed as I realized that when he arrived in the United States and he found no work, or he found himself trapped (like so many immigrants) by custom, culture, racism, and fear, inside his own national community, he would realize again how little his sacrifice had earned him.

At four o'clock I began to get nervous. I could see the tightly knit neighborhood closing in on us, and hear the strange murmuring reverberation of our action. *What are they saying?* I made an excuse for leaving, got up, and said goodbye. I am impassioned about politics in my kitchen and at parties, but when it hits me in the face I am painfully unnerved. What in the world could a man who cultivates orchids and speaks in such a gentle tone, have done that was so criminal? I wanted to get away as quickly as I could.

But I couldn't. Further down the road, at the Mimosa Cafe, I sat by myself watching foreigners write in diaries and postcards, read travelbooks, and discuss itineraries. A woman from the hill tribes stood outside the window, smiling and holding up her bag of handwoven scarves. I was eating a croissant when the waitress came over to talk to me. It was a casual conversation that went on longer and got deeper than I expected.

"You came here from America? To live?"

"I'm a teacher," I answered, "and I like to travel."

"You Americans like to wander," she said, "we Vietnamese cannot go far. We are like a large family." It wasn't said with sentimentality. She didn't particularly admire this trait; she had simply observed it.

"How did you learn English?" I asked.

"I went to school. I was in college for a year, but I stopped so I could work. A big career is not so important. I like working here and talking to people."

People like to take strangers into their confidence. They feel less vulnerable when they talk to you, as if they are speaking into darkness, talking only to the night. From the time I arrived in Viet Nam, I felt like Nick Carraway, of *The Great Gatsby*, "privy to the secret griefs of wild, unknown men." Most of the confidences are unsolicited: A university colleague told me about her early "retirement," another confessed to adoration of Western culture and jokingly called me a "high priestess" for the next generation. People seemed to believe that as a Westerner, as an American, you have an extra capacity for understanding.

"Your English is excellent," I told the waitress.

"Really?"

I didn't expect a country girl to speak so fluently, to talk so smoothly. We sat together for hours. She had her story, too. Like the pilot I met on the street she wanted to tell it to the American. She would spill the family secrets, air the laundry while she leaned across the table speaking English.

"My father was a South Viet Nam military officer. He was a very good man. He was abroad once, but he told me I must stay in Viet Nam, that I am Vietnamese. He was put in reeducation after 1975." She paused for a moment. "It's funny, on April 30 he was happy the war was over; he thought he could live with the Communists. The old regime was so corrupt and the Communists talked so much about fairness for everyone." She shook her head in disbelief, "April 30—that was quite an extraordinary day. We were in Saigon and were going to try to get out on a navy ship, and just as we were leaving an army tank passed by our driveway and we knew we would never get off the street." Eventually her father was imprisoned, and she was allowed to visit him for one hour each month.

"One day at school I heard an announcement for me to go and see the school director. He told me my father was dead."

"That's how you found out?"

"Yes, then he sent me home."

"Were you alone?" I asked.

"My mother was at home."

She paused then, because she wanted me to understand something very important; there is a mystery:

"You see, my father was a very strong man. He was an athlete his entire life. He rowed a shell on the river everyday when he was in Saigon. We believed he would survive above all others. We think someone poisoned him."

It all came spilling out. I hear these stories all the time—in America, in China, in Viet Nam. Sometimes when I hear them they seem just another story. A colleague tells me she was denied admission to medical college because of her family history. Families are split up by distance and political ideology; children are raised without parents, fathers emasculated, mothers denied. There is the repeated refrain: "We had to burn everything when the Communists came. Everything."

My Dalat friend continued, "My mother decided some time later that we would leave Viet Nam by boat. On the day of our departure the police came to the house and we were all arrested. My brother and I were in jail for a week, my sister was released after a month, and my mother was sent to reeducation for two years. When I turned eighteen we got desperate. We told people we would bribe someone to release my mother. An officer came to my house to talk about it one day when I was alone. What he said . . . the way he talked to me, I was very afraid. You know I didn't know when my brother would be home and this man . . . he . . . he touched me in that way, you know? Finally, I agreed to change places with my mother, and then my brother came home."

I am not usually moved by these stories. I know it sounds callous to say that, but I believe that in order to be genuinely, sincerely moved we need to be able to recognize and relate to the language and circumstances of the speaker. In so many ways these stories about police states and government persecution are unimaginable, and we in the United States look at them with the curious eyes of international news watchers. However, on this day I was taken with so many elements of her story that it became painfully real. I saw her father rowing on the Saigon River in the light of early morning; I heard the treads of the tanks rolling by their house before they had a chance to escape; I saw her mother telling the family to go casually through everyday rituals on the day of their second escape attempt, and I saw the growing darkness of late afternoon when the officer cornered her.

She did not go back to the prison camp ("I believe the memory of my father gave me strength") and her mother was eventually released.

"But I have never told that story," she finished, "I was too ashamed, be-cause I allowed the man to touch me."

"You were very brave."

She snorted a soft laugh, "Oh, come on. That is not brave."

I finished my coffee and walked back to my hotel. On an unlit street refreshing winds turned cold, and I sighed back tears. I sighed because my mother sent me a card and it made me homesick; I sighed because I walked a block with a man, and that made him feel brave. I sighed because I saw myself in the face of a beggar girl—I am clutching a penny and thinking of food. I sighed because I missed my family, and I sighed because I felt un-speakably sad that a young woman could not recognize that at such an early age she had already lived bravely and generously.

It was the last day of the trip, and we were not going to go anywhere any-more. The next morning I climbed into the van and Mr. Lam and I laughed about how tiring children can be. We began our controlled conversation.

"The sun is out!"

"Yes," I replied, "no rain today."

"No rain today. Ah-ha-ha-ha. No rain today," and we went home.

Twenty kilometers down the road the driver stopped at a shrine.

"It is for safe journey" Mr. Lam explained. We passed a giant Jesus further on, with affected casualness he asked if I'd like to stop. I paused.

"No," I said, "but thank you for asking."

"Thank you for asking," he said.

Chapter Six

It turned out that pronunciation and voice were the simplest of culture gaps to overcome, or at least tolerate.

"Have you noticed your students will call you 'Miss Edie'?" Ms. Nguyễn the English department chair, asked one day at a university luncheon.

"Oh, yes." I said, "I've heard that before. It's OK."

"It's not proper English!" The Australian volunteer teacher added to the conversation.

"Mmmh, yes, well," Ms. Nguyễn mumbled in reply, then added something that I couldn't decipher.

I smiled. The Australian woman was having the same experience I did. She clearly disliked the use of *Miss*, or *Mrs.*, before a first name. She did not say why, but I could tell from her tone that it was similar to a struggle I often have with the many courtesies of Asia. There is much attention given to decorous behavior, and these manners drain the patience of a Westerner. Honorifics before names, founded on the Asian concept of personal respect, place our pupils and peers in a position that is far too submissive. Taken in a Western context this practice is turned into a racist stereotype. "Miss Edie" makes the speaker sound silly and childish, it echoes the voices of plantation slaves.

Linda, my colleague, wore glasses, had close-cropped hair, and a serious demeanor at all times. "G'day," she'd say, as if it was an order. She walked fast, spoke bluntly, and always looked directly at me. Talking to her was often like an unexpected cold shower. She was authoritarian in her classroom, students referred to her courses as "for our own good," and when she walked into the English Department office people scattered.

Linda and her partner Mary Ann were in Viet Nam on a two-year contract with the Overseas Service Bureau in Australia. It was part of a larger 'round the world sojourn they were taking in the second half of their lives. Their house, a corner apartment wedged in an alley between the Hai Ba Trung market and a string of pancake houses and coffee bars, became a way station for travelers and volunteers passing through Saigon. Sunday evening was the one night each week when most of the foreign volunteer community was off, and that became the dinner party evening. Linda was a fabulous, if strident, vegetarian cook.

"Are you a Buddhist?" a Vietnamese colleague asked at the department luncheon.

"No, I'm an atheist, but I don't eat anything that has been killed," she explained.

The entire table mumbled in reply. I smiled and took a sip of the crab and asparagus soup. In contrast to the awkward and overly polite interactions I was having with the Vietnamese, Linda was refreshing. I'm blunt myself, and I liked the idea that there was someone in the neighborhood with whom I could talk and argue. When Linda called Americans "Yanks," I laughed at her and referred to Australia as "an island off the coast of New Zealand."

"I just want to travel and teach," Linda told me one day after the luncheon. They had come to Viet Nam from stints in Egypt, Turkey, and Eastern Europe. Much of the work was on a volunteer basis, but like so many EFL teachers they did teaching on the side that funded their trips between semesters.

"We work for ELT International," Linda said.

ELT is one of a number of companies around the world that provide English language training for employees of multinational corporations. In most developing countries the lessons are considered part of a benefits package. The workers get the lessons for free and are almost always happy to attend.

"Are they hiring?" I asked, looking for a little cash.

"Yes," she said, "but he won't hire people who aren't certified. And I don't think he hires Americans."

I let the subject drop, not wanting to battle the rebuff.

"Where did you get your degree?" I asked.

"Mary Ann and I did a certificate course by correspondence. Of course, you know that's a load of crap, but it helps you get jobs. You can check with Glenn, the director, about work. We're getting $18 an hour."

"I'm not sure I think those certificates are worth much," I said, "and I don't want to be working somewhere where I'm not welcome."

"Well, . . ." she said, then dropped it.

I didn't want to get into the politics and defensiveness of the EFL profession. I don't have a degree in language instruction. I have an MA in English literature and I've always swung between sheepishness and irritation about the response I get from my teaching peers.

Conversations with Linda and Mary Ann weren't for the timid, but their house was a vegetarian, feminist haven for me once each week, full of discussions and arguments that ranged in subject matter from the rules of Scrabble to the androgyny of Vietnamese culture and its gay underground. We talked a lot about classroom success and failures, but most of the time we simply complained and griped about the shadow dancing that we had to do when we interacted with our students and school administrators.

In Asia, Western individualism and openness, our disdain for pretense, are all aspects of character for which we are greatly admired and welcomed, if not completely understood. In a sense, we are very amusing to people who center their social interactions on form. We speak loudly, argue openly, laugh often, and like to make others laugh as well. I always open my classes with a joke about the American social presence, how I speak and teach very actively. I walk up and down rows, sit on my desk, sit on empty student desks, put my foot up on a bench. In a cement building with no windows and a tin roof, desks that are oversized and crammed together, these habits are quite a sight. As I talked about American history in terms of dreams and ideals my arms waved in illustration. When I asked the students to imagine the life of a nineteenth-century Irish farm girl, then imagine her arrival in America, I did it to a soundtrack of trucks and motorcycles on the nearby street. My voice rose, then rose again,

"Clare," I said to a young woman in the front row, "you're from a *place called County Clare!*"

Students brought their hands to their mouths then looked away to giggle, as I tried to walk up and down the cramped aisles while I was talking; I tripped and continued talking; I dropped papers and chalk, then picked them up without stopping my lectures. I teased the students who weren't paying attention. "*Gentlemeeeen!*" I called to the group of boys in the back of the class, then made a silly face at them. I was a giant cartoon character— Miss Edie: American. In the end, I don't recommend strolling around the classrooms of Ho Chi Minh City University while speaking. The cement floors are riddled with holes, and I was constantly talking to the silent, amused crowd, and would twist my foot. I tried to be graceful, but my students were startled every time ("Oh Miss!" they said with nervous laughter). The blackboard was no safer. It was set above a lecturing platform covered with broken chalk that acted as vaudeville banana peels one day during a serious lecture on westward expansion.

In the classroom, forthright, Western behavior startles the Vietnamese. In student responses to our questions Western teachers find odd, obscure ideas. In composition class I asked my first-year university students to answer a letter to a Miss Lonely Hearts column. I had invented the letter, which was a tale of contemporary marriage difficulties: A woman marries a man who becomes a millionaire and he begins to spoil their children. He is rarely at home to take part in their moral education, and when he returns from his many trips he brings only expensive presents and indulgence. She claims that the marriage is falling apart because of him, that they are arguing and she is frustrated and angry.

I was rather pleased with myself for inventing this task. It is not a particularly unique assignment, but it can often be fruitful in the language learning classroom. I sat back and waited for answers that were messy and complicated. I thought I had given them a nice tangled ball of yarn that we could spend time teasing.

I was stunned by the answers I got: "Don't be angry!" I could hear a collective gasp coming from students, especially females, at the idea of a woman expressing anger. This phrase showed up in nine out of ten letters, and as I read I grew amused at the naiveté of the advice—did they really think that was possible? The element of anger took on tragic proportions; they truly believed it would only bring about disaster. It is this attention to decorum paid by the Vietnamese that I found so amusing, admirable, and irritating all at once.

"Above all, we are polite and calm," one student wrote.

"A woman must bear these burdens," another wrote.

"Woman have their clever ways," students told me over and over again, "you can speak sweetly and softly to solve the problem."

I felt defeated. I wanted action. I wanted the situation to be changed and changed immediately. In interviews and classroom discussion I asked the students if the husband in the story had any responsibilities, wasn't he part of the problem? I thought I had created a boor, an irresponsible father. In my eyes, it was easy to see that the husband needed to be shaped up, told to get in line; their children's future was at stake. I will remember the blank look on my students faces forever. Him? His fault? No, no, they told me, women take care of everything in the family. That's a woman's job.

My initial response to this advice was irritation. It was overly simplistic, even childish. For me, a brash American, this politeness, this refusal to argue openly, is bothersome and frustrating.

The next week, as the project came to an end I asked the students to hand in their final copies, and the earlier responses—the drafts. They broke up into giggles.

"What's the matter?" I asked. Some students continued laughing, and one young man was shaking his head.

"What is the matter?" I repeated, in "foreigner English."

"Oh no, Miss," he said, "we cannot."

I could see that giving me their drafts made them very nervous.

"Cannot?" I asked, though I knew what was coming. For many students, deletions, editorial marks, and translations are a source of shame.

"Miss, the drafts are dirty."

"They are all messy!" a female student added. "We make many errors."

"It's OK," I reassured them, then put my hand out to take the papers. A look of alarm swept over their faces. It was as if I had sprung a pop quiz on them.

"We must clean them first," someone said.

"No, no," I continued, "messy is good!"

Looking at drafts would help me to see how they worked out the problem, not just the neat package they put it in. I wanted to see them thinking on paper. In addition, I could see error patterns and trouble spots they had on a technical level. They laughed as if I were joking. I began taking the papers from students and continued reassuring them that "dirty" papers were OK, that they would not be graded on their drafts, I simply wanted to help them improve their English. Students asked one more time if they could clean the drafts, then sighed in resignation as I refused. One young woman became agitated and panicky. She slipped a sheet of paper into her notebook and told me flatly she didn't have a draft. I smiled and said, "OK." The lesson ended with this quiet but stubborn battle, and I went home with a pile of "dirty" papers.

It is a thousand and one small things like this that give the Western teacher a headache. There is a painful contradiction between the ancient forms of decorum and everyday life. These interpersonal practices appear to be the only highly structured elements in the society. Streets and offices in Saigon are chaotic, there is a strange form of discourtesy in shops and the market; it was a benign neglect I called un-courtesy. And everyday the Vietnamese must struggle to keep up with the new economic hustle. Foreign teachers violate codes of culture; we violate codes of behavior, and we refuse to do things we don't want to do.

"Will you teach an extra course this term?" an administrator will ask politely, "the students love you so much."

"No, I'm sorry, I haven't got time to prepare for another course," we reply over and over. To us this is a polite answer, since it is honest. But principals and deans will persist in their gentle, sometimes playful, persuasion.

"Of course, you can teach extra classes! You are a native speaker! Prepare what?! Just go in and speak!"

This response is important, because it is true. Students want only to hear your voice, to have exposure to your pronunciation. They will imitate it, repeat it, they will mouth words while you are giving lectures.

"... expansion ..." you'll say.

"ex*ban*sion" you'll hear whispered softly by someone in the crowd.

Students will take your voice and learn from it.

In addition to the weight of history and the enduring heritage of manners, Viet Nam has absurd inconveniences that come from an overcrowded, over-burdened society in the midst of change. On the day I scheduled a listening exercise, they were drilling and digging outside my (windowless) classroom; during a final exam in the heart of the city a cock crowed for twenty minutes; during a Sunday morning class a pig wandered around outside the class-room door. Students didn't show up for class because of the rain; students showed up late because of traffic and "crowds." No one got my messages; everyone got my mail.

Finally, when I gave tests, either for general assessment or as part of a course, disorder and anxiety met to create a frustrating, absurd scenario. Spoken and written instructions were ignored in deference to the single most important question occupying the mind of my students. As I recited the directions, it began, "Listen to the brief speech. After it is finished answer each question by choosing the appropriate response from the column." Students whispered and pointed, held the test paper up and hypothesized. They were talking about it, whispering to one another, doubting the an-swers, looking at what was written on the board and still not believing. I walked slowly, repeated my guidance, asked them to "please listen," and they continued whispering.

Students lose sleep over this question, and no matter how many times they took exams, no matter what their instincts told them, they can think of nothing else. The problem hung in the air like fruit weighing down a branch. It must fall or be plucked. I walk again, reciting the directions, with what I hope is the appropriate mixture of care and authority. The students' jitteriness annoys me—they chatter and talk with impatience and fear. When the whispers overwhelm me, and I can no longer suppress my irritation, I say tersely, "What is it? Is there a question?"

"Miss," a voice says from the back, "do I circle the answer or put an X through it?"

Above all else, test takers want to know The Rule. At least one weekend a month all of this drove me around the bend, and I was a demanding, raving lunatic. My students turned into empty-headed, poor listeners; they were *stupid*.

At our weekly gatherings I would share dinner and complaints with Mary Ann and Linda and our other Australian colleagues. Trish and Emmie-Clare taught at two key middle schools in the city—Nguyen Trai and Le Hong Phong. They looked strikingly like the models in the Western clothing catalogs the Vietnamese circulated around the country in a perpetual recycling of exotic images. Emmie-Clare was brown-eyed, with thick long hair, and an enchanting smile. Trish, with blond hair, make-up, and a personality that verged on "bubbly," was like something out of a movie. Her attempts at Vietnamese were charming, not plodding, like mine; she made friends easily with vendors, shopkeepers and workplace colleagues. Trish's ready laugh was infectious and her classroom stories aroused envy in me.

"We were reading *Romeo and Juliet*," she said, one evening, "so I taught them the Dire Straits song. They loved it."

Emmie-Clare was also immensely popular with her students, but when we met she had just ended a three-month tussle with school administrators over their requirement that female teachers wear *áo dài* to work. We all considered this a victory, since the *áo dài* has been transformed from a piece of "traditional" attire into an uncomfortable, inconvenient, form-fitting burden.

"Traditionally it wasn't cut like it is today," Nick, a volunteer from Melbourne, said one evening. "It wasn't as tight through the top, and not cut as high up the side."

"Oh, I can't stand them," I added, referring to my experience wearing one on National Teacher's Day. "I felt like the snaps were going to pop open if I breathed." I raged on, "O God, and those pants! Geez, how's a gal supposed to ride a motorbike with those billowy trousers on?"

"I guess she's not," Nick said, laughing softly at my temper.

"I think this really has made a small, but important difference," Linda added, referring to Emmie-Clare's experience.

"Oh, I guess," I said, dismissing the topic with my hand. "I hate those kinds of arguments. I mean, it's not like they aren't just going to go back to whatever they want to do when she's gone."

These dinners were our chance to blow off steam. One evening, looking for sympathy and understanding, I entered their apartment raving, "THIS PLACE IS DRIVING ME CRAZY!" That week my classes felt like a tug-of-war. It seemed my students cast forth their quiet, courteous behavior like it was knotted silk rope I should pull on, and I obliged. I asked for answers; they gave me giggles. I asked for questions; they gave me silence. I lectured dully on U.S. history, talked obtusely on English composition, wrote on the board and then erased it. "Any questions?" I asked each class, my voice edgy, for I knew their answer. It was always silence.

In contrast to that, my eighth graders, whom I met with only once every few weeks were riotously out of control.

"I've got it!" I announced as I entered Linda's kitchen, "the next Nobel Peace Prize gets awarded to every eighth grade teacher in the world. I mean, even if you've only subbed once or twice you get the prize."

Linda laughed at me, "Can't handle 'em, eh?"

"I keep thinking of my friend Sue, back in Boston," I said. "She's been handling kids this age for twenty years. I can't believe it."

"It just takes some getting used to," she advised.

There are so many ways we step over the line innocently, and so many ways we get alienated by Vietnamese behavior. I had problems with students, never with administrators, but Mary Ann and Linda were always complaining about supervisors and administrators.

"I'm beginning to think," said Mary Ann one evening, "that honesty is a Western concept." Mary Ann is a large woman ("from New Zealand, not Australia"), with salt-and-pepper hair and pale skin. Most of the time she wore baggy trousers made from tie-dyed cloth and slouched comfortably in her middle age. At home I would have jumped on her statement as racist, called her uninformed, but I had been lied to that very afternoon and I was irritated. "I know!" I agreed.

She continued. "Today I asked Minh a question, and I knew she'd lie to me, and she did . . . and I knew she was lying, and she knew I knew she was lying, and I thought . . . 'Why bother!'" Her hand went up in the air and she dismissed Minh summarily.

"Oh, yeah," I mumbled, "the courtesy lie. Donchya hate that?!" My eyes began to squint, my head nodded disapproval. Surely courtesy here was a conspiracy.

We aren't wrong, but we're not right either. If I ask a student if he's done his homework (when it's clear he hasn't), he'll still say yes and he'll give some poor, pathetic excuse for why he can't give it to me. You see it would be impolite to say "No," it would be an offense to the teacher. "No" is simply not courteous, one never uses it. So you see, they're not really lying. Sort of.

My university students did not often do their homework. One afternoon they claimed that Linda gave them too much, so they had to do her homework instead of mine; another afternoon they said there was a movie showing in the English Resource Center and they didn't want to miss it; another day a student concert was being held downtown. They had a bagful of poor excuses that I hated, but much of the time these weren't the real reasons they couldn't hand in the work. Many of the fourth-year students had hustled up work as translators, many ran small businesses, most were forced to work second jobs to support families or to earn a living stipend for themselves. At one point in the term I said that if they came to me with this information I could have integrated the work somehow into my class lesson, but this request for "honesty" was greeted with disbelief and we got all tangled up in a game of manners and confusion.

The higher-level students at the middle school often ignored my class, too. But they were forced to remain in school by a handful of adults who shooed them into my room after the bell. These English language textbooks that taught students about W. B. Yeats, Langston Hughes, and Emily Dickinson, made me happy. I lit up over these poetry-filled chapters, embraced these structured exercises, and enthusiastically said: "Listen and Repeat." It didn't go over. The kids liked me—I was "beautiful" they said, and "very nice"—but English was boring. I'm a lover of English literature, so in all my classes I tried, in a desperate manner, to generate enthusiasm for poetic language. But most students seemed to feel only that English was simply a practical matter—a necessary skill in the twenty-first century, the keys to the kingdom of prosperity.

Late in the fall term, as winter exams were approaching, I was tossed each day from class to class without schedule, one morning it was 11A, the next 9B. This was done for no other reason, I think, than that the school didn't really know what to do with me. Though I found it frustrating, I smiled and agreed most of the time. I suggested that the students would learn nothing from me if we didn't meet regularly. To the school director this didn't matter; the students needed to hear a native speaker. I didn't have to teach them anything, I only had to talk. After running up against this attitude day after day I simply yielded and allowed them to guide me from room to room.

"Open your books to Unit 12," I announced to class 10A one morning. The lesson began with W. B. Yeats poem "When You are Old." This is one of my favorite poems.

"Ooooh!" I said dramatically, "Yeats! A wonderful Irish poet."

There are approximately forty students in each level, and they all looked up politely, but blankly, as the lesson began.

"Listen and repeat," I announced, "When you are old and gray and full of sleep."

They chorused a response. The intent of this old-fashioned exercise is not thorough understanding and literary appreciation, it is exposure to rhythm, pronunciation, and intonation. But that doesn't matter. It's boring.

"And nodding by the fire, take down this book," I continued. They began with a polite chorus, and then petered out to mumbles.

From where I was standing I saw that a male student in the back row had his book propped up against the chair in front of him, but it was upside down. I walked to the back of the class and stood near him.

"take down this book," I repeated. The class's reply was garbled. I stood closer to the boy.

"tade down this booc," he recited sheepishly.

"take" I said.

"take" he repeated.

His desk was covered with notes from a science lecture. As I stood near him, he struck a silly pose of intense concentration on his upside-down English book. But when I moved away, he was rewriting his science notes. He wasn't the only one in the class to do it. They were all nervous about exams. I was angry, but I didn't want to turn into a nag, and surely I would appear that way if I started lecturing them about paying attention in class. I wanted to take a different approach.

"take down this book," I continued.

"take down this book," he said.

I stepped away.

"And slowly read," I announced.

"And slowly read," the class parroted.

Again I stepped closer to the distracted student. A giggle ran through the room. Papers shuffled behind my back as his classmates stuffed their science notes into their bookbags. The boy looked up. "and dream of the soft look," I said with a smile.

"and dream of the soff loos," he said nervously.

I paused. Students began to look at their hands in shame. I realized I was carrying on too long. To break the chill, I fingered the papers on the boy's desk, leaned forward, and repeated the phrase I had heard so many mothers around the city say,

"Làm gì?" (What are you doing?)

The class erupted into laughter, and the boy smiled as he piled his papers up and put them away.

In general my students suffered these repetitive exercises graciously. They were rewarded by games and competitions in the second half of class. But the tendency to stray into other coursework remained, and as their team-mates raced to the chalkboard to write out English sentences many of the tenth graders sat studying and rewriting their math and science homework.

*   *   *

"Kim Thư," I said one afternoon during lunch, "what is this romance with science and math in my middle school students?"

She smiled and nodded. "They're taught this," she said, with a touch of scorn. I knew she loved poetry, and she spoke English exquisitely. "They're taught to value sciences above other fields as 'practical.'"

Kim Thư, I discovered, loved science too. As a young woman she fantasized about becoming a medical doctor, but after high school her government exam results set her field of study for her—she would be an English teacher. In the 1980s this was not a field considered desirable, but Thư said, she did it—grateful to have a university education at all. "I did not want to," she said about her appointed major, "but you see, it has become the best thing for me." Thư translated for visitors often and, since she was around campus after I finished my morning class, we often had lunch together. She became the cultural interpreter and translator I often needed.

We were eating at Tin-Tin restaurant. Like so many shops in the city it is a converted garage, fronted by a charcoal grill and prep table, crammed full of folding tables. In the back a bookshelf, converted to a display case, is lined with the locally manufactured cola Tribeco, Pepsi, Coke, 7-up, and three different flavors of Youki, a soda made with tropical fruit flavors imported from Singapore. Thư eyed the waitress.

"Hai chạo tôm nem nướng," she said.

We ordered the same thing every time we had lunch together: vermicelli noodle salad, served with shrimp and pork, leaf lettuce, bean sprouts, mint, and chopped peanuts, then topped with hot oil sauce.

"Thư," I said, pouring the hot sauce over my salad.

"Oh, be careful!" she said, putting her hand forward. "It's hot!"

"I know," I said, "it's OK. I like hot sauce."

She cringed slightly, and spooned the sauce over her bowl. Whenever we were together, our gestures betrayed our upbringing. She spooned her sauces, I poured mine; she took timid, small, slow bites as she ate; I tore through the salad, swallowing whole lumps of sticky noodles and meat. To watch it probably looked comic, but we got on well and I was often in need of her honesty and guidance.

Thư mentioned that she taught in the evenings at the university Learning Center. "I come home at the end of the day and don't have time to eat dinner with my son. I must rush off to teach an evening class."

"Oh, your son?" I said, "how old is he?"

"He's three years old," she said, her eyes lighting up. It was the first time I saw an animated look on her face. She smiled as she continued, "I cannot imagine a child could be so energetic." She put her hand to her mouth as she laughed.

"A three-year-old!" I said, in awe, "you're the same age as me!" It's so young to have a child, I thought. Her career was really just starting. She was on the faculty of a major university, and her skills were in demand at many of the night schools in the city. Under the new "Open Door" policy she quali- fied to do graduate research overseas on scholarship. A three-year-old? I looked at her healthy, round face. How did she manage a kid, work, house- work, marketing, and what seemed like a burdensome amount of cooking? Furthermore, what was she doing taking me to lunch? Suddenly, I felt I was a burden. I had only requested her company the day before as an offhand comment. I wanted to get to know my colleagues. She was, perhaps, too gracious to say no?

"Shouldn't you—um—shouldn't we go home?" I asked, worrying that I was contributing to the creation of a latchkey kid.

"Do you want to leave?" she replied.

"No, I mean, do you?" I asked.

"It's up to you," she said. This was no answer. She was being polite.

"I mean, do you have to pick up your son? Who's with your son?"

This seemed an odd question to her, and she looked at me with a puzzled expression.

"He is with my mother. I will go home after, and we will rest in the afternoon."

"Oh, right, right," I said, remembering the extended families of Viet Nam. Thư, her husband, and son all lived together with her parents in a downtown apartment. It was crowded but, no doubt, loving. I relaxed a bit, and enjoyed the meal.

"Thư what's the name of the really beautiful student in third year?" I continued. I was thinking of the Mariah Carey fan who was beginning to irritate me in class.

"Which group?" she asked. "Is she in A or B?"

"I think it's B," I said, "but anyway, she's very pretty, sociable, sort of bold?"

"She talks back in class?" Thư asked, tensing a little in recognition.

"No, mostly she talks to her little friends, but sometimes she talks to me. She *never* does her homework," I said with a laugh, "know who I mean?" I picked up a mouth full of noodles.

"I know who you mean," Thư said disapprovingly. "Her name is Hùynh. It means depth or subtlety."

I started coughing, and said, "mmmmhh?"

Thư dropped her chopsticks. "Oh! I told you, the sauce is hot!"

I continued coughing and tried to smile so she knew it was brought on by laughter.

"She's so different," I said finally. "I like her."

"I don't like her," Thư said dismissively. "She is so saucy."

I laughed at her word choice. "Well, I'm saucy too," I said, teasing her, "so I like her and her friends. We're all saucy girls together!" I popped a bean sprout in my mouth and smiled at her. Thư put her hand in front of her mouth and looked down, a smile restraining her enjoyment.

The ambition and pragmatism of all my students was disheartening to me, but completely understandable. In the developing world, science, economics, and now English, represent the future. They are the last Imperial Court. To memorize scientific manuals and translate for foreign businessmen is to rise out of a poor, uneducated past and take part in the rest of the world. Learning for pleasure, for beauty or aesthetics, is a luxury of the wealthy. Bình, with her high energy and determination, tells me she is not like me; "I cannot sit around all day." With my bookish ways, I am "Princess not laborer." I made faces behind her back when she said this, and among my friends I accused her (and many others) of being an automaton student.

The Vietnamese, like us, are more than a simple sum of historical parts. In their culture math and science and memorization are a part of ambition and enthusiasm. With astonishing commitment my students—children, teens, and adults—took what they needed each step of the way up a ladder they built for themselves. No one I met wanted to be poet laureate, which saddens me, but they will certainly soar. They were soaring before I arrived.

"I'm a far cry from a pioneer here, at the end of the twentieth century," I wrote in my diary one evening. Each time I banged my head against the elements of Viet Nam's multicolored history and culture, the line between student and teacher blurred. People thanked me profusely for teaching them English, but most of the time I couldn't say for sure who was learning what.

On occasion a student would come up to me, asking for advice on understanding English poetry, or an explanation of a phrase in some dog-eared history book. Then I was free to wax rhapsodic about the accomplishments of the women and men of history or "ooh" and "aaw" over the rhythm and form of Frost or Dickinson. And in the evenings, when things got quiet and it was time to rest, Bình would look up from her books, weary but not exhausted, and recite the poem she had memorized:

> But I have promises to keep,
> And miles to go before I sleep,
> And miles to go before I sleep.

In any classroom these are rare moments, full of a different kind of hunger. We all light up. We all speak the same language.

Chapter Seven

> As for me, I confess that when I arrived in Cochinchina
> and when I heard the natives, especially the women, speak,
> I had the impression of hearing the twittering of birds, and I
> despaired of being able to learn it. All the words are mono-
> syllabic and one only distinguishes their meaning by the
> various tones which are given to them in speech. The same
> syllable, for example Dai, means twenty-three completely
> different things, owing to the various ways of pronouncing
> it, which has the result that one only speaks by chanting.
>
> —Alexandre de Rhodes, 1681

Quí wore khakis. We traveled down the Mekong Delta, to Chau Doc in Ân
Giang Province, to administer language proficiency tests, and my colleague
Nguyễn Phú Quí was looking crisp and sporty in a polo shirt and khakis. A
descendent of the last emperor of Viet Nam—Quí is a mix of quick wit, good
looks, and Vietnamese culture. He has long hair, a small frame, and big eyes;
he likes jazz and hangs out with painters. An English teacher at the evening
school of the university, he's "hip" in a way Westerners admire, but so graceful and polite that he is also consummately Vietnamese. Sitting in a cafe on a
hot afternoon in Chau Doc I noticed his crispness over a glass of coconut
water. Quí was following a conversation between our colleague Kiều and
Philip, a social science researcher from Australia. They were debating tones.

"Sử is history."

"Sự is polite."

The variation is infinitesimal to the Western ear, but one *su* rises and one
falls.

"No, one falls, then rises," said Philip. He told Kiều that both her *sus* rose.

"Sử."

"Sử."

Meanwhile a boy of four or five stood next to another colleague, Ms. Hạ,
chanting nonsense and waiting for her to give him money. Chau Doc is
swarming with beggars.

"*Shoo!*" our driver Mr. Hồng snapped, and I cringed.

The university Language Center was administering examinations for private language school students in rural areas who had just completed A-level courses in English. During the week I heard about the trip through a colleague and asked if I could tag along; I wanted to see the countryside.

A week before I was told by a colleague that Quí is descended from royalty. It was a charming piece of gossip about a very charming guy. Vietnamese who knew him smiled when they referred to him; he is Bảo Đại's relative. But it isn't his royalty they smile at—it's him. He is not quite 5′5″, and has long hair. He leans forward when he talks to you and with his soft features, his almost female eyelashes, you are certain he is listening. "Yeah," he says slow and smooth, "yeah."

Early in my stay I made a trade with Quí because I found him so interesting. The deal was: music for language lessons. I gave him two jazz tapes (one Ella Fitzgerald and one Miles Davis), in exchange for teaching me Vietnamese. We got around to the lessons two months later. Still dragging my heels on the idea of formal lessons, I told friends they were simply information sessions. Since I carry a notebook with me everywhere, I had a record of the everyday sounds and phrases that were staying in my memory. This is how I studied. I often liked to sit with Vietnamese friends and repeat phrases I found useful, pretty, amusing. I asked about sounds I heard over and over again. I don't remember the patterns now, but I can still recall my silly questions . . .

What is tat ca? tat ca cac ban?

"Tất cả" is everything; "tất cả các bạn," everyone. Each afternoon I lay under my fan during lunch hour and listened to Bình talk with her sister and her friends. They started soft and slow, then, in laughter or anger, fast, fast, fast. In between my notes about markets and landscapes, I have these language and listening notes: "*Thea,*" Bình says . . . or "*vung.*" In some there are cartoon drawings made by Quí, in others there is an odd romanization as I tried to record what I heard. The notes of this symphony puzzle me. There were so many words I could neither see nor say. By this time, I knew "Cám ơn" with its delicate c/g ("Gam?" I ask over and over), and I love "Ơi"—easy, this one—it falls like confetti on the streets . . . Ơi goi ơi, trời ơi, Anh ơi, Edie ơi . . . But I cannot connect the sounds between my ears and my mouth. I cannot connect Quí's cartoon picture of me and the words in the bubble over my head: "mệt lam!"

"Oi vei ha?" (Oh, really?), I stuttered one day during our lesson.

"Good!" Quí replied. "That's great! Now say it fast—*oi ya ha?*"

"Oi ya ha?"

"Great!"

I tried it the next day with Kim Thư in her office, she crinkled her brow in misunderstanding and said, "What? What are you trying to say?"

Driving me home on the back of his Honda that afternoon Quí gestured to the Museum of American War Crimes and yelled to me over his shoulder.

"Don't go to that museum."

"Why not?" I asked.

"They make it seem like the U.S. are the only ones who did anything wrong."

"They're probably pretty close to the truth," I muttered in reply.

"What?" he asked.

"Nothing, never mind," I answered. I had already made up my mind that I would not be visiting the museum. The American War was one of the few things I *could* imagine about Viet Nam, and I didn't want to follow up on it. There would be many pictures there I had already seen in the United States, and much suffering I encountered here. I wouldn't go there, and I wouldn't go to Cho Ray Hospital, where the walls are lined with the aborted grand-children of Agent Orange.

Insisting that Viet Nam is a country, not a war, is a stance taken in-creasingly by younger Americans. There were more than a few moments when I sided with this seemingly callous outlook. It wasn't that I wanted to disregard recent history, it was that I wanted to break free of it as the packag-ing of Viet Nam. If we say it is only a war, then we say that Viet Nam has only *one* past, and that past is defined by us. The Vietnamese have much longer historical memories than Americans do. For me Viet Nam was becoming a beautiful place our society had wrapped in hideous, self-serving packaging and we referred to that packaging again and again as the real society and culture. When I thought about this issue from inside Viet Nam, my hands got tied with shame and confusion. There is so much more in Viet Nam—in Asia—that evokes a sense of wonder in the traveler. I wanted to spend most of my time there.

Quí turned on to Hai Ba Trung Street, then quickly pulled to the side of the road.

"What happened?" I asked.

"The cops."

"Oh, terrific," I said, seriously. I wanted to see police and citizens interact firsthand. Quí saw the officer signal him from the sidewalk (it was a small gesture that I didn't even notice, but it was enough for most Vietnamese). Quí pulled over and said, with a hint of drama, "I gotta go talk to the cops."

He walked over sheepishly, like so many other people I'd seen stopped in the city. This is part of body politics in Viet Nam. *You* approach power (police) and authority (elders) and you stand when you talk to them. I smiled when I finally recognized this body language; my students and colleagues were no longer strange beings sitting on springs, ready to pop up when I spoke to them. They stood, like Quí with the policeman, out of deference and respect. As he talked with the officer, Quí put his hands in his pockets, he leaned "just so" (the cop has the power, you lean toward him). I stood nearby waiting for a raised voice and watching for the payoff. Quí kept his hands in his pockets and talked. And talked. And talked. When we left I asked what happened.

"We just talked," he said.

"About what?"

"You know—I was very friendly and flattering. You have to flatter the cops in Viet Nam."

He played stupid. *Light? What light?* He told the cop he was smart. *You're right. Yes, you're right.*

"Then we talked about you," Quí continued. "I told him you teach at the university. I think he wants to study English. I told him I'm a translator for foreigners . . . you know."

"Did you get a ticket?"

"Of course not." He waved the incident away.

He was smooth, he was sooo smooth. I laughed to myself as I imagined the vague promises, gray references to English lessons, introductions to the "well connected," and the strange, new exploitative power of being a language teacher. Quí had played the game right, but that wasn't surprising to me; it wasn't exactly a rock and a hard place. He had worked his way out of tougher situations. One day, when he was younger, Quí, like so many hundreds of other residents of central Viet Nam, packed up and took his savings (eight dollars) with him to the big city. He was a small town schoolteacher who had argued with the headmaster.

"I guess he thought I was too much of a rebel," he said.

As an amateur artist, he "found work doing anything, and living anywhere anyone would let me." In Viet Nam migration to the city is not the same as in the West. In the United States a place to live establishes residency, in Viet Nam residency isn't legal without a government-issued place to live. Who's gonna give a house to a rebellious artist-schoolteacher? He lived illegally for years. But still, he stayed, painted a lot, taught English a lot, saved his money, and then asked his wife to join him in the city. They both taught at the university, where Quí also worked as a translator for American college groups. He learned a great deal through this work and peppered his conversations with words and phrases he often heard. Saying goodbye to him one evening, I added that I'd see him again during the week. "Yeah," he replied, "that's cool."

He had practiced that reply, I could tell; it was delivered with perfect pitch and excellent timing. He never stumbled over English slang. I listened to his story one night over noodles. I prodded him and he continued while we ate dessert at the fancy ice cream shop near my house. "But enough about me," he said at the end of his bowl of chocolate chip, "what about you? What do you think of me?"

Quí and his wife, Bình, were a handsome couple. She was the consummate country beauty, with long hair, fragile features, a soft voice, and clothes that were fashionable and refined at the same time. You met Bình and were immediately taken with her sincerity; you were certain she would never put one over on you. When I imagined these two wandering through the Imperial Court in Hue, I couldn't help laughing. It was the Joking Emperor and his soft-spoken wife. Quí—who once told his students, in a moment of frustration "Oh, Please! Get out of my face!"—was always in search of an open mike. And Bình—mother of his child, another no-longer-royal heir— was a vision of smiling patience.

On our drive down the delta to Chau Doc and Long Xuyen, Quí felt that my presence was an opportunity to practice the slang he recently learned. He leaned forward like a kid in the back seat of a station wagon, and went through all the phrases for vomiting. Listening to his lilting pronunciation, it occurred to me that "blotto" sounds a bit like a dance when it comes from him.

"Have you learned the Blotto?"

This was not a good time for me to practice or teach slang, as I was suffering from nausea brought on by the driver. Highway One is not the best road in the world, and it is particularly unbearable when the van sways back and forth and side to side as a result of Vietnamese driving techniques. With no speed limit and no thought of tomorrow, the driver careened, rocked and rolled down the delta, horn blaring peasants out of the road, wheels scattering rice laid out for drying. Even on a good day, traveling in this environment is difficult. The atmosphere is marred by the smoke of slash-and-burn agriculture, and the population's dependence on wood for fuel. Peasants working on the sides of narrow roads are swung in and out of danger by drivers bent on arrival. Bridges used beyond endurance clunk threateningly as we race over them, and the heartiest traveler is easily nauseated.

If you began in China, at the head of the Mekong, and floated downstream you would enter Viet Nam through Chau Doc and Long Xuyen. On the way there you would pass through Thailand, Laos, and Cambodia, and before you reached the South China Sea you would arrive in this corner of Viet Nam. Located on her border with Cambodia, these two towns are an hour apart and full of houses on stilts, villages made of boats and bamboo (monkey) footbridges that oversized Westerners cannot cross. The energy of this corner of the Mekong Delta—believed by many to be supernatural—is a combination of the many cultures of Southeast Asia.

But I did not float into Chau Doc and Long Xuyen. I took Highway One. Westerners always recall overland travel in the developing world with amusement. There are moments when its discomfort reaches such extreme proportions that you laugh hysterically after it's over, believing you've just had a brush with death and won.

Philip from Canberra had been down this road about twenty times. He hitched a ride with us so he could do further research. Ten minutes into the journey I was pale, my Vietnamese friends were alarmed, and he was reading an article from an academic journal. As a seasoned traveler, he knew all the highway hot spots and graciously acted the tour guide. He showed me the smuggling road from Cambodia (it's just after Mytho), explained the landowning laws for southern farmers ("basically it's theirs in twenty years if they grow rice on it"), and was, in general, bubbly and excited about the prospect of being in the countryside again. You meet researchers like Philip a lot when you travel. Like lab scientists, they are absent minded and saturated by their subject. When researchers are in-country they're odd company. They get a dazed look when asked to undertake everyday activities, but bring up something as obscure as indigenous religions and cults, sociocultural tendencies, or the migratory pattern of the eighteenth-century peasant and they're a house on fire. They may know the meaning of everything you're looking at, but conversations are never quite finished. "Well, it's hard to explain, it's very complicated," they may say. Philip and I turn in different universes; and when he explained migration patterns as we made our way through the countryside, all I could think in response was: "Am I supposed to keep my eye on the horizon or not?"

My colleague Kiều was devoted and concerned about my nausea, offering sips of water, then touches of tiger balm, and inquiring frequently: "Do you feel as if you want to vomit?" When Kiều talks it seems as if she's hiding a tape recording inside herself, with perfect, crisp enunciation, and a preciseness that makes it seem as if words are targets and she is determined to hit them all perfectly. I looked at her:

"Do I look that bad?" I asked.

"Yes. Quite bad."

Bad news is always funny from someone as devoted to the concepts of honesty and kindness as Kiều. She hates to tell you that you look terrible, but she cannot lie either, so she delivers the truth with a gentleness and simplicity that shatters you.

"Do I look *terrible?*" I pressed.

"Yes, I'm sorry to say you do."

You have to laugh. In a desperate attempt at distraction I began complaining about giving exams the previous week. I rambled on rudely about cheating in Viet Nam, and arrogantly explained the uselessness of the university's practice of grading according to final exams.

"blah, blah, blah," I finished.

Kiều said "Oh," gave me some more tiger balm, then told me the tale of the Betel plant and the Areca tree:

"The Mandarin Cao had sons who looked exactly alike. Tân and Lang."

"Twins?" I asked. She leaned toward me; her cheeks expanded, and her nose flattened, as if it were behind a wide-angle lens.

"Yes, thass right. Twins. That means no one could tell the brothers apart. They were also very close and they loved each other a lot."

I watched the horizon. White tombstones raced past my line of vision, like tiles in a mahjongg game. I closed my eyes, remembering the story I had heard about the old man who refused to leave his home during a wartime evacuation. Kiều reached over while she talked and softly placed menthol oil on my forehead.

"The brothers never left each other. That means they were very committed."

"Right," I said, with an exhale.

"But they were handsome and beautiful and . . ."

The menthol relaxed my forehead. Turns out a woman comes between the brothers. It was inevitable; one of them had to get married sooner or later. After the death of their parents, Tân and Lang went in search of work and came upon the home of a mandarin with an enchanting daughter.

"They could not part through marriage, even. That means that neither one would marry the daughter." Kiều's eyes looked softly at me, but she pressed her lips together tightly to reflect Tân and Lang's determination. I smiled and imagined the brothers tripping over one another with politeness, insisting, in that very Asian way, "No, you go, I insist . . ."

"What did the father do?" I asked.

"He tricked them. He was very clever," she said with a smile. "He left two bowls of rice on the table, but only *one* set of chopsticks."

"The younger brother would defer," I said.

"Thass riight," Kiều said. "So he chose the older brother according to cultuwal tradition. It was Tân."

"That *is* clever," I said. The van swerved, and my eyes widened briefly.

"Do you feel as if you are going to vomit?" Kiều asked.

"No, I'm gonna be OK. What happened next?"

After some time everything began to fall apart, and Lang left.

"What could he do?" Kiều asked. "He was broken-hearted. He walked until he reached the ocean."

"The ooocean," I mumbled, understanding Lang briefly.

"He cried until he was transformed into a rock. A white rock," Kiều said.

But that's not all. The Vietnamese *love* "love and devotion." This story is the perfect example of their cultural ideal of fraternal and conjugal love. Tân runs to find his brother, following the same path, ending up in the same spot; and weeping until he too dies of grief, he is transformed into the Areca tree, a tall, thin-trunked palm with a frond on top. After following the two men, the bride, too, weeps until she becomes the Betel plant, which twined itself around the stately trunk of the areca tree.

It's a pretty story, and the areca tree is very stately. It stands rather majestically above the raggy coconut palms and banana plants in the delta. But in my nausea I could only look out the window and look at Kiều, then say, as enthusiastically as possible . . . "Oh. That's nice."

When we arrived at the dock for the ferry to cross the Mekong River, I stood in the crowd waiting to board and thought about the opening scene of *The Lover*, and the landscapes of the film *Indochine*. I paused to look around at the real world romance: a young boy with a basket of bananas on his head looked at me and said "Hello Banana," a man standing in the boarding line began a rapid-fire conversation with a peasant woman. He told her he could get her a seat on a bus to Bac Lieu . . . "I know people . . . cheap price, good seat, Auntie." Old women selling meat sandwiches stared at me, and a little boy danced T'ai Chi through cooking smoke. He waved a white shirt over his head and swung his arms about in a dance I imagined titled "Crane

Rising from Fog." He was doing very well until his sister came along and shoved him (Ơi!). It all became this strange blur of coconut vendors, migrants, ride brokers, and locals. There were jade peddlers and monks, motorcyclists with girlfriends, peasant women scolding barefoot kids, and little boys making loud noises to get my attention. I started laughing and wondered if Catherine Deneuve suffered from motion sickness when she came to Viet Nam to make her film. I wondered if she, like me, stood "head and shoulders above the crowd" like her exotic character and couldn't rid her face of the look of suppressed retching.

The five-minute ferry brought me the relief of open sky and moist air. I was charmed by the "pocketa-pocketa" of fishing boats, and I breathed deep to regain my feeling of balance. I told myself that this trip would come back to me one day in a vision of sampans and sunsets. But I could not lean romantically on the rail, my head hung from traveler's fatigue, and I kept hearing Kiều's voice saying, "Do you feel as if you want to vomit?" The ride broker was fighting with the bus driver; the Auntie sat by the window, knee up, foot on the seat, like country women do. Such a deal. I felt better as we debarked. I watched schoolgirls in white áo dài float by like butterflies, giggling under their conical hats and egging each other on to speak English with the very tall, very white foreign woman.

In spite of all this, I realized that the Mekong Delta is beautiful. In twilight (we had to stop for a blown tire), the sky turns pink, red, and gray, and fishing nets hang behind houses looking like abstract art (beige and brown against fields of emerald green). Two bamboo poles stand at right angles to a third, supporting the corners of the net hanging out over the river. When the water is high the net goes in, and comes up soon after full of fish and shrimp. With their five-minute bounty, vó hang in the sunset like eternal guardians of family prosperity.

The road was intermittently filled with the blare of truck horns and the manic rush of van drivers; they came and went like trains in a film. During the quiet, footsteps of children created a murmur as they were hurried home by their grandparents. Crickets and cicadas managed to sing above all of it, and with the light they prompted people to speak in hushed, quiet tones, as if the atmosphere had a spell that could not be violated.

"Đi con . . . đi, đi" (C'mon now . . . hurry up), an old woman tells a child, and a bicyclist stumbles along the dirt in the moonrise. As we got closer to Long Xuyen the road narrowed, and I imagined the gray van in the middle of the overgrown brush as a rhinoceros trampling through the jungle. We crossed—I was certain—every single wooden bridge on the Mekong Delta.

Horn blares, ker-plunk-clunk, we cross a bridge—thumpthumpthump-thump-clunk, a safe arrival on the other side. Another slow, heavy ferry brought us to our final destination.

Long Xuyen has more homes on the river than the road, and evening light is cast by lamps on the boats of tea sellers who look like Halloween skeleton figures paddling, dancing, and singing in the dark. It's a strange song, with only a few familiar words.

Cà-phê đa, sửa đa, tra đa, hông. . . . Cà-phê đa, sửa đa, tra đa, hông . . .

✻   ✻   ✻

We arrived at the hotel, and I explained to my colleagues that I was tired. After dinner I only wanted to sleep. But there's always a problem on these trips. In this case it was the heat.

Sleeping in Viet Nam takes some getting used to. In New England, after winters that leave you chilled and reticent, there is a tendency to dramatize warm weather. When the summer heat arrives, New Englanders moan and complain about humidity. Even weather forecasters join in with dramatic phrases: "Heat wave!" "Hazy, hot and humid!" "Phew!" "Watch out!"

Average humidity in Saigon was 80 percent. It just was. There were no comments made, though many cloths crossed damp brows. There was no bemoaning the thick air like it was a cursed fate. Women wore conservative trousers and skirts. Men had shirts that were neatly pressed, with collars they didn't often pull at, and sleeves that stayed in place. Hair stayed unruffled. I often came home from the university or middle school with my red cotton cloth tied around my neck to catch sweat; I'd rub it along the back of my neck and head, over my ears and brow, trying to rid myself of moisture. In the kitchen Bình stood over a cooker, stirring a pan of sauteed pork or garlic and spinach, without an ounce of discomfort. Thảo sat in a wooden lounge chair wearing beige cotton pajamas that fit loosely on his thin frame. Thanh often wore colorful LaCoste shirts that seemed to maintain their brightness in a way that mystified me. Often I migrated upstairs, and in an attempt to break through the sweat and mental haze of the day, I showered and exercised to a drip-dry under my fan. I wanted to stretch and breeze my way into sensibility. I tried to roll away from the frustrations of my cross-cultural and cross-linguistic struggles.

Covered only in sweat and this dreamy state, I tried to rid myself of the haunting faces of street children, the veiled scars of the country's modern history and all the sensory stimulation that sent me spinning. There was the lingering aroma of foods and fruits, the tart spring onion, chopped into tiny bits, the ground pepper sitting atop crab meat, overwhelmed by diced and stringy asparagus. With the shower I hoped I was rinsing away the oily, pungent smell of fish sauce; it is a condiment so important to the Vietnamese diet I felt it must ooze slightly from their pores, like the vital presence of oil that spreads mysteriously through a machine. I wanted to rinse away the slippery feel of *bánh cuốn*, a rice paper salad I sometimes had for breakfast. The small white squares slipped around my mouth mildly, before I was socked with the bite of the fish sauce and bits of shrimp. I wavered constantly between the heat of this seduction and the sense that I should somehow be more clear-headed in this strange, crowded place. "I'm a teacher," I thought, "it's my job to be clear-headed and sensible."

As I tried to rest or sleep, clothes and sheets weren't doing me any good at all, and though a mosquito net was a necessity it was stifling. So, restless and bored, I read my books, wandered in and out of the cool of my shower, and lay under my ceiling fan as if I were worshiping a goddess. In the middle of the night there is nothing to listen to in my neighborhood; I could smell the evening flower (Queen of the Night) from the patio, and hear Nục growl and bark at the rats in the alley.

In the Mekong Delta it was not so easy. I shared my hotel room with Kiều, and had to toss and turn my way to sleep in my black silk trousers and tee-shirt. I faded in and out of sleep, startled awake as I recalled my conversation with Quí about the War Crimes Museum, and imagined some of the photographs there. Then, memory swinging my mood, I giggled about his English slang. There were bicycle bells outside the window, and on occasion, the distant sound of a motorbike horn. I sweated and stared at the wall geckos as they swallowed moths and mosquitos. To add to my discomfort, my mosquito net had only one hook, so I couldn't hang it without wrapping myself up in it in my sleep. I finally arranged an odd isosceles triangle shape and curled up in a ball. At 3 a.m. I rolled over and sighed; nothing was working. Kiều turned the page of the book she was reading by flashlight.

"You look like a bug," she said.

We wouldn't have to give exams until Sunday, so the first thing on Saturday's itinerary was Sam Mountain in Chau Doc. It was an hour overland and, as they always seem to do, the women had arranged things very quietly and I was invited to sit in the front seat to avoid a repeat of the previous day's nausea. While we were driving Philip mentioned that An Giang is the richest province in Viet Nam, that they have the fastest growing birth rate, and the lowest level of education. He turned around to the local school director at one point and asked: "Why do you suppose that is?"

The man, a former ARVN soldier with excellent English and bad *lý lịch* (family political history) let the cigarette hanging from his lip burn, and stared at Philip like he had just asked him the Dow Jones Industrial average.

"How the hell should he know?" I mumbled softly, clicking my tongue over Philip's silly remove.

In fact, the man probably knows all too well, but you won't find that in any academic journal. The Mekong Delta provides 90 percent of the rice for Viet Nam, but the single largest source of income for the Vietnamese there is smuggling—everything from cigarettes to cars. That weekend the marketplace was full of products smuggled from Cambodia and Thailand. Western food and chocolates lined up next to Japanese cigarettes and oh-so-desirable military-issue instant foods. The gray plastic envelopes, with their instructions ("Add water and stir"), looked bland and tasteless amid the supermarket colors.

In addition to income, this area of the Mekong is rich in religion. Like most peasant areas, it is also full of folk superstitions and religious distortions. There are Taoists, geomancers, fortune tellers, and faith healers; there are magic monks, pure monks, corrupt monks, Confucianists, Khmers, Siamese, Vietnamese, Chinese. It has the only range of mountains in the entire delta, and they are said to house untold amounts of power. In addition, it is the birthplace of the Hoa Hao religion, a movement both spiritual and political—an odd mix of grand ideas and ancient superstitions.

Buu son ky huong (Strange fragrance from the precious mountain) is the poetic phrase borne on amulets worn by Hoa Hao followers. It is a powerful combination of words. Each word introduces one line of the poem that is their spiritual text; it is a strange stanza that is uninterpretable in any language. The founder of the sect was said to be a human incarnation of the Buddha Master of Western Peace. He was a nineteenth-century peasant who lived in the region and was struck by illness; by virtue of circumstance—no home, no money, no medicine, no help—and study—he was said to be versed in Buddhism—he established a religious following based not on elaborate ritual, but on frugality and virtue. It was not monks the Master thought special, but laypeople.

Hùynh Phú Sổ was the twentieth-century prophet of the Buddha Master. Also a sickly youth, Sổ was enlightened during illness and became a practitioner and preacher of the strange, fragrant, seven-mountain sect. The ideology is both complex and simple because it involves the salvation of laypeople, not monks, and its ritual is deliberately sparse. The French colonial government laughingly referred to Sổ as "The Mad Bonze," accusing him of all sorts of crimes and insanities as he walked around the delta talking to villagers, prophesying, and preaching.

But it was no joke. And matters became horribly complicated when a link was made with politics; after all, this man was empowering simple people. The French colonial government declared him insane and put him in jail in Saigon. The plan was a flop; he converted the jailer and the attending nurses. Then he went on to dance with the Japanese occupiers during World War II, escaping again when things got tight, and preaching and preaching until the Viet Minh found him. They didn't like him either, so he was assassinated.

Add to this odd and fleeting movement the fact that they leave no relics behind, that there are no temples left, none of the garish monuments to goodness that I saw in the Mekong's Cao Dai communities, no robed follow-ers, no continuing elders. To me it's all a very romantic drama, and standing on the hillside near Sam Mountain I look over toward the areca trees of Cambodia to see flooded rice fields shimmer magically in the sunlight.

The various temples of Chau Doc's other religions are more colorful and carnival-like than spiritual, with a range of statues erected in worship to mandarins, monks, and gods. It seems all mixed up as a statue of Shiva stands alongside Shakyamuni and Guanyin, and a mandarin from the four-teenth century is worshipped as a bringer of development and a protector of the population—a middleman between the people and the court. The largest, most elaborate temple belongs to Lady Chúa Xứ, who is a source of prosperity, a granter of wishes. Her statue is said to have landed at the foot of Sam Mountain after being carried part of the way by Siamese troops in the early nineteenth century. The soldiers had wanted to transport her to Thai-land, but as they attempted to do so the weight became too great, and they were forced to abandon it. Villagers later found the statue and were in-formed by its visiting spirit that she could only be transported by forty virgins. At the base of the mountain the girls were unable to go further, so the people concluded that this site was the one selected by the spirit for the construction of a temple. Lady Xứ is a big jolly-looking goddess who is wrapped in colorful robes and prayed to by believers, for children, riches, and family safety. Each year, on the twenty-third day of the fourth lunar month, the town fills with country pilgrims who take part in the annual festival and parade celebrating Lady Xứ's powers. The temple complex becomes a crowd of peasants carry-ing sleeping mats and wishes, throwing sticks to divine the future, making donations, and dressing Lady Xứ's likeness to parade through town. In my intellect I find all this slightly amusing and very interesting. But these ideas and rituals, the wish-making and the wish-granting, the garish colors of temple robes and the gaudy lights used to grab the attention of those who reside in heaven, are the alternative to smuggling your way out of poverty. The thought pulls at me as much as the beggars.

Chau Doc, like much of Viet Nam, has something else besides this color. In almost violent contrast to the wealth of the landscape, there is an army of beggars. On every street there are poverty-stricken children and elderly people; toddlers carrying babies beg for coins; the limbless and the blind mutter and beg with their hands out, as do those with weeping sores and burdened with madness. The persistence of these beggars is painful and irritating. A Westerner, no matter how hardened, is not accustomed to the desperation of this poverty, and as they tug at your arm, repeating nonsense over and over like an incantation, it is nearly impossible to suppress a violent response. To give money to one (as I did) is to invite flies to a honeypot. "Madam," the girl says tapping my arm, hip out to carry a baby half her size, "Madam" she repeats. Tap, tap, tap. Hair stringy, hands dirty, she is the same girl I see all over the country. I'm not Mother Theresa—I haven't got that much in me—and like many others I was overwhelmed by the filth and despair of these migrant poor. And, like others also, I began to shoo them away—like flies. Mr. Hồng snapped loudly at them and motioned dramatically, to send them away, and I cringed in recognition.

*   *   *

Sunday was exam day. Like many of us, the Vietnamese take institutional exams as the first step up a career ladder. In Viet Nam today schools base their language exams on a Western model. I think these tests (often bought from British and Australian publishing companies) have no more merit than the memorization and recitation required in the Confucian model used for so many centuries. Students memorize answers for exams, and we can't really ever measure their underlying skills. But as in Ho Chi Minh City, my blanket condemnation in the countryside is dwarfed in the face of student's mastery. They recited sounds that came out like words and doubled up into sentences, and it was all in English. In my language. In the language of money.

Language—specifically English—was viewed as a pragmatic tool that, once acquired, yielded the fruit of prosperity. The A, B, and C Level English (and Chinese) exams help residents of the countryside find work opportunities in the city, where the standard of living is higher. Farmers and middle school students, housewives and high school graduates file into the evening schools hoping this room, this paper, this conversation with a foreigner, will be their ticket up and out. For these exams I would be speaking briefly with a long line of eager and anxious students. The Vietnamese had to stand and wait for what must have felt like hours as I asked their classmates questions like: "Can you tell me about your childhood home?"

The students stared at the floor most of the time and when I spoke—slowly, clearly, simply (like the voice on the tapes they studied)—they paled if they didn't understand, or they giggled with excitement if they did. Up close the process is slightly absurd and while it is under way communication appears hopeless, virtually impossible. As a student of foreign languages, I am empathetic and awed by the efforts of the self-taught and the energy of night school students who listen to these strange sounds and try to make sense of them. As a student of Vietnamese I didn't remember any of the sentences I learned from Quí, but that half-effort was doomed from the start. I wouldn't memorize. I need to learn in the way I want to teach. Through context.

Language is organic, like the dirt under your feet in the garden, like the sand that sticks to your toes on the beach. It is tea cups "clinking," parents "kissing," children screeching ("Eeeek! Cô Eeedieee!"). When we language teachers are forced to become observers and students we shake our heads in wonder. How can we teach this and do it justice?

In the Mekong Delta I am listening. Vendors are singing, children are shouting, in my presence people say "Cô la người gì," my friends reply for me: "Mỹ." Young students swallow words in English, their vowels roll like pebbles pushed and pulled by waves. There are six tones, I know, and if I am not careful with them I will say things like "nhà gà" (chicken house) instead of "nhà ga," with which I mean to say "railroad station." But I love the flowers outside my door, Nguyệt que, I can smell that word when I say it. In Saigon I want to say people's names. I want to please my student, so I will say her name correctly. "Ngọc." And then there is Thảo, whom I can hear speaking on the phone from my room. His voice stays muffled beneath the ceiling fan and the sound reminds me of my own voice echoing in a dixie cup on the beach at home. Thảo makes me feel sentimental. The tone falls and rises . . . "Thảo." Bình comes home from the market, walks quickly into my room, flourishes his purchase—a pair of trousers—says his name, and I can hear the fall-rise tone: "You see, I bought this for Thảo."

I am listening, I am listening. I do not hear "th" but "t." I cannot see the shape of the words of the woman collecting trash, but I can see the sway of her shoulder basket. I am listening to vendors sing. There is a porridge seller with a call so strong I couldn't reach a sound like that if I tried. It is a language so deep inside her that we can't reach it—where is that place inside one? (In secret one day I tried to call like that—to have a voice like a big woman—the sound got stuck in my throat, quivered and faded.) But I can say "phở," a warm sound for noodle soup, and "gối cươn"—that is the sound of craving, it is quick and delicious spring rolls. For most of the year I had a good hold on the cooling phrase "cà phê sửa đa." I throw it around like a native speaker. "Môt cà phê sửa đa . . . hai cà phê sửa đa . . ." It means iced coffee with milk.

The students who were coming to sit and talk with me on Sunday morning in the Mekong Delta took an ever-changing, untouchable tool, language, and used it in the service of their most valuable resource, their lives; the poorest among them have already gained my unending respect.

At the morning meeting Kièu and I were partnered to proctor and interview forty students for the A-level certificate. This is the lowest of the three exams, so already nervous students shudder as I walk in knowing they will have to speak to me—a native speaker!—in English. We began with listening. I wrote instructions on the board. I repeated them aloud.

"Listen to the tape. We will play it three times. After you have finished listening, answer the questions in Section One. Choose the correct answer by circling it with your pen." The class mumbled; hands went up. I pointed to the instructions on the board. Kièu wrote a sample answer. The students continued talking among themselves. I gestured to a young man who had his hand up.

"Yes?" I asked, smiling, knowing, waiting like I do in the city, waiting for the fruit to fall.

We spoke in unison: "Miss, . . . do we circle the correct answer or put an X through it?"

"Miss, . . . what if we want to change our answer?" someone added.

Like my students in the city these students were not stupid. It is just that directions are far less emotionally engaging than fear and anxiety. They became wrapped up in the energy and ambition of the moment. I wondered what would happen if we made students "listen and repeat" the phrase "I am afraid," to get rid of this unidentified obstacle, then hear the directions again.

Kièu and I walked around the room during the first section. I don't care about concepts of "face" during exams, so in my loud, Western, policing way I ran around the room chasing voices like they were flies, trying to stop the ghostlike whispering of answers, trying to separate people, trying to intimidate the middle-aged man who was clumsily looking over the shoulder of a twelve-year-old. Kiều stood next to his desk, but to no avail. We decided that I would report him to the director, while Kiều made him change seats for the next section. This is not as easy as it may sound to you and me; it was authoritative and explicit. She had to look him in the eye and say: "Move."

"Did you move him?" I asked when I returned.

"Yes," she said, "but now"—she put her head in her hand—"they will hate me."

After lunch there were oral interviews. As A-level students there is not very much expected of them, but they must pick a topic at random and compose a handful of sentences about it in the space of five minutes. This is scary, and nearly all the students began by apologizing to me because they cannot speak my language very well. I smiled most of the time, waved away their anxiety and asked easy questions. "Where do you live?" "Can you tell me how to get to the market here in Long Xuyen?" The first student, a father, chattered on about his childhood, and the formidable task of parenting his own children.

"How many brothers and sisters do you have?" Kiều asked.

This threw him . . . "Pardon?" he replied.

She repeated coldly: "How many brothers and sisters do you have?"

Silence.

Kiều clicked her tongue. "Oh, come on. It is an easy question."

He blushed. I thought he made a good recovery eventually and gave him twelve out of twenty points (ten is passing).

"Oh, come on," said Kiều, "aren't you being easy on him?"

I was a little taken aback by this. Let's take it easy, I wanted to say, this isn't multiple choice, or short answer. This is night school, this is self-study. This is hard.

A young woman came in. She was covered in jade and gold, and she had very nicely manicured hands. She told us that her parents were goldsellers. She could not say much more than that, only "my English very bad." She was polite, but we failed her. Gold is a more universal language than English. She'll be fine.

I was worried about the farmer, though, and the housewife who started to cry out of nervousness. The middle school students rattled on in textbook English and talked about studying French also. I never thought I would find myself sitting in the Mekong Delta face to face with a twelve-year-old debating the merits of learning French over English. There I was.

"Kiều," I said in the end, "let's pass the farmer."

She stared at me a moment; I had created a gray area. Why would I so aggressively pursue anxious whispers, then pass a man whose English bordered on incomprehensible?

"I felt sorry for him," I said sheepishly.

She snorted. "Tst. You are so soft-hearted."

I looked at her button nose, and her grade failing the farmer.

"I am?"

*   *   *

It is Monday. I am waiting for a ferry to cross the Mekong River. The driver gets out to smoke a cigarette and pace. I'm alone in the front seat when an elderly woman appears at my window. For three days I have been followed by the incessant whining that begging children use, the relentless cry and soft touch. This woman's face is unbearable to me and I turn away. When I turn to my left I realize that an old man, teeth gone, blinded in one eye, has approached in utter silence. He is only an arm's length from me and I am taken aback.

There is so much chaos and sensory stimulation in this country that at times I feel exhausted by the atmosphere alone. These silent gestures send me spinning backward, and there are hundreds of them—the old man, the child, the flower seller, the beautiful woman, the thief . . . "Cô," they say softly. But the eternal contradiction, I wake up every day looking for more. "It is as if," I wrote to a friend, "a heartbeat dictates the rhythm of everything and everyone. . . . As I try to understand why I am drawn to Asia, I think maybe, when I'm out in the traffic, out in the chaos and noise and heat, maybe I hear that heartbeat too."

My memories of the Mekong Delta are light and sound. They are endless shades of green, they are the beige-brown of river houses, bamboo bridges, fishing nets, and floating villages. They are pink and golden from sunsets, and they are the soft yellow of drying harvests. Beneath the hum and whine of the beggars, the uneasy presence of smugglers and thieves, the sadness and longing of country people heading toward the twenty-first century, the towns on the Mekong sit in my memory accompanied by the light of early evening and the continuous music of river sampans.

Tuk, Tuk, Tuk, Tuk, Tuk

Chapter Eight

The history and religion of this vanished people is now exposed to the eyes of the incredulous, so that they can no longer deny that . . . the Cambodia we know once nourished and might again nourish a great artistic and energetic race. They can no longer deny it when they see what was created here a few hundred years ago in this land so well favoured by nature.

—Admiral Bonard, *Revue maritime et coloniale* (1862)

Later, we all said we saw it coming. Karen was sitting perfectly still on the back of the Honda, then—bounce, bump, plop—she was in the puddle. Like a doll falling off a table, her arms bent, her legs spread, she fell backward and hit the ground before any of us could gasp. It's difficult to tell how deep puddles are on country roads; we had driven a long way through the mud, and still we were inside the wall of the city Angkor Thom. But we felt far enough away from things to be lost. Parts of the road were completely impassable, trucks rolled by full of . . . what? soldiers or guerrillas? There were long stretches of nothing, then we would stumble onto an overgrown city gate, a doorway that led nowhere, steps rising from a stream to a platform guarded by stone lions. There were buildings made of brick and buildings made of sandstone, there was water everywhere, and in what passed for neighborhoods there were young children screeching and splashing in puddles and ponds.

A few days before, on a sunny afternoon in Saigon, I was sitting in a noodle shop with my American friend Dave and came up with the idea of visiting Cambodia.

"Let's go to Angkor Wat," I said suddenly.

He smiled. "OK, when?"

"Next week, let's leave on Wednesday."

"All right."

It was sort of a lark, a jaunt to ancient ruins for the weekend. We smiled at each other over the spontaneity of the idea.

"I know!" Dave continued, "let's try going overland, we'll take a bus through the Mekong Delta and into Phnom Penh."

"No, no," I said, my memory still fresh from the drive down the delta. "Let's fly."

We spent the remainder of the week running around Saigon trying to get our visa status changed. I told my students at the university that classes would have to be rescheduled, and I explained to Mr. Lam at the middle school that I would be away visiting Cambodia for a week. His eyes widened momentarily in shock. "Oh," he said, with a worried expression.

Two days before I left, I explained to Thảo and Bình that I would be away for five days visiting Angkor and Phnom Penh. Bình crinkled her brow,

"Cambodia is very dirty and poor!" she said loudly. "It is not safe."

"I think it's still safe," I replied, "and I don't get upset about the dirt."

"Bình is right," Thảo said, quietly, "the Cambodians are . . ." he paused. "They are . . ." I shot him a serious look that said I didn't want to go further with the conversation. The Vietnamese all wondered why I would want to visit Cambodia. "It is such a poor and troubled country," they said. They were right, and their government's own recent history with Cambodia lent a certain weight to their words. Not too long ago Viet Nam and Cambodia were at war with one another. The country was—to use an American analogy—their "Viet Nam."

What could I say? "I'm going to Cambodia to *see*. I'm going to Cambodia to *learn*." Everyone was nervous about the idea of our trip, except Dave and me. "It's not safe!" the Vietnamese said. "They're poor!" After a few days of confronting their nervousness, I sat down with Dave for lunch and brought up the subject of the civil conflict.

"Do you think it's safe?" I said.

"Well, as long as we don't take the train to Angkor," he said.

"What are you talking about?" I asked.

Dave has red hair, very pale skin, and a rather absurd sense of humor. He's sarcastic, observant, and quick-witted. He comes from California, but swears his sense of humor has destined him for a life on the East Coast. He can find a laugh in the darkest of situations, which he was doing at that moment.

"I just met a guy," he paused to laugh, "now, this is true. He says if you take the train in Cambodia the first two cars are free."

"Why?" I asked over his laughter.

"Well," he put his hand up to explain the reasoning, "apparently they use those two cars to set off any landmines that might be on the tracks."

My heart sank. "Why do you want to go overland?" I asked.

"Let's fly," he said.

"From the news I've seen I think things are relatively quiet right now, and the UN is still there, which, for some reason, makes me think we'll be OK as long as we go now, instead of after they've left entirely," I reasoned. "Still, . . ." I paused for a moment, in case he wanted to back out, "you know, it's the middle of the rainy season and it can be pretty messy in the countryside."

Dave looked at me for a moment in thought. "Well," he decided finally, "I think the rainy season is infinitely preferable to the civil war season, don't you?" I laughed out loud. It was settled.

When we arrived at the airport at Siem Reap, the town closest to the ruins of Angkor, we were surrounded by guesthouse owners and pitchmen who haggled with a type of anxiety and desperateness that provoked both irritation and sympathy. The four of us, Dave, Rob (a traveler we met in Saigon), Karen (whom we met on the plane from Phnom Penh), and I were the only ones not being met by guides. This meant we were the only customers available, since there was only one flight a day from Phnom Penh.

Since Karen knew a few words of Khmer she began the haggling. One man seemed to have her cornered, and she kept smiling and laughing softly. The charming pitchman snagged her quickly and we decided to stay at the Mahogany Guesthouse, of whose woodwork we got an extensive description during the taxi ride. I thought he must have heard once that tourists were enchanted by the wooden architecture of Cambodian homes and had an adoration of mahogany that would sell his place.

"Is very nice, all mahogany walls and furniture," he said, gesturing with his hand, "and carving too. And we have beer!"

"Well, there ya go," said Rob, "sold. Just tell me, where's Angkor Thom from your place?"

"Should we change money?" Dave asked.

"I'm not," I said, "just negotiate in U.S. dollars."

"What's the rate?" Rob asked.

"Like a million to one," I said dramatically.

"Million to one, eh?" he replied.

"OK, so I exaggerate," I finished.

"Mr., uh, I'm sorry what's your name?" Dave asked the guesthouse manager.

"Prouen. Call me Mr. Prouen," he said from the front seat, with a kiddish smile. He handed us his card. THE MAHOGANY GUESTHOUSE. MR. PROUEN, OWNER, MAN, SIEM REAP, CAMBODIA.

"Karen," I said, handing her the card, "is that Prone or Prune?"

"I think it's Prawn," she said.

Like the Vietnamese, Cambodians are deferential and respectful in reference to one another, and when guests trip and stumble over pronunciation they smile politely. Mr. Prouen had a slight build and a high-pitched voice. He waited on all his guests hand and foot, and then sat and talked to you with a charming curiosity. He did not have the sadness and longing I so often found in people when I traveled. They seemed to thrill vicariously in your freedom and economic power, living only for the day they can leave where they are. Standing in the middle of war-ravaged Cambodia this isn't exactly difficult to understand, but for me it is tempered by the knowledge of the strange and lonely life of the refugee/immigrant, spurned everywhere because of his poverty.

Mr. Prouen was about to get married, he had a good business going for himself, he took care of his family, and he expressed no desire to leave Cambodia. It seemed that he missed the profitable presence of soldiers who need housing, but he would wait until the tourists came again. He read an English textbook every morning, making him another in a long line of small businessmen in Asia who taught themselves a foreign language. In general we had simple, polite conversations, but I asked him once about the United Nations.

"There were a lot of soldiers here, Mr. Prouen?"

"Oh, yes."

"Did you like UNTAC?" I pried. I wanted to hear local gossip.

"UN is great. I love UNTAC."

This statement surprised me. The journalistic scuttlebutt in Saigon bars said UNTAC was a mess, there were terrible stories about soldier's drunkenness, reports of rape and robbery.

"Bandits still run the towns," an Australian worker said one evening with beery bravado. "It's a complete failure."

"Why did you like UNTAC?" I asked Mr. Prouen. "Didn't they bring trouble?"

"No, no. When we go to vote . . ." he paused. "They are great." He mimed a soldier armed and at attention. "Always very good, very clean. They are great."

"Really?" I ask, unbelieving, almost condescending.

"Yes." He was firm on this. His hand went up (to settle the conversation), like a native English speaker's. His palm was forward. He was telling me he knew what he was talking about.

"I love the UN. They are the first people who come to Cambodia who don't want to take something."

I've learned not to argue with people who know history better than I do. The conversation was finished.

Not too far from the Mahogany Guesthouse was the reason people had come to Siem Reap for centuries. The ruins of Angkor are described as "the most spectacular man-made remains in the world." They are the structures of eleventh- and twelfth-century Khmer Empire, and like the Egyptian cities dragged piecemeal across the seas and displayed in museum showcases, they are a compelling wonder. Over the course of four centuries Angkor expanded as the Khmer Empire rose and fell. The ruins are a series of temples, mausoleums and, built at the peak of the empire, the walled city Angkor Thom. The site, and Khmer history, have inspired countless books and theories that range from the plausible to the outrageous. Angkor Wat, the best-known of the buildings is said by one authority to have taken 300 years to build; another work estimates the building time to be thirty years. In the nineteenth century a French archeologist was told by the Cambodians that the Wat built itself. In order to cover the entire terrain known as Angkor (the Grand Circuit), the traveler needs three full days, but only if you are seeing it by car. The roads, most of which are unpaved, bend and turn through overgrown jungle and forest, then narrow and wind through small villages. If you are seeing it by motorbike, as we were, it is easy to get lost.

The complex nature of the area's layout is matched only by its history. At the end of the twelfth century, it spread as far east as Annam (Viet Nam) and influenced the Malay Peninsula, Burma, and Siam. The Khmer kingdom reached its apogee under Jayavarman VII, but like so many overextended, overindulgent kings, he also brought about the decline of the empire. A twelfth-century attack by Siam initiated two centuries of war and destruction that left Angkor virtually desolate by the end of the fourteenth century.

As a record of the lives of the god-kings, Angkor is a strange mixture of the reverent and the egotistical. The Angkorian personal cults elevated the local, earthly "Lord" to "Lord of the Universe" by putting up statues that blended the figure of the prince or king with a corresponding deity. Thus, Suryavarman II, the king entombed in Angkor Wat is an earthly form of Shiva. In what has been called a mixture of Indian religions—Hindu and Buddhist—the Khmer cults established an aristocracy that ruled two universes: the lives of the earthbound and the kingdom of the dead. Walking in sandstone palaces and tombs built by slaves in tribute to a self-appointed god-king does inspire awe, but it is difficult to say of what sort. Is it the craftsmanship or the arrogance that takes your breath away?

Because the kings claimed they were at least semidivine, they were forced to build their kingdoms according to the cosmic design of Indian mythology.

To insure harmony all structures had to create a duplicate of the layout of the cosmos—to create a microcosm of it. The kingdom had to realize a micro/macro harmony so the souls of the kings would be insured peace. To do this it was necessary to recreate the mountain of Meru (the Magic Mountain) and the ocean around it, to make all buildings on a strictly rectangular plan, and have doors facing the cardinal points. This blueprint, with its towers and moats, its causeways measured by footsteps, its walls built of stone (because wood was for humans) was a vision of the center of the universe. It was meant to be heaven on earth.

From the tenth to the twelfth century the god-kings convinced the population that they were the human gateway to nirvana. Thus, their souls needed to be provided for after they passed away in order to protect the lives of those left behind. This meant a continuous stream of grand and complex architectural tributes. Thus, buildings, sculptures, and stelae were created full of high praise for these rulers and their chiefs. Many of the ruins in the area are funerary temples, but other evidence confuses archeologists, who report the presence of inscriptions making tribute to the living. It seems that the desire for the Divine led to runaway spiritualism and ended in gluttony.

The builders of Angkor operated on an elaborate map of the universe that dictated the location of every wall, tower, and doorway. Ancient architects reported to the god-king that the universe was designed *just so*, and that the temple he would one day inhabit must accord with that cosmic plan in order to produce the requisite harmony. Operating on these designs, imagining the ultimate tribute to the universe and himself, each Khmer king probably enslaved thousands (overlooking a small detail about compassion). But Jayavarman VII, the Buddhist ruler of Angkor Thom, did create a mystical fortress, a city with a haunting quality that comes, perhaps, from the contradictory presence of the spirits of the reverent and the enslaved; it shows both extremes of which human beings are capable—the tyranny of the personal cult, and the genius of cartographers of the universe.

This stone empire—with its distinctive lotus-shaped towers, its haunting Buddhist and Hindu faces observing centuries of conflict, struggle, and desire—is stunning. Every morning it was a pleasure to wake up and ride our motorbikes through the empty, dark country roads until we rounded one last corner, made one more turn that brought us to a southeast approach to Angkor Wat, and, catching our breath, shook our heads in wonder. You look over the moat to the outer walls, imagining the walk down the inner causeway and smiling at the symmetry of the five towers in the Wat's center. I made this pass twice a day for four days, and my wonder never dimmed.

Angkor Wat, the mausoleum of Suryavarman II, is the best maintained of the ruins. According to the cosmic architects, the moat surrounding the mausoleum is the ocean, the first wall the Wall of Rock, and the center Mount Meru's five peaks. Add to this ponds, libraries and courtyards, stairs that rise straight up, like the face of a mountain, and long cool hallways shaded from the sun by intricate window designs and arching roofs.

On the second day of our visit, my friends and I were part of a group of eight travelers sitting at the bottom of the inner causeway, staring into the center of the Wat and eating warm bread in the half-light of the sunrise. In the mist and quiet the green of the land and trees glistened with dew, monks walked in saffron robes to nearby temples, and cowbells rang softly in response to the prodding of herders. Add to this a German man who couldn't stop talking about his camera, a college kid from California who wanted to figure out a way to bring his guitar down in the middle of the night, "play some tunes," and sleep in the center of the Wat, and an Australian woman who kept clicking her tongue because people were walking on the causeway, ruining her photos. All of us snapped pictures, each one hardly distinguishable from the next.

Finally, as the sky was changing from gray-blue to pink, Dave—overcome by some unnameable inspiration—decided to run the length of the causeway, go to the interior of the Wat, and climb the fifty-five meters to the central tower. He came back when the sun was high, exhausted but satisfied. I looked at him, and then at the group. The German man was still talking about bargain prices for cameras, and the others looked slightly bored. I smiled and laughed softly; we had missed it. We stood standing staring from the outside, taking photo after photo, trying to capture "the light," as if it were holy, while Dave was in the middle of it all, climbing around "the five peaks at the center of the universe."

The Wat was the greatest of all Khmer monuments, until Suryavarman II died and the kingdom changed hands. Eventually Siem Reap (as the capital of the kingdom) became the Center of the Universe, Angkor Thom the city in tribute to the new king, and the Bayon the monument at the center of the city.

The Bayon was meant to be the meeting place of heaven and earth. This is a temple built in a hurry. Formerly pyramidal in shape, it now stands alone in the tropical foliage with forty-nine towers, and an endless number of hallways on three different levels; its walls are broken in some spots, moldy and blackened in others. The pyramid shape is gone and it has taken on the air of an elaborate chess set abandoned mid-game, with spiderwebs, vines, fallen sandstone blocks, and the sad acceptance of abandonment. As the spiritual center of the city, it stands alone, with only a circle road to surround it, and dew and shadows in her empty halls.

Jayavarman VII, the impatient Buddhist king who created the Bayon, built and attacked with reckless abandon. The Khmer Empire was to extend from Angkor Thom outward in the ten directions. His conquests, made in the name of religion, include the Cham kingdom (south of Annam) and parts of northern Burma. At one point he made a valiant attempt to capture the Malay Peninsula. Naturally he created a lot of enemies, so Angkor Thom was designed to be not just holy, but impregnable. Fronted by a moat eight miles in circumference, the city wall was supported on the inside by an enormous earth embankment. Because it was a serpent that protected Shakyamuni Buddha during a storm, fifty demon guardians holding seven-headed serpents line the causeways in front of the five tower-sized gates. The serpent rose up during the falling rain and spread its hood, forming an umbrella over Shakyamuni's head. In an abandoned room inside the Bayon, a stone sculpture of this moment sits in the cool shade. In front of the figure are offerings made by Cambodian pilgrims and travelers. The Bayon, like Angkor Wat, is not a temple, but the figures and sculptures inside hold religious significance for the peasants who live in Cambodia's countryside. Even the tall, thick foliage that surrounds the monument's ring road seems to provide shelter.

It's difficult to get your mind around the details the architects had to take into consideration when they planned the city and this monument. I was constantly approaching things at the ruins with a childlike curiosity, only to be taken aback by their enormity. The city gates don't intimidate on approach, but then they dwarf you as you ride through. One morning I looked to my right to discover the columns I so admired on each side were the trunks of elaborate elephant sculptures that served to support the top of the gate, a bust of Lokeshvara, the bodhisattva of compassion. The close second look these sculptures inspired always left me awed.

"How did they do that?" I mumbled to no one in particular, and someone nearby would murmur agreement. Sometimes it was Karen or Rob, sometimes a stranger, but always people were drawn together in friendly curiosity and wonder; it's so quiet, so misty, there is so much that you cannot identify.

The wall panels of the Bayon tell a hundred different stories in sandstone bas-relief. Historical record and gossip blend to reveal the lives of the people in Angkor Thom. Each panel has intricate carvings that record the everyday life of the ancient Khmers. Battles and births are followed by a face-off between soldiers of competing empires; there is a parade of animals, then villagers at feast and a circus, all carved in extensive, intricate detail. The monument rises up from these first-tier walls, making a courtyard here, a dark and narrow hallway there, ending in a series of forty-nine towers. It's a complicated, confusing design, the meaning of which is not clear. Hallways sometimes lead nowhere, stairs go up, but the traveler is easily led astray, losing her direction in the mazelike interior.

The monument was made, some archeologists suggest, without tools. There is not much support for this theory, but nor are there hammers uncovered from the site. Nor are there chisels or wire. There's nothing; the pieces aren't even held together with any form of cement. One writer suggests that the reliefs were *rubbed* into place. This idea is astonishing when you're standing in the mist and recognize the figure of a woman washing her hair, or notice the detail in the line of a bird's throat as it swallows a fish. How did they do it? On a cloudy afternoon I sat in a courtyard, thinking about this question, listening to the voices of my friends rise and fade as they groped along the darkness and tripped up stairs. When the afternoon rain began, I moved to shelter. I huddled in the doorway and then, as if for the first time, I saw what archeologists have described as: "blood-curdling," "eternal," "leering" "fantastic," "eerie," "absolutely unique."

People can't quite get a handle on the towers at the top of the Bayon. They are the peak of this monument in the middle of the universe, and on all four sides is the recurring motif of Angkor Thom, the face of Lokeshvara. The womanly face has eyes half-closed, as if in meditation, her nose is wide and flat, her lips are in a soft smile. The carvings appear not to have been cut *into* the stone, but instead to have been pressed outward from the middle, like masks shaped by the repeated pressure of fingertips. Hundreds of hands must have rubbed soft circles for hundreds of hours to make the round cheeks and the full lips. I did not find the faces frightening, but instead, in the moisture and warmth, omniscient. It seemed as if the towers were chanting an eternal mantra and they swept us up, in an embrace. The face of the wise woman looks into you and repeats again and again, as if soothing a hurt. . . . *I know . . . I know . . .* When we walk around, when we look down the hallways and into the courtyards of the building, even when we leave Lokeshvara is watching us, smiling placidly.

The irony of history is that Jayavarman VII is now said to be the most ambitious, not the most compassionate, of the Khmer kings. Angkor Thom contains some of the most elaborate, and elaborately maintained, temples in the world, built with the labor and genius of the Khmer people. But he was reckless, greedy. The Khmers had already built Angkor Wat. Jayavarman VII pushed for more. He demanded that thousands of villages provide masons and laborers, sculptors and decorators. He kept the city walls up by enslaving the population, taxing them, and then conscripting youth for his royal army. Yet there is evidence of hundreds of hospitals and rest houses for Buddhist pilgrims. And his chief queen, Jayarajadevi, is said, by court historians, to have "filled the earth with a shower of magnificent gifts."

Much has been made of the health of this colorful king. Though "the facts" are always open for debate, it is said that like Yasovarman, the founder of the Khmer Empire, Jayavarman VII was a leper. The only real evidence is cosmic: the thirteenth and fourteenth centuries are marked by a horrible, wasting, and deteriorating decline of Angkorian civilization. The assault by Siam, marking the beginning of the end, may have been a series of conflicts involving weary, jaded, pathetic Khmer troops, just a little tired of all this worship and ready to accept the introduction of Hinayana Buddhism, of which there were many missionaries. This was not a court-imposed god-king cult. It was a popular movement, and has been with Cambodia ever since. But the transition was not so simple, the change of kingdoms violent. Cults dictated that god-kings were buried with their earthly riches as well as their less tangible "essence." French archeologists discovering the ruins of Angkor Thom six centuries later, noted that they were marked by the destruction of both nature and ancient looters. Statues were destroyed in an attempt to find the gold and jewels buried beneath, then strange additions were made and carvings altered in a new rush to reach God. All this before the painful course of modern history in Cambodia. In the end, by the time you, the modern traveler, wander around the Bayon, the monument has been sacked and redesigned, looted, bombed by guerrillas, occupied by soldiers, pilgrims and peasants, studied by archaeologists and anthropologists, wrapped in a weblike growth of vines and weeds, and photographed from all angles. What is still standing, exactly as they were centuries ago, are the faces of Lokeshvara, looking and knowing. . . . *It will all pass . . . It will all pass . . .* The mere memory may cause a visitor to look over her shoulder, but she's not quite sure why.

When you walk around Angkor, when you ride through the gates of Angkor Thom, or wander in and out of the Bayon, you are transported through a type of time warp. The quiet of the jungle, the moisture in the air, you wonder again and again; "How on earth did people design and build this place?" And what is its power that people would fight so over it? The second question occurs again and again as you make your way past unmarked police patrols and ride through armed motorcycle gangs. On our last sunrise visit to the Wat, I trailed behind Dave, Rob, and Karen to take some pictures of the guardian lions on the outside walkway. I jogged to catch up after I finished, only to bump into a Cambodian teenager in the entranceway.

"Oh," I said, startled, "I'm sorry."

He looked at me for a moment, then continued on his way. I watched him over my shoulder, then continued on to the second causeway. I stepped into the light, and his figure, with its small frame and what I thought was a rifle strap hanging across his shoulder, suddenly became clear in my immediate memory. The rifle rose too high and its muzzle was too large.

"It was a little dark in the doorway," I said to everyone, "but was that kid carrying a rocket launcher?" There was a long pause. Dave turned and looked at me, "Is that what that was?"

Without taking my camera out of the bag, I sat and watched the sunrise.

Chapter Nine

"You come from a very happy place," the driver said. "This is not a happy place." I usually disagree with people when they talk like this—"Oh no," I say, "Oh no, your city is beautiful." But I was in Phnom Penh; I had a scarf tied across my face because the smell of garbage was so strong; my skin and hair felt burnt from the sunlight, and I was irritable and disgusted because the city—war-torn and ragged—has a Mercedes Benz dealership but no refuse collection. We arrived at the street where Karen was living. I got off, turned, and gave the driver 1,000 riel.

"No, no," he said "two thousand."

"No way!" I snapped.

"We take you very far."

He crossed his arms. He had that look of frustration and anger that hungry people get from living too long hand to mouth. He makes his money by riding around the city on a Honda—borrowed, bought, or stolen I don't know—and giving rides to Cambodians and foreigners. I'm sure he has to argue like this a lot with people. There is no set fee for rides, only this endless bickering. I was told Cambodians pay only 500 riel for the same ride. I knew what the going rate was and, as always, I used that knowledge to be strong in negotiations. In America the hungry and desperate would call me a "cheap bitch," but he just stared hard at me from behind crossed arms.

"Don't pay him extra," Karen said. "I already paid my driver. It's only 1,000 riel."

I was in a jam. Two thousand riel isn't that much. But I was irritated, so I shoved the two 500 riel notes into his hand and turned away. I waved away his protest and yelled over my shoulder, "That's it buddy." Phnom Penh is like this. It is irritating, frustrating, dirty, and unexplainable. I wanted to get out as soon as possible. I was staying with Karen and her family. Like so many Australians and Europeans, they live and work in the city. I had two days before my flight back to Saigon, and that meant more rides on Hondas and a not-so-comfortable itinerary. After four days imagining the power of ancient Khmer culture, we would re-witness and reconsider the thing Cambodia is most famous for: genocide.

Before I left Viet Nam I told people I would not visit Tuol Sleng or the Killing Fields at Choueng Ek. I thought it was a vulgar gesture to do so; I thought I should avoid being a "rubbernecker." But ideas change, thoughts happen, and they lead to conversations. One afternoon in Saigon, during a rambling overseas call from my sister and her husband, I pondered the idea of visiting, with the intention of writing about it. "Maybe it would be interesting," I said.

"I think an article like that would be fantastic," my brother-in-law said, "it sounds great. I mean I'd love to read something like that."

Wouldn't it be interesting?

The same day I thought about my friend Susan, who is a junior high teacher in Belmont, Massachusetts. We have had the same conversation about my travel for years. Before I leave on one of my extended trips overseas, she says: "Oh, when you get back you can do a special slide show for the kids in social studies. They'd really be interested. They love this stuff."

"Oh yeah," I replied each time, "it would be fun."

I imagined myself showing slides of China, the Great Wall, and the Forbidden City. From Viet Nam, I would show the basket fishing boats of Danang, and the riverways of the Mekong Delta. I could show them the conical hat my Vietnamese students in Ho Chi Minh City gave me, and the beaded slippers that are part of Vietnamese dress. In Siem Reap I thought of stories I could tell them about the Khmer kings and their battles for the expansion of empire. I tried to think of ways to describe the awesome gates of Angkor Thom and the haunting faces of the Bayon. I wanted to show them the old maps of Indochina I found in antique stores, and the place names that have changed again and again. I imagined their chubby hands running across the paper and the soft mumbling sounds they would make as they tried to imagine a hot, humid place halfway around the world.

Wouldn't it be fun?

I went. It wasn't exactly a lark, but I didn't know what I was in for and I wasn't sure if I was right. Was this just some sort of vulgar moral thrill ride?

Tuol Sleng was a high school once. It was called Tuol Svay Prey Middle School and located at (what is now called) 113 Street, just off 350 Street. It became S-21 in 1975 after the Khmer Rouge takeover of Phnom Penh. Then it became a torture chamber. Literally. We've all referred to our adolescence as "torture," but now imagine . . . Classrooms built to expand the horizons of young minds shelter demons. Hallways once full of giggles and flirting echo with the sound of chains binding ankles, heads hitting wood, teeth hitting brick, and the involuntary screams that come with electric shock.

The four buildings of the compound have been left almost entirely as they were found by the Vietnamese in 1979. All photographs contained there were taken by the Khmer Rouge as a form of record keeping. I walked through the gate, a nondescript stone wall with a heavy iron door. It is an everyday entrance, one that frightens all the more for its mundaneness. There is no giant doorway, no large sign—it is steps away from an apartment building. I went to the left, entered the first building, and took myself from bad to worse.

At first there are three empty rooms, in one there was a street mutt who, people said, was there every day. The absurdity of it fits; he is nestled in the corner under a poster-size photo of the mutilated bodies of torture victims. Beneath my feet the dirt and pollution of the city barely cover blood stains. I begin to feel the first strains of discomfort and start mumbling stupid questions. What is that? . . . is that . . . uh, is that . . .? The buildings form a horseshoe around the school playground. I'm thinking twice about everything I encounter . . . Is that a swing? It is not a swing in the middle of the "playground," it is a scaffold from which people were hung by their wrists . . . . . . which were bound behind their backs.

The second building contains records of the takeover of the city and the imprisonment of the "enemies of the revolution." This Maoist attack targeted the educated and the middle and upper classes; the Khmer Rouge forced them to relocate to rural areas, then proceeded to torture and execute them. Survivors made their way on foot across the country to Thailand where refugee camps had been set up by the Red Cross.

On one wall are photos from 1975. Everyone is gone from Phnom Penh. The United States has abandoned its odd and illicit mission, the UN hasn't arrived yet, reporters have run from the chaos, the well-connected have fled; it is a ghost town. The black-and-white city streets are completely vacant. Apartment blocks are abandoned; hundreds of empty windows and mortar holes look like mouths agape in horror. I'm trying to imagine the forced evacuation of an entire city by men holding guns and riding the running-boards of trucks. I'm trying to imagine looking out a window and seeing this.

I was reminded of a nightmare I had in my mid-twenties. It was long and full of symbols: There were flowers and lawns, a man and a woman; there were scientists and intellectuals; there was a dark house and a spacious laboratory. And there were killers. Killers were chasing me through underbrush and city streets. I analyzed and tried to interpret the dream for years and came up with nothing. I remember the sound of my breath and the pushing away of branches and leaves. After time the only thing left in my memory—clear as a photograph—is the image of me squatting in a doorway sweating and scared because a car full of killers is chasing me and there is nowhere to hide. These photographs frighten me, and I think that if pictures could make sound. . . . Well, I think that these pictures are scary, and that the streets look like some clichéd western, with the painful, eerie rustle of paper traveling on the wind, the unreal echo of fleeing footsteps and screams before death.

There is another photo next to this portrait of the city. It is a mountain of clothing taken from the genocide victims. Like a photo of a pile of bodies this might first strike you as just another news item, just another part of the record. But in this room the pictures are fronted by a glass case with actual pieces. I'm saddened and sickened by the worn, moldy, stained fabric, and I'm shocked, as I would be again and again, by the size of the children's clothes. The room is full of pictures of different size, and the back wall is dominated by an exhibit recording the capture, confession, and execution of three foreigners. I should be taken by this, but I am not. I am drawn to a photo of a woman by the door. Later, when I spoke with Dave about his journey through the building he recalled the same thing. "I noticed her too," he said, "I don't know why."

She has the look of an educated city woman. She has no flatness of face, no weary expression, her skin is not browned from tropical heat or field work. Her expression is neither resigned nor rebellious. She does not wince from the light or look shocked. She seems to gaze right at you in a type of emotional coma. This woman's face strikes me—I think—because of the size of the photo; it is a poster, like so many others. But I wander over again and again to this corner, stare long at the face of this city woman and the nearby photo of her with her child. I don't know why I am touched by her—I am not saddened. On my third pass I understand. She's beautiful. The bloodied clothes in the case to the right do not diminish it, the blankness of her expression does not hide it, the immediate memory I have of what a tortured body looks like does not override it. This is the beginning of my trip through this weird maze, and I feel myself take shelter in her grace and poise. For a time I held on to it so I did not have to see what was ahead of me.

As I move from room to room the number of pictures increase, until I am standing in a room wallpapered with faces. A wall of women stare out at me. I can still see the face of one woman in her cell. It repulses me. I cannot say why. I want the dignity of the first woman I saw, but I cannot see it. This woman, in the small 4″ × 6″ photograph is not hideous, not fearful; her face has not been beaten. But she has a surprised look. She sits up, stunned by the light from the open door of her cell, her baby asleep on the mat beside her. Maybe she has been woken from sleep by a flashlight, by someone pounding on the piece of wood that acted as door to the brick box she was placed in. Maybe she was looking in question—"Yes, what is it?" "Do I go now?" "Is it my turn?" Maybe inside she was hoping this would be her turn to get killed; maybe she was thinking that luck would be with her today and she would get a bullet in the head. I walk away from the picture and a sick thought rises . . . but I suppress it. I look at more faces, some startled, some angry, some numbed. But hers will not go away; I try to think of the woman in the first room; I can only see the eyes of the other women and babies papering the wall of this room. I am overcome by nausea as the thought of this woman's experience takes form. . . . I can hear the pained realization today as I recall her face, and the small body that lay beside her. . . . *The baby will be tortured too. Maybe they'll take it from her and torture it first.*

At home when my migraine headaches strike hard and furious, I put my hands on my face. I warm my hands and place them on my head, the thing that feels like it will shatter. In Phnom Penh I hear this sentence that is separate from me but completely my own and, overcome with grief, I place my face in my hands. There is no comfort. Feeling claustrophobic I begin to back away, to turn here or there, but I only encounter more faces, I cannot avert my eyes. I move to the next room only to encounter more walls with more people.

The third building of Tuol Sleng contains torture rooms and holding cells for victims. Thrown together quickly in order to accommodate the 17,000 people seized from Phnom Penh, the brick and wood cells are so small that if you rock your body from side to side you will repeatedly bang your head. Holes were knocked in walls to make doors between rooms, and moving in the darkness and silence, breathing in the dust and pollution it is easy to get unnerved. I've come up to the second floor—walked up the consummate schoolhouse stairwell, wide cement staircases with heavy metal edging and sturdy handrails that are broken up by room-sized landings. I've walked down the caged hallway, stepped into the darkened rooms, peered through the wall holes. I've even squatted in a cell. But I will not touch anything. I walk down the center of halls for fear of brushing against barbed wire or brick; I won't step through the wall holes because I see myself tripping and imagine my head hitting the floor. I begin hyperventilating because the dust and rust is sticking in my throat—so I stop breathing.

As I entered the last building I realized that it was where I should have begun. I mistakenly walked through the maze backward, starting at building four and moving to building one. It contains exhibits detailing events in historical order. The faces of the recently dead are shading my vision as I look at the scrap-and-paste exhibits, the photos made by Khmer Rouge and the paintings made by witnesses. These wall-size testaments to history make the viewer cringe. They are testimony given by survivors and painfully done with bright colors and a childlike hand. Lifted from this place and put before psychoanalysts the paintings and pictures might be called the work of psychotics. But the vicious gleam in eyes that watch bound women scream over the presence of scorpions on their bare breasts, the wicked twist in hands that electrocute beaten victims held in vats of water, is no melodramatic act of imagination. All of it—the signs written in awkward schoolchild English on pieces of scrap wood with red and black paint (there are no pens, no paper, no printing . . .?), the weird explanations (wire nets cover all balcony areas to "prevent the insane committing suicide") have a way of searing through all your sensibilities until you're mute.

When it came time for me to consider these images, I was hot and thirsty and exhausted. I walked out after staring at a plaster-of-paris map of Cambodia hanging on the wall, bottom-heavy with skulls. Karen was waiting for me at the gate (she said she couldn't come in; she had seen it before). She was laughing with a young man trying to sell her something. She didn't try to make conversation; she just took me home.

✳   ✳   ✳

The next morning we went to the Killing Fields at Choueng Ek. Fifteen kilometers away from the center of the city these grounds were the site where the Khmer Rouge continued their crimes and disposed of the bodies. Today a stupa stands two stories high, filled with the 8,895 human skulls excavated from the ground beneath. The remaining thousands will stay buried throughout Cambodia. On the bottom tier of the stupa are the children's skulls they are all cracked in three directions. Karen put her hand on the glass.

"Look," she said, "they're all exactly the same."

"Yeah," I murmured.

"That must be . . .," she paused.

"What?" I was dazed and overwhelmed.

"how they, uh . . ." We looked at each other.

"How they died." She said, "They bludgeoned them."

As the shelves rise up, the skulls tilt forward, and empty sockets stare down at you. Some are missing jaws, some, mouths agape, fall backward. Then, rising up still higher, the heads can only be viewed from the bottom. We stood staring up at an endless number of holes that held spines.

Months later, at another dinner with Linda and Mary Ann, Trish began to talk about her plans for a trip to Angkor.

"Don't go to Phnom Penh," I said. "It's so upsetting."

"The Killing Fields?" Trish asked.

"I still don't know why I went," I said. "I think . . ." I paused. They waited. "I don't know, I don't know," I ended, awkwardly.

I couldn't articulate it, but I was grappling with my growing belief in the need for witnesses. It wasn't a moral thrill ride. It wasn't even close. Linda and Mary Ann had also gone to Cambodia around the time of my trip. They took out their photos to show Trish.

"You took photos?" I asked, shocked.

"I thought I should," said Linda.

"I couldn't bring myself to do it," I told her.

We couldn't share much more. But they remembered meeting an American doctor on the road.

"He was on leave from his job," said Mary Ann. "His wife teaches in Viet Nam and he was traveling for a few weeks. He said he had come to love and admire Cambodians, and thought about working there."

"Doctors without Borders?" I asked.

"Well," she continued, "he's an optometrist and he said he wanted to somehow raise funds to open up clinics for eye care. 'Then,' he said, 'after seeing the Killing Fields it struck me what a huge leap of faith I was asking so many Cambodians to make.'"

We paused. I leaned forward, trying to get Mary Ann to elaborate, trying to understand.

"He? . . ." I asked, then stopped suddenly. "Oh! They . . .," but I didn't finish. Glasses, a symbol of intellectualism in a Maoist revolution, were a death sentence for Cambodians. Trish continued looking at the photos.

"Here. Look," Linda said, handing me the album. "I wish someone had told, or would tell them how to write signs in English."

She showed me a photo of a piece of wood painted white, like the signs in

Tuol Sleng. The black-paint lettering identified the hole over which it stood: ON THIS SITE THE POL POT CLIQUE KILLED THREE 300 WOMEN AND CHILDREN ALL OF WHOM WERE NAKED.

"What's wrong with it?" I asked.

"I just wish someone had fixed it. I mean I can see so many people reading it and giggling."

"You think people could actually laugh there?"

I imagined the sign done over in the tile plate style of museums. On this site lay the tortured, naked bodies of 300 women and children.

"I like the signs as they are," I said.

Next to a stupa of bludgeoned skulls and a $7' \times 7'$ hole full of bone chips, the quality of print is completely academic.

"I want them to leave things as they are," I said.

The ground behind the stupa, a series of holes and pathways, looks like— is—an archaeological dig. Under your feet, the earth is quilted with white bone fragments and, rising silently, the ragged clothing of the victims. I remembered Tuol Sleng and the pieces of clothing taken from dead bodies: there was a small blue jacket, a black shirt, trousers torn and piled up like rags. There were work trousers and the robes of monks. There were shirts that covered shoulders that were beaten and broken, there were robes that wrapped around bodies that were starved then electrocuted. If the monuments of Angkor testify to the grandness of the ancient Khmer civilization, these pieces of fabric rise up in silent testimony to madness.

I walked around in the silence of this countryside setting, and fought off the irrational fear that I would slip from the narrow pathways of the dig into one of the holes. I kept wrestling with the nervousness aroused by my imagination. I saw myself slipping and falling into a pit and then trying to climb up walls quilted with the bone chips of children and the rags that bound their mother's mouths. In my vision I am hysterical and incapable, a silly, screaming figure rolling around the detritus of a calamity. So, I walk, very slowly, back to the base of the stupa and sit near the cola seller.

How could I have thought that I would be able to teach people about this place? I wondered. I saw myself standing in front of Susan's junior high students who sit and smile from under their Champion sweatshirts, who cry over social snubs and lost athletic competitions. . . . *My mouth is opening and closing, but there are no words coming out.*

I kept hearing children's voices. "I know I'm not crazy," I mumbled.

"Is that a school?" I asked.

"Yes," Karen said, "the local children go to school near here."

In deciding to go to these places, I mistakenly assumed myself capable of a clinical detachment. I thought it would be "like the movie, only more real." I assumed that I would never understand this, that it would all appear so distant. I put my head in my hands again.

A group of four tourists arrived with cameras and began taking pictures. As if to keep something between themselves and us, the Cambodian guides gathered on the back side of the stupa. I knew they were strangers because they had not greeted each other, but they talked now because they had much common ground.

*   *   *

That night, trying to sleep in a large, beautiful house in the center of the city, I was afraid of the dark. I left my hall light on, paced around my room, looked out the window at Phnom Penh—a city half-blackened because electricity is rationed. I thought about our guide, who said he had never seen the Killing Fields.

"It make me very afraid," he explained. But he drove us there. I suppose he needed the money. He sat with us while we stared at the horizon and said: "I miss my family."

In my memory I can still see the Cambodian interpreters talking to each other at the back of the stupa: four thin, dark-haired figures with voices that made soft, beautiful sounds, talking, perhaps, about the unspeakable. I wonder if their language is more resonant than English. Is it like Vietnamese, where meaning ripples outward, getting bigger and bigger? I wonder if they had words big enough to explain this place. I know that I never will. In the half light of my room I listened to the darkness and felt terrorized by the silence that Cambodia engenders. I felt horribly unsafe and haunted by the wall of faces. I climbed into my bed, pulled up a sheet, and curled into a ball. I cried myself to sleep thinking about empty city streets, bombed out, vacant buildings, hundreds of thousands of bones, and the ghosts of torture victims sifting slowly through the piles of clothes they once wore. Weeping and sobbing, I wished, for the first time in my life, that I had never left home.

Chapter Ten

It is not good for the Christian health
to challenge the Asian brown
For the Christian riles and the Asian smiles
and he weareth the Christian down.
At the end of the fight lies a tombstone white
with the name of the late deceased
And the epitaph drear: "A fool lies here
Who tried to hustle the East."

—Rudyard Kipling

Olivier thought they were overdressed; he shuffled through business cards, rattled on about "must sees," and took off his tie.

"Are we overdressed?" he asked me.

"Yeah," his business partner, Kim, added, "what do people wear here?"

"It's hard for me to say," I replied. "I don't turn much in business circles, but it seems that people here are pretty casual."

Here's something new: today in Ho Chi Minh City small groups of Western investors can be seen sitting around hotel lobbies, playing with name cards and having conversations that begin: "Do you remember what this guy does?"

Olivier and Kim were researching Viet Nam's business climate. It is an understandable impression to wonder about the atmosphere. Vietnamese businessmen ride around the city on Hondas, wearing white tennis suits and Ray-ban sunglasses, and Western investors stroll in from New York and Hong Kong wearing Armani. They drink gin and tonic, or Heineken, in hotel lounges and they talk about Taiwan imports and Mekong Delta factories. They listen to people say they love it in Viet Nam, and they listen to people say they hate it in Viet Nam.

At a quick, page six–style glance the city looks like this: There's a Viet Kieu from Los Angeles wandering around looking for capital, and a venture capitalist from New York looking for investments; billionaire bankers arrive daily from Europe, chic restauranteurs from California. There's a fancy bar called "Q" where expats gather, and a club called "Buffalo Blues" that has real jazz, pool tables, and Bass Ale on tap. Oil men ("the boys from Castrol") are dating local girls, and energetic and wealthy Eurokids spread corporate rumors. Outside Asia international newspapers and magazines write about per capita consumption, Viet Nam's literate labor force, and the hardworking nature of her population. They tempt foreign investors with language more appropriate for the travel and style sections than the business page. Investing in Viet Nam, it seems, is very chic.

I didn't know what to say to Olivier about the logistics of doing business in Ho Chi Minh City. I was having a difficult time trying to accomplish simple tasks. Only a few days before I had placed a call at the post office to my brother and his wife. I grudgingly gave the woman in the yellow *áo dài* a week's salary, then sat in booth number eleven and waited fifteen minutes for the call to go through. It was the middle of the night in Boston so I woke up Brian and his wife, Sue.

"Hi!" Sue said. "How is it?! What's it like? Did you get sick?"

We went through a strange series of pauses and exchanges, saying a lot of nothing and then she passed the phone to Brian.

"Ede," I heard him say, in a tone that told me he was eager to talk.

"Hey!" I replied, my voice cracking.

Then the line went dead.

I hadn't calculated properly, and I didn't have enough money to pay for more time; I had wasted the money already spent. Brian's voice echoed in the booth. We didn't write to one another, and it was hard hearing a familiar voice like that, as if it had echoed from a dream.

"God damn this country," I muttered as I slammed the door of the booth.

I rode home trying to think of ways to get access to a phone with international lines; I tried to think of people I knew teaching in foreign companies; I thought I should start cultivating good relations with some Vietnamese businessmen. I was looking for the "gonneggtions" that Meyer Wolfsheim so crudely offered Nick Carraway in 1920s New York.

＊   ＊   ＊

"Mr. Phương would like you to teach him English," Bình mentioned at dinner, a few days later.

"Phương?" I said, "Oh, God, no. I don't want to teach Phương!"

Phương was the rich restauranteur that I met on my first night in Ho Chi Minh City. He was a friend of Bình and Thảo who had struck out on his own after years of working for the government in the National Biochemistry Research Lab. He was certainly colorful, but I had no interest in taking on a new student who probably wasn't very serious.

"Phương is going to England in two months," Thảo explained, then he laughed nervously. "He would like you to teach him English."

"I'm sorry," I answered. "I understand he's your friend, but I really only like to take on serious students." Thảo and Bình were quiet for a moment. I realized a flat "no" would embarrass them.

"OK, look, I know what will work. Tell him I charge twenty-five dollars an hour." This was a new trick I was trying, to sort out the committed students from the newly rich out on a lark. Twenty-five dollars is a little less than the going rate elsewhere in Asia, and it is standard pay in the United States for private lessons. So far the trick had worked well, a month earlier it scared off Bình's boss who showed up at the house late one evening, drunk and demanding. He kept insisting he would study English, even if it meant beginning our lessons at 6:30 in the morning, wouldn't I please teach him? I kept giving him a cold stare and a flat "no," and Bình translated politely that I was very busy with my university work, and (I inferred this from her gestures) I had just returned from Kampuchea and the trip had made me terribly sick and worn out.

"Tell him I charge twenty-five dollars an hour," I said, with my first smile of the evening.

"What?" Bình asked, with a blink and a smile.

"Twenty-five U.S. dollars an hour," I said, looking at the man's face, which was flush with a beer buzz. "Eh. . . ." Bình tried to explain.

"Never mind," I said, getting up, "he understands."

Thảo and Bình continued politely with the conversation until he could be persuaded to leave.

"How could you be so polite to him?" I demanded of Bình later. "He was horrible." She started laughing.

"Dốt lắm," she said. "Edie, I hate him. He is a farmer boss. He is *dốt lắm*." He was a fool, but he was her boss. Thảo and she were smarter and more polite than I because they had to be.

Phương, however, would be a different story.

"He can pay whatever you like!" Bình proclaimed that night at dinner.

"Really?" I asked.

"Oh, yes," Thảo said quietly. "Phương is very wealthy businessman."

We went to his restaurant the next evening, and the enticements began. "You'll come to my factory," he told me. "I am going to London. I will study

English with you." He began to ply me with food, taking a serving spoon and placing chicken on my plate, using the chopsticks to de-bone the fish in the center of the table and ladling brown sauce over it before he placed it very delicately on top of my rice. He explained that he had a chef at the factory who would prepare my lunch three days a week, and then we would spend one and a half hours studying. This would last for approximately one month before he left on his business trip. Because I wanted to go to Burma in the spring, I needed money, so the lavish enticements of the banquet were unnecessary.

Phương is part of what the *International Herald Tribune* called Viet Nam's "inherent entrepreneurial vigor." He has a round face, he's a little fat, with a loud laugh and lousy English. He has all the accoutrements of success: a car and driver, Western sportswear, a Rolex watch, a government official of his own, a wife *and* a girlfriend (she's Chinese, it brings him luck), an office on the road to Chinatown, and a fashionable court time at the city tennis club. When he talked, he leaned forward, and said "yeah, yeah, yeah," so I could see he was listening.

In all our clumsy conversations I tried to imagine Phương playing tennis in the wild way I had seen Vietnamese play at the Cercle Sportif on Nguyen Thi Minh Kai Street.

"They play tennis like me," I told Trish one afternoon, which is to say they have the unrestrained enthusiasm of the untaught. Spindly figures take oversized strides, arms flying, ball high, they misjudge shots and swing like cartoon characters swatting air. Extreme bursts of effort created the occasional swan song shot, but energy expended, players were unable to reach the return and stood panting and helpless at the front of the court as the ball landed, ever so lightly, a million miles away.

On the sidelines people chat casually, make mental notes about fashion, sip iced coffee, and smoke cigarettes. It reminded me very much of Wimbledon, with parading, nodding, fashionable drinks, and not the least amount of interest in tennis. By the time I left Viet Nam the entire crowd was beginning golf. I never saw Phương play tennis (the fashionable court time is 6 a.m.), but I often imagined his bouncy gait, his "Yeah, yeah, yeah" and his "HA HAHA" rising up in the shadows of the French colonial buildings that make up the sports complex and I smiled.

He has an ear always cocked for the latest trends, the most fashionable thoughts.

"Oh," he said to me one evening when rumors of a Saigon Stock Exchange were circulating, "The Dow." The phrase hung empty in the air. I smiled and repeated it. "The Dow." He never seemed to drink alcohol ("I'm getting too fat! Too much beer! HA HAHA!"). I theorized that he didn't drink because he was bullied by his girlfriend, but at some point he must have realized alcohol dulls the senses and in such a gray and crowded place as the Vietnamese market he knew he needed to keep his wits about him.

As it turned out things were often too chaotic at his office for the English lesson, never mind the meal. I arrived on the first day to find him yeah-yeahing on the phone. He hung up quickly when he saw me, laughed, and boomed: "TEACHER!" He looked at his "boys"—his runners, drivers, lackeys—and nodded toward me, giving a satisfied, adolescent look of accomplishment. He had acquired an American English teacher. This is very impressive; it is an important new connection in a connection-conscious culture. Like nouveau riche the world over, when Phương ran out of things to buy, he tried to acquire people.

Like elsewhere in Asia, today's Vietnamese millionaires come from one of two places: the street or abroad. Viet Kieu return from abroad for reasons of sentiment and smarts, the government encourages investment by former citizens with tax incentives and land-owning privileges. Some Viet Kieu have MBAs from Harvard or degrees from New South Wales in Australia. They wave their diplomas like flags, but when you are in Viet Nam it is the "something from nothing" business that grabs your attention, the locals who stuck around and stuck it out. I can see them today on the tennis court, or at one of the many new golf courses popping up in Viet Nam. Playing these games of success Vietnamese men and women may repeat too jovially—like laughter in the dark—a joke that circulated through the country in the early eighties.

> The war is over, and Hanoi sends a telegram to Moscow:
> SEND MONEY!
> Moscow replies: TIGHTEN YOUR BELTS!
> Hanoi wires back: SEND BELTS!

It's cute, Ah-ha-ha-ha, except that its so painfully, terribly true. Viet Nam starved through the eighties. That awareness, like some all-consuming primal urge, fuels every business person in the country today, from spring roll seller to factory owner. The more I looked the more elements of post-1975 Viet Nam rose like images in a violent, surreal dream. Thus the black humor. In my mind I could see Viet Nam as a pawn stranded on the edge of a chess board, small, useless, and deserted. In daily life hunger lurked everywhere in people's memories. It was behind the lavish banquets; it was what made the gold letters of the Tet decorations glimmer; it gave speed and weight to the gesture of taking money from a tourist. I could hear its urgency in mother's voices when children refused to eat—too young to remember the stark dilemma of trading meat for oil or having to choose between a pound of meat and two pounds of bones. "I became accustomed to having only the marrow," a friend said casually during an afternoon lunch. "Now, I prefer it."

Phương worked his way up from those streets. Here's how: he went through a scrap heap, pirated engineering plans, and set up a noodle factory. He was dirt-poor once, but he decided one day that he would stay in Viet Nam instead of leaving, like so many others. He told me he knew he'd never make it overseas. "If I lived in America today," he said, "I'd be washing dishes. In Viet Nam I am rich." He's right. He's got virtually no overhead in his factory. Every month he clears . . . if I tell you you'll think I'm exaggerating; Twenty thousand? Thirty thousand? Believe it.

What's the story? Where's the miracle? It all began with a visit to Japan. A Japanese food company was looking for entrepreneurs to begin a chain for its brand of instant noodles. They conducted meetings, showed Vietnamese how they could start a franchise, what kind of equipment they would use, and how much money they would need. Phương liked *all* their ideas. He especially liked the idea that he could be a factory owner. A boss. If he worked hard enough, he could be a noodle king. He didn't like the initial outlay though; there had to be a way around that. He called a friend in government. He went to a scrap yard. There were piles of American weapons and steel scrap. He had studied enough engineering to know how to build an assembly line, so he took American weaponry and did just that. He broke canons off tanks, and made them into presses; he took pieces of steel and built covers for ovens and oil vats; he took springs and wires, wheels and rubber and he slapped together an instant noodle factory. First one, then two, and so on and so on. He got foreign investors, so he could expand. He now runs factories in Russia, Korea, and the Philippines. He's a millionaire.

Our first class was a tour of the factory. He showed me his two assembly lines and raved about the quality of American steel; he laughed at his own ingenuity; he repeated his monthly profits and told me about all the other factories he had set up in the same way. His noodles are immensely popular; he dumps them in city shops and pays the owners not to sell other brands. This is a very effective distribution method, he told me just before he repeated his monthly profits. We went back to the office and the classwork began.

"Phương, let's practice introductions, OK?"

"Yeah."

"Hi, my name is Edie Shillue. I'm from the United States."

"Yeah, yeah. Hi, I am Mr. Phương. Saigon, Viet Nam. I very pleased to meet you."

Western courtesies are an odd stumbling block for the older student. They can't glide along like young people—they're too embarrassed. Introductory lessons and minor detail, smack of baby talk for the adult. Their built-in syllabus leaps from "Hello," to contract negotiations and diplomatic missions. Phương was like the adolescent piano player who doesn't want to play scales, only wants to perform concertos. With him, a "How are you?" would segue into a comic series of stumbles that neither of us could get out of . . .

"Now? now what?" he asked.

". . . No, Phương, *how.*"

"How?"

"No," I tried to rescue the conversation, "I mean, How . . . are . . . you?" I pointed at him. He paused a long time.

"Oh! . . . Ha, ha! a very easy question! Ha, ha! Fine, thanks, and you?" By this time I'd lost my rhythm, too, so I rattled off, "Fine thanks, and you?"

Phương smiled and said, "Fine thanks, and you?"

Conversations like these often usurped a good part of the lesson. I pestered him on pronunciation—I told him to drop the "yeah," and tapped the table every time this fossilized habit popped up. The result: His sentences became a staccato of words, taps, and "yeahs." The office became a reverse Pavlovian, Henry Higgins torture chamber.

"How are you, Phương?"

"Yeah, yeah."

Tap Tap.

"Oh, yeah."

Tap.

"Fine thanks, and you?"

In our first lesson I explained noun-verb agreement, and the importance of using the right gender in pronouns (thus avoiding phrases like "He is my wife"). He smiled a lot, told me I was a good teacher, and, at the end of the hour, handed me a hundred dollar bill.

There is no stronger evidence of the contradictory relationship between the heart and head than the foreign language lesson. With every new word from this other world, we simultaneously discover and reinvent ourselves. Schoolteachers are princesses; noodle kings become diplomats. We do not want to learn "Hello," or "I'm fine thanks, and you?" We have too much to say. I knew that with my taps and prods, my insistence on saying it right, I was taking all the fun out of it for this flashy, ambitious guy. I went home and bet Bình five dollars that he wouldn't last the month. I won.

Phương wanted to talk business, but he couldn't. He spoke clearly and loudly when we toured his factory and, if I had had a chance to ask, he may have told me one of the stories I'd heard about him. I was told he was from a poor family with a questionable political history, that his family home in Danang was gone, that he survived the eighties by doing what he was told and that, when he wanted to strike out on his own no one would "allow" it, but he did it anyway!

"Phương make me very nervous," Thảo said one evening a few weeks later.

"What do you mean?" I asked.

"He would have people killed, you know, over business."

"Terrific," I mumbled, "now I'm schoolteacher to a mafia boss."

Phương gave up on his schooling, but whenever he saw me I was known laughingly, as his "teacher."

With his street smarts and his political shadiness Phương is thriving in what the business press might call "less developed administrative environments." For those accustomed to order and consistency, this market is a carnival ride, by turns thrilling and terrifying. Anyone with a spare dime looks at the Asian bazaar and sees gold. It's goods being sold by eager merchants, it's millions of workers who perform repetitive factory tasks for pennies, and it's governments that ignore regulation. It's heaven. Or it's hell. It's factory goods that come out "just a little off," it's a marketplace full of dumped merchandise, it's problems that aren't addressed by the law but by bribes, and it's crowded. It's very very crowded.

A few days after my lesson with Phương, during one of our lunches at the restaurant Tin-Tin, Thư invited me to accompany her to the market. "My sister and I are going to An Dong market to buy material for a new áo dài, do you want to join us?"

"Sure," I said, happy to tag along.

We hopped on her motorbike, went down Vo Van Tan Street to the center of the city, then went on to District 5. An Dong is a large, modern market located next to Cholon, Saigon's Chinatown. It has a bargain basement atmosphere, and is part of the growing Asian investment in Viet Nam.

"Don't buy anything," Thư advised me, "tell me what you like and I can come back and get it tomorrow. They will give me a better price for it."

This is an appealing proposition that my Vietnamese friends frequently offered. I seldom accepted because of the trouble coming back the next day meant for them. Since Thư is Vietnamese, she would always be negotiating from a lower price than I would.

"Are you going to go up to the third level?" I asked Thư and Van, her sister. "Yes."

"I want to look at some backpacks, so I'll stay down here. OK?" I said, referring to the second level.

"OK," they agreed.

Today, the single largest investor in Viet Nam's economic future is Singapore, but not too far behind are Taiwan and Korea. Everywhere in the city there are Taiwanese financed shops, cafes, and computer firms as well as a thriving guesthouse industry. It is the presence of the Asian manufacturer, and pirate, that is so apparent to the traveler. In An Dong vendors hawk hot sneakers from Korea, try to palm off Live's Stress jeans, Nick's athletic wear, Polo sports shirts ("made in the USA"), and hundreds and hundreds of goods that have stolen labels sewn on them. Men buy leather jackets that say Victoria's Secret on the pocket, or wear baseball caps and T-shirts that say Adibas or Rebok. An Dong is mountains of things that symbolize prosperity (sort of) and it's all dirt cheap. Or at least negotiable. Thư's offer to help me make purchases was more than a friendly gesture. The negotiating game that is sales in the Vietnamese market is part of a culture that is both ancient and modern. Vendors live double lives in developing economies; there are a million unwritten regulations for both the legal and the illegal business person.

The next day I wandered down Pasteur Street near my house, looking into the block of shops that specialize in housewares. It's a colorful area, the sidewalk is lined with plastic products in bright red, blue, yellow, and purple. There are forests of coat racks and matching closet hangers, there are wall hooks for kitchen pots, and trash cans large and small. There are milk crates and tupperware-style food containers. It's a Habitat, a Crate & Barrel, chi-chi products sold on a chi-chi street.

"How much is this?" I asked, in English, to the owner of one shop. I looked stupid, when I did this—we always do. Americans, and Europeans, say, very loudly, to people we know cannot speak English *How much is this?* The vendor told me it was 60,000 đong. That's six dollars for a tiny trash can. I paused; I theorized that they had a copy of a Crate & Barrel catalog in the back, that's how they set their prices. I got irritated.

"Gimme a break will ya, buddy?" I muttered. "Six dollars for a trash can, geez!"

But my irritation did not last long. There was an atmospheric shift. It felt like a drop in barometric pressure. The traffic didn't slow, the conversation didn't stop, but something was different. A man across the street gestured; he said something in a regular tone of voice, which to my American ear is too soft. I shrugged, maybe it was my imagination. A moment later I noticed all the vendors doing the same thing. They walked out to the curb, grabbed a handful of goods and carried them indoors. Further down the street, peasants rolled up their blankets and hustled down an alley. Everyone kept talking, they didn't change expression, they didn't even look frantic. The light at the end of the block turned green and the traffic in the cross street began rolling. It was the police. They cruised slowly down the street looking at the shop goods for "illegal" products and unlicensed vendors.

"The cops need money," a friend told me. "It's our version of highway robbery." I smiled and thought about restaurant licensing in the United States.

On Pasteur Street, in Viet Nam, it's a coin toss. One day you're in business, one day you're not. When the police tried to exploit their power, I saw the Vietnamese moving gracefully in the spontaneous choreography of evasion (it's a little hope and a lot of hustle). Just as the police were turning down the next block, I caught on and tried to act cool. But the moment had passed. The Vietnamese talked and worked. I stood in the sunlight with my dark glasses and my Western sportswear staring at a tiny trash can like it was a physics question, trying to blend.

Westerners cannot blend. Even where capitalism is concerned we don't turn in the same universe as the Vietnamese. We like efficiency (I want what I want when I want it); they are bound by courtesy. We are ruled by regulation (and how to get around it); they are tied up by corruption (and how to pay for it). We take the direct route; they work the long way round. We like to get to the point; their interactions are dictated by face and formality. Ceremoniousness accompanies capitalism here; politeness is the policy, no matter how brutal the intent.

The foreign teacher is not the only person to stumble over the courtesy block in Asia. Personal and business interactions witnessed reveal the comic and tragic capacity for conflicts between Asians and Westerners. In the reception offices of countless guesthouses in Viet Nam, there are stories of fiery interactions between guests and personnel. It happens over and over again, The Ugly American/Australian/European makes an appearance and creates a scene over the smallest of misunderstandings.

The evening of my Pasteur Street adventure I was watching CNN in the University Guesthouse lobby, and a textbook example of cross-cultural disaster walked across the threshold. A redheaded American businessman came in and gestured to Thúy, the young woman who was trying to make a long distance call for him. She saw him and said softly, "It's still busy." He would have to wait.

"Try again," he said. It was loud, and he didn't say please, and—I could tell by his voice—he didn't believe her. She hadn't tried hard enough, or had made a mistake. Thúy dialed again and the connection failed. The man nodded as if all his assumptions were reinforced; *they don't know what they are doing here.*

"That's not a busy signal," he said, pointing to the phone. Thúy looked at him, not blankly, but she had a muted response that frustrated him, and he began to spit out an adolescent nastiness.

"Do we have to tell these people how to do everything?" he muttered. I smirked at him and left. Five minutes later I reentered the office to find him yelling into the phone receiver.

"Yeah, terrific, mmh, and . . . and Harry, thanks, . . . hmmh? Yeah . . . thanks for your hard work."

It was a mundane conversation, but it looked absurd. It was so loud and harsh.

I taught that woman behind the counter, and, in so many ways, I know that man too. Now, he wasn't really yelling, not by American standards, but in Viet Nam, he was yelling. Thúy wasn't stupid or rude, but through Western eyes she looks a little . . . uninformed? It was all so strange; he wasn't a large man, but he appeared so vulgar and intrusive; he was so terribly unlikable. Thúy's silence, her placid face, her failure to take the bait of his display, made her look manipulative. What was she up to?

These two aren't alone. Cultural misunderstandings are often started because of the way we underestimate our hosts; nowhere is this easier than Asia, where decorum and face are the first order of the day. The uninformed work under the impression that "these people" are easily handled, they do what we tell them, and they will learn our ways. But this is wrong. Western business practices are well organized, thorough, and dependable. But it's not so simple in Asia—success in the West is not success in the Orient. You'll see and hear it everywhere: There is no *Just do it,* success means you are able to *just wait.* When combined with the urgency and anxiety that come from being out of place, the impatience of Westerners transforms everyday requests into unreasonable demands. We want to make a phone call or meet a company director. They ask us to wait. We get riled.

It is not just personal interactions that may frighten off the sheepish Westerner. It is sheer abundance in the midst of poverty. The modern world, assembled and packaged in this not-so-small corner of the planet, is made up of machines and technology that make our lives easy *and* dangerous. Phương built his factory from scrap, but today people in Viet Nam are high on gadgetry and consumer goods. They regard technology with high esteem, they love computers, television sets, cars, and tall buildings. They find all this so pleasing, so representative of an advanced society. Like other developing countries the Vietnamese saturate themselves in what they believe is a type of salvation. Phương's card read: "Chairman, Advanced Technology Development Corporation." Government television has twenty-minute programs showing how local factories work, how goods are packaged by machines, how foods are frozen, snacks made; imported products are showcased in the most modern houses owned by smart, young couples. In labor-intensive countries hard-working people want relief. Household and business technology, with its ease, with its sleek appearance, with its status, is relief. With technology Viet Nam can develop economically. People can open factories and offices, they can own stereos and computers, they can have jobs in factories building more machines. People can get rich.

But when economic development gets out of control there is an increase in industrial accidents and a shocking carelessness in the operation of machinery. I noted in my diary one day: "A man was killed today on the electricity wires on Hai Ba Trung Street." I remember the incident clearly. Riding home from university one afternoon, I saw a traffic jam at a stop light. I began muttering complaints: Why was everyone so bunched together, going so slow? There was a crowd at the gas station across the street from the Que Huong Hotel. ("Oh terrific, what's all this?") I followed their eyes to my left and saw a man hanging from the electricity wire, his leg tangled in a cord. It was not a utility worker; it was a peasant. His body hung limp between the wires, one leg bent, head and arms thrown to the side.

"It *is* getting wild here," I wrote. "It is not a cultural carelessness, it is something else, something almost psychic—as if the society is determined to race forward uncontrollably in response to its years of authoritarian regulation and deprivation. There seems to be no course for it to take but this veering, breakneck gallop. To where? Everywhere in the world people hurry toward tomorrow. But here, now, people run around like dogs just unleashed, racing and circling uncontrollably, giddy with freedom." The peasant looked like a migrant worker. I theorized that he had been killed trying to connect some lights that decorated a tree growing up around the wires. I thought the restaurant below had hired him to climb the tree, hang the light, and run the wire off the main line providing electricity to the street. In the local newspaper the restaurant owner said it was an accident resulting from his climb up another tree, a nearby palm. The paper reported the incident this way: The restaurant hired him to climb the palm tree and break off the dead leaves. He fell from the top onto the wires and was electrocuted.

Whenever technology and old cultures meet there are funny factory and development stories: pirates take machinery apart, and can't put it back together; sneakers are sold in pairs with two left feet. But a dead peasant on an electricity wire is not funny. In this out-of-control atmosphere, welders handle blow torches like they are cigarette lighters and use eyeguards only on occasion. Construction sites are haphazardly marked, and construction materials (steel rods, wooden beams, glass) are precariously transported by cyclos. Regulation-happy Americans are shocked by this environment, regulation-sick companies are lured by it. "O Pioneers!" I finished my diary entry. "It's the Wild West all over again."

But Asia *is* a hard-working labor pool. There is a certain awe aroused in the traveler who sees workers bending steel rods by hand, mixing cement with a stick, and digging ditches. We slap the sides of finished columns and shake our heads in disbelief ("Yep, it'll hold"). Things are getting built, projects are being finished, and workers keep coming back for more. On the road to Chinatown, there are crowds of men ready for hire, with bicycles and wagons to transport your television, your refrigerator, your construction company cement. Lines of young women bearing shoulder poles unknowingly strike picturesque poses while carting goods down city streets; lean bodies lift blocks of ice in the summer heat, steam rising from their shoulders and water dribbling down their backs. There are old women who lay rock and spread gravel for the paving of roads; there are crowds of country people hanging off the backs of trucks going to work sites and factories; there are people who wander, like ghosts in the night, selling food, beer, T-shirts, and newspapers. And, as if these things aren't enough, that army of the disenfranchised, shoeshine boys and street kids, walk around until midnight with their persistent musical sales pitch. *Whatever you want, whenever you want, for less than a dollar.*

The Vietnamese are very ambitious people. I teach English to factory owners, hotel workers, and university students, some of whom have learned through sheer force of will. Many will continue their work by going abroad on scholarship. Who they are in the classroom is impressive, but when I stood in-country, it was the shop and factory owners who grabbed my attention. I admired the cosmic poetry of the quick-witted, clumsy, and questionable businessmen who struck it rich and laughed loudly about it. These small companies are based on the "If they can do it I can do it" approach to manufacturing. They're pirates and hacks, but they're rich pirates and hacks.

Modern Asia was built by a thousand and one noodlemaking millionaires, junk buyers, and their middlemen; their children were educated by all the money that traded hands and—just to distribute the wealth evenly—entire neighborhoods were entertained by their parties, given jobs, commissions, and "gifts" that helped them realize the glories of wealth. Asians shrug. Who needs regulation? Weeks after my lessons with Phương were done, I had dinner with Dave.

"Dave, it's true!" I said, dramatically. "I was schoolteacher to a mafia boss!"

"Now you know why this place makes me nervous," he said, smiling.

"Well, his mafianess didn't make me nervous. I was just too amazed by his moxie, and, you know, my university students love that word 'clever'—he was so damn clever!"

"Now you know why this place makes me nervous."

Chapter Eleven

I steered my bike through traffic on the way to Linda and Mary Ann's. It was Christmastime and the sidewalks of Hai Ba Trung Street were filled with vendors; there were Christmas trees, card stands, and Christian artwork. Outside the gate of a Catholic church a man was selling paintings of praying Jesus, the Sacred Heart portrait, and cards depicting the manger scene in Bethlehem. A particularly good seller was a plastic portrait of the Virgin Mary with a halo of white lights around her head. It was almost a duplicate of the Bodhisattva of Compassion that I saw in Buddhist temples and altars all over the country.

I pedaled on, nodding to a bread seller that I wasn't interested in buying. On the right was the alley to Linda and Mary Ann's; I tried to work my way over to that side of the street. Two teenage boys on a red Honda braked, then leaned on the horn to stop me from turning; I glided past. The neighborhood pancake house was doing a booming business. The alley was full of motorbikes, and the surrounding families had converted their front rooms into small parking garages. An old woman put her hand out as people slowed, then she gave them a small slip of paper and they pulled off the street into a parking spot.

I slowed to watch the woman at the pancake house working in front of cooking fires. A sizzle rose as she spooned oil into a steel pan, then lifted and lowered it from the flame. The other hand moved from pot to pot, first the batter, then onion, then garlic and seasoning. The mixture began to bubble. She placed another pan on the second fire, ladled oil on it, and started again. As she grabbed the first pan and flipped the pancake I moved on. I stopped my bike at Linda and Mary Ann's house and banged on the metal accordion gate.

"Yoohoo! Laaaaddiieees!" I called, playfully.

"Coming!"

Mary Ann opened the door with a shove.

"Hellooo," she said, waving me in with her hand.

"Hi. I'm here again," I said, wheeling my bike into the front room and sliding it out of the way of foot traffic. We walked into the kitchen and I sat at the table.

"Hi Edie," Linda said from where she was working by the stove. "Brandy and soda? Beer? Water?"

"I'll have a beer," I said. "Here you go," I added, handing a book to Mary Ann.

We were often trading books and music; they often passed on the remainders of departing Australian volunteers. I had just finished *A Place Apart* by Dervla Murphy, an Irish travelwriter who has written on much of the developing world. This book was about Northern Ireland. It was my first time reading her, and I had a great deal of enthusiasm.

"Never read her?" Mary Ann asked.

"Never even heard of her!" I replied. "She's wonderful."

"I haven't read this one," she continued.

"Her narrative voice is very original, and it's just a fabulous, intimate portrait of the nature of the conflict," I said. Mary Ann read the back cover of the book.

"Did I tell you my latest drama with 3B?" I asked Linda.

"What?" she said.

"American culture," I said. "We're doing Westward Expansion—Oh, it was classic Subtlety."

"Which one is she again?" Linda asked.

"Thu calls her the Saucy Girl!" I said.

"Oh. Yeah, keeps throwing her hair back?"

"That's the one."

During the week Subtlety and another student, Lotus, were distracted and distracting in class. They sat in the front row, rolled their eyes in boredom, and leaned forward in dramatic gesture. When I asked the class to break up into groups, they huddled together.

"For the remainder of the class," I announced, "your assignment is to think about what a government has to do to develop land. I want you to work together in your group to come up with a plan of action. You are going to go to an area in central Viet Nam and help develop or redevelop a town. What will you do first?" I turned around to write questions on the board, and the class started to talk. "Electricity? Education? Infrastructure?" I announced to the air.

The students got to work talking and writing, and I sat down to write in my journal. Subtlety and Lotus groaned dramatically as they worked. Finally, Lotus raised her hand to get my attention. I walked over to where they were working.

"Yes?" I asked.

"Miss," she said softly, "people don't go to central Viet Nam."

"I understand that," I said, "but that is your assignment."

"Miss!" Subtlety said from behind crossed arms, "*No one* goes there! It is poor! Everyone in Central Viet Nam is coming here, or going to Hanoi! . . . Ttt," she turned her face away in a huff. The nineteenth-century poet Hồ Xuân Hương once dismissed troublesome students as "little goats brushing your horns against a fence." They were irritating me now with their petulance. I knew they hadn't done the reading. My anger peaked and I asked sharply, "Did you do the reading homework this week?" They both looked at their hands.

"Now look," I said coldly, "this is directly related to the reading. Furthermore, it's part of what is happening in your country today. You know what the assignment is. Now please stop complaining."

They looked away again and crossed their arms stubbornly. It is not a pleasant topic certainly, given the gargantuan task developing nations face. It is tantamount to asking suburban American kids to come up with the solution for urban violence. There are infinitely more interesting things for a nineteen-year-old to consider.

"They haven't got the least bit of interest in work like that," Mary Ann said, in reference to Vietnamese university students.

"I had the same problem last spring when I tried to teach that group the short story 'The Yellow Wallpaper,' " Linda added. "They didn't have the least bit of interest in trying to think about the story and the issues it portrayed."

"Isn't it too bad?" I said.

"To them it isn't," Mary Ann said.

"Oh, Edie," Linda said, "before I forget, I wanted to invite you. We thought we'd all go to Madame Đai's for dinner on Christmas Eve. Nick, Emmie-Clare, and Trish are going to Nha Trang on the weekend, so we thought we'd get together Thursday. Care to join?"

"Yeah, terrific, I've never been to Mme Đai's."

"Neither have we, so it's all a guess, but tomorrow Mary Ann is going to stop by and make the reservations."

Madame Đai's Bibliothèque is a Saigon restaurant run by Nguyễn Phuoc Đai, a lawyer and former member of the South Vietnamese National Assembly. The building that houses her restaurant (and former library) is in the center of town, around the corner from the post office. Like most buildings in the area, its design is French colonial, with jalousied windows, wooden shutters, and a cozy, mahogany interior. The books that lined all the walls were from her former legal career, but she has added a Vietnamese touch by making the rest of the decor traditionally Asian. We were seated in the back room, around the corner from a staircase and across from a small mahogany door that led to the kitchen. There were tea candles at each table, and, perhaps as the finishing touch, Mme Đai—petite, gray-haired, and elegant— floated around the room in a pastel-colored *áo dài* speaking French, English, and Vietnamese.

We ordered. I started with asparagus and crab soup, then followed with the shrimp and lotus root salad. This cold dish was becoming a favorite of mine. Large boiled shrimp, served atop a salad made of shredded lotus root, and mint, topped with a sweetened vinegar dressing and served with fried shrimp chips. It was easy to find in restaurants and food stands all over the city, and it was tasty and filling.

"Do you have vegetarian food?" Linda asked the waitress.

"Vegetarian?" the waitress repeated.

"*Com chay,*" Linda said, using the Vietnamese for "vegetarian."

The waitress looked alarmed and mumbled.

"Maybe!" I said, using the English response I had come to accept as "no" from the Vietnamese. Mary Ann smiled.

"Do you have cheese?" Linda continued.

"Yes," the waitress replied, relieved.

"Could we have a plate of cheese and vegetables?"

"Yes," the waitress said, happy to be finished. She turned and went back to the kitchen.

"Where's the rest of the gang?" I asked.

"Trish and Emmie-Clare will be right along. Nick is going to be late. He said around eight o'clock." Mary Ann said.

Just as she finished speaking, they arrived. Trish broke into a wide smile and held up a bottle of wine. She sat down and in the soft light her smile was enchanting. She is tall, with short blond hair, and a way of laughing that made me think of Daisy Buchanan. "Helloooooo!" I said happily.

"Oh, good," said Linda, referring to the bottle. "I forgot they don't serve here."

Emmie-Clare said hello to Mme Đai, and asked her to bring some wine glasses to the table. Mme Đai called out to the waitress, and pointed to our table.

"Goods from Grog Alley!" Trish said as she opened the Beaujolais and poured. When she was done, Emmie-Clare held up her glass.

"Happy Christmas, all," she said.

"Happy Christmas."

*   *   *

"I'm reading Lewis again," I said during the meal.

Norman Lewis is a British travelwriter whose work I came across on Linda and Mary Ann's bookshelf. I looked through *A Dragon Apparent*, about Viet Nam, Laos, and Cambodia, and was glancing at his work on Burma.

"Which one?" Mary Ann asked.

"*Golden Earth*, the one about Burma."

"What did you think of his work?" Linda asked.

"Well, I think he sure gets his history down well. I mean he covers all the details of the place and fills you in well on things, but then he goes and ruins everything with these horrible comments! I can't stand it! This sort of 'Aren't the natives interesting?' attitude. He called Cambodians, 'clever, lazy people.'"

"Oh, I can't stand that British disdain," Mary Ann commented.

"I'm pretty sure I'll be going to Burma in the spring," I said.

"Burma?" Nick said from across the table. He was wearing a purple mandarin top, and his eyebrows rose in question.

"Burma," I said, then I made an exaggerated face, raising my brows up and down, as if the word could seduce him, "Burma. Care to join me?"

He started laughing. "I'd love to, but I haven't got a cent."

"Well," I replied, "it would hardly be a financial burden. I mean it's not Paris. Besides, I'm not going until the spring." He smiled and said he'd think about it.

"Well," said Linda, "we just read that they have new entry requirements, so you know you'll be giving money directly to SLORC."

SLORC is the acronym for the State Law and Order Restoration Council, the military junta that has been ruling Burma, now called Myanmar, since its violent crackdown on the free election movement in 1988. The junta, corrupt, bankrupt, and isolated, was demanding that all tourists lay down 300

U.S. dollars at the Rangoon airport, to be converted into foreign exchange currency that had no value outside Burma. Linda was right, the directive had no purpose whatsoever except to line the pockets of the generals with American dollars. It was just another obstacle to keep people out, though they claimed to be encouraging tourism. Tourists in Burma were restricted to fourteen days, recently changed from seven, and while the country was said to be "open," travelers I met said that the Burmese suffered a great deal if they spent too much time with foreigners, that it was in fact dangerous for them to be seen with you. It had been many years since the crackdown, but still few people in the West knew anything about the junta, or the freely elected leader Aung San Suu Kyi who was jailed and had been under house arrest since 1990.

"Well," I replied to Linda, "I really believe in the role of the witness. People have to be there to say 'It's like this or that.'"

"Oh," she dismissed me. "You can rationalize it any way you like."

"Listen," I said, "you're on your way to China. Now, you've said before that you won't travel or work in Muslim countries because of the way they treat women. I got news for ya, honey, women have virtually no reproductive rights in China. Tibetan women have been sterilized against their will, for years!" I raised my voice. "And there's a whole lot of Viet Kieu in the U.S.— probably in Australia too—who think we're Communist sympathizers for being *here*."

The argument went on through the meal. Emmie-Clare said traveling in China wasn't the same as traveling in Burma, neither was traveling in Viet Nam. Trish reasoned that since none of us had backed the United States (and her Australian supporters) during the war, we shouldn't care about the response of politically motivated Viet Kieu. We were in Viet Nam to teach, and we were traveling—to Burma, to Cambodia, to China—to travel. It was all done out of love, curiosity, interest, and pleasure. None of which made any sense to the Vietnamese or Cambodians we met. "Why would you want to go to poor places, when there was so much to see in the rich countries you come from?" they asked.

"The other day I was at the Uni," Linda said, "and Bích Hạnh walked up to me and said, 'We have some Australian visitors, would you like to meet them?' and I turned to her and said, 'Lord, no! I left the damn country to get away from them!' I'm sure she had no idea what I was on about."

"I know. I always try to avoid visiting Americans, too," I said.

This snobbishness was anathema in a country like Viet Nam, where people referred to the population as "like one big family." But it seemed, to me, to be part and parcel of our trip. Viet Nam had lured me through the character of my Vietnamese students in the United States. I wasn't interested in meeting people from home; I'd be there soon enough.

Nick poured out the remainder of the second bottle of wine. I wanted to change the subject.

"Linda, do you know when the Uni breaks for Tet?"

"I haven't the foggiest," she said with a laugh, "not that they know much more! I went to the department office," she put her glass down. "Do you know that I couldn't get an answer out of anyone!"

I turned to Mary Ann, perhaps she knew. "Well, when does the Poly-technic let out? They must be on the same schedule."

Linda made a wifely face at Mary Ann, and used her hands to prod the answer.

"I don't know," Mary Ann said, only mouthing the words.

"No one will tell her!" Linda finished. She gave me a these-people-are-so-infuriating face. I started laughing.

"Well . . ." I continued loudly, "when's Tet?" Everyone paused.

"First full moon," Nick said, dryly.

Most of the time I found it soothing that the university administrators (and often my Vietnamese friends) were vague about committing to schedules and dates. On a personal level it gave a loose feel to life; it was a refreshing change from the stridency and anxiety of the social consciousness at home, where you are constantly committing yourself so far in advance. The Viet-namese seemed to wait until the last minute to decide things. But profession-ally this habit was terribly irritating. I often felt I was flying by the seat of my pants.

"When do classes start again?" I wondered.

"Whenever we want," Linda said, dismissively, "could be over a month."

"So, you'll be away in China for Tet. Too bad."

"Not really, it's Chinese New Year, we're going to be in Shanghai that weekend, I think. What are you doing?"

"I'm going to Hanoi. A friend of mine is doing research there." I sipped the remainder of my wine. There was an extended silence.

"There's that pause," Trish said in a whisper. "It must be five before the hour."

I looked at my watch. It was five before eleven. "Let's go downtown!" Emmie-Clare suggested. My face flush with wine, I smiled and agreed.

It was a wild evening in the street. The Saigonese, many of whom are Catholic, poured into the streets and turned the late hours of Christmas Eve into a massive parade. People sold stuffed toys, balloons, Christmas cards, and gaudy holiday novelty items. Families wandered through parks, posing for pictures in front of Santa and Mickey Mouse villages, and singing Christmas carols on karaoke machines. Shop and restaurant owners sped through town on motorbikes laden with products. The noodle shops ran out of noodles; the spring roll vendors ran out of rice paper; the pancake houses lit their fires, poured their beers, and flipped cakes again and again and again. People hurried you along with their excited footsteps, and crowded around you with their goods for sale. Like American kids borrowing the family car, teenagers were piled in fours on expensive new Hondas. On others families squeezed together, toddlers sandwiched cozily between two parents. People swooped down on us in both the streets and the sidewalk.

My favorite vendors were the glitter men. Young men were wandering everywhere selling plastic sandwich bags full of glittery rainbow confetti for a penny. College kids, street kids, country kids, city kids—they had all tapped in to this one-night sale, bought a kilo or so of glitter, bagged it, and sold it on the street. The Saigonese threw it in the air, threw it at each other, and got a real kick out of walking up to the foreigners and rubbing it in our hair. It felt like some strange version of the Burmese water festival, where tossing water at people is a way of blessing them, and wishing them good fortune.

"Mua đi" (Come buy), an old man said, holding up a bag of confetti.

"Không," I said, then cringed with embarrassment as he walked away. Even drunk I knew that "Không" alone is a rather rude utterance, and I had recently realized the Vietnamese don't often use it. "Không" is a blunt "No." There are a variety of ways of saying "No," that use "không" with something else, an "ah" or a "yah" or a "phai." The additional sounds soften the blow of the "No." Then there was the use of "chua," a truly polite way of saying no, since it means "not yet." It was another little practice that I had noticed, but never been taught. I don't think the vendor cared, but I hated the ungainly nature of my Vietnamese. I had the curiosity of an eager child, but my practice and pronunciation sometimes felt like my heavy footsteps. I thought I was a clod.

A teenage boy rode by on a mountain bike and threw confetti at me. It splattered across the side of my face and down my neck. The crowd was so thick on Dong Khoi Street. that we got off our bikes and walked.

"Oh, God," I said to Nick and Emmie-Clare, "even a little drunk I don't think I can handle this."

"Oh, it's all right," said Nick, "I think it's rather fun. Here," he handed me a joint.

"Well, if it's not all right now," I said, taking it, "I suppose it will be in a few minutes."

We walked a half block. I handed the joint to Emmie-Clare and turned to talk to Nick.

"Where'd ya get it?" I asked.

"Just ask for a pack of cigarettes at Phương's Cafe," Nick explained.

I took the joint back from Emmie-Clare. Linda and Mary Ann rode ahead on their Honda, Linda shouting plans from over her shoulder.

"We're bound to get split," I said to Emmie-Clare, referring to the crowd. "Are we meeting at the Rex lobby?"

"No, the roof," she said, looking at me. I took another hit from the joint.

"Teacher!" a voice called from behind. Emmie-Clare's shoulders went up. My eyes widened.

"Oh, Jesus," I coughed, and promptly handed the joint to Nick.

Four of Nick's students wandered up behind us. He smiled and held the joint casually while the teenagers sprinkled him with glitter. We lost them with a quick right-hand turn onto Le Thanh Ton Street.

The Rex Hotel, like the Continental, is a landmark in downtown Saigon. It was a big, old building, with one of the tackiest roof patios I had ever seen. It was decorated in one corner with a giant king's crown, and full of ornate, white wrought-iron furniture. In spots the tables were surrounded by topiary bushes covered with small white lights. From the street I knew it would be crowded.

I looked around. The confetti fell thick as snow in the streetlights. The traffic rotary was a mob of revelers circling the block in an inexplicable giddiness. A little boy holding an orange balloon threw flakes at me; they stuck to my clothes. From behind me a motorbike horn blared and then, as the driver pulled around me, a hand reached up and pressed a pile of confetti aggressively on my head.

"C'mon!" I said, irritated.

A drunk-looking young man in jeans and a white T-shirt walked quickly toward me from the sidewalk. I gave him a look of discouragement. He raised both hands over my head and showered me with glitter. I shook my hair out, and the pieces stuck to my eyelashes. I tried to brush them away, and they stuck to my lips. Trish and Emmie-Clare waved to me that they were parking their bikes and yelled that they would meet me on the roof. A street kid tried to sell me some Coca-Cola. "No, no," I said with a soft smile. He stared at me for a moment, then walked away.

We all split up, unintentionally, I never made it up to the roof. I stood on the sidewalk, felt a growing discomfort with the push of the crowd, and (importantly) remembered the price of drinks at the hotel. Fatigue set in.

There were some shoeshine kids sitting on stools in front of a closed news-stand, and across the street, in the small island in front of the Opera House young couples and families posed for photos in front of topiary bushes and a statue of Ho Chi Minh.

I went back home after the pot wore off. Nguyen Thi Minh Khai Street was a traffic jam up until Reunification Hall, the darkened gates of which were full of young women and men coupling on Hondas. I turned right at Le Duan Boulevard and then left onto Pasteur Street. The noise began to fade, and the street sellers switched from novelty items to food. For two blocks wire stretched between trees connected single light bulbs that lit snack stands. Peasant women napped in lounge chairs seated next to small charcoal fires heating duck eggs. Houses began to darken and as the street quieted the shadowy effect was soothing. I stopped my bike outside my alley gate, reached in to unlock the chain that went on late at night and opened it. It groaned in the darkness and Nục began to bark from the end of the alley. I rode my bike to the house.

"Nục, ơi, Nục," I called softly.

I heard his paws go up against the gate, and he began to whine.

"Nục Nịch," I said as I put my hand through the latch to unlock the housegate. He let a sound roll out of him and began to lick my hand. The gate made a loud noise as I went in. "Shh," I said drunkenly to it. Nục circled around and lay down in his corner. I walked gingerly into the house, sup-pressing a giggle as I imagined my shadow something akin to Inspector Clousseau. Thanh was asleep on the couch, his mosquito net tied to chairs and lamps. I paused a moment to adjust my eyes to the darkness, then stumbled forward, hands out in case I tripped. I went into the kitchen for a glass of water, then retired to my room.

I turned on the bathroom light and began to take off my clothes. The glitter fell out of my hair like dandruff. It stuck to the back of my neck, fell down my shirt, clung to my ankles and feet. My clothing had the smoky, garlicky smell I noticed after I went to restaurants, so I decided to take a shower. The water felt good. I rinsed and remembered the work I had done that week. In composition class two days before I used a Scrabble game to provide a break from work. There was a knock-off board that was selling well in the city. For the students it was a welcome relief from the dreary rewriting I often asked them to do. In the class the game went well. I settled three arguments about spelling, and quietly advised a shy young woman about the art of strategizing with double word score boxes. I bought a second set to give as a gift to Thảo and Bình for Christmas.

I finished showering, and the bite of garlic and smoke faded from the air. I was happy. I was happy to be a language teacher, and I was happy to be living and traveling in Viet Nam. I walked slowly across my room. It was Christmas Eve, and I was slightly drunk. With the wine I had room for two languages in my head. Words pushed in on me like the crowds in the street. "Chị mua đi."

I am listening. When people are celebrating, arguing, drinking, and singing, I am listening, and listening to Vietnamese. Some sounds I can make out, and others I cannot. I have learned "cha cá" (fried fish) by going to a tiny restaurant hidden in a block of alleys and advertised with paper signs and small arrows. "Cơm chay" is Linda and Mary Ann, and the vegetarian restaurant on Vo Thi Sau Street. I can hear it all clearly, but not clearly. I am listening . . . to "Chi khỏe, không?" (How are you, Miss?). "Khỏe." This word has become charming, reassuring, familiar. Khỏe, "I'm OK." Khỏe . . . I am listening . . . to late night snacks served in garage restaurants, and sold from bamboo baskets. I am listening . . . to directions, and questions, and walking out of Mme. Đai's earlier that night, coming out the door, and turning left, I laughed, because after all that resistance, I could finally hear, see, and say "Bưu Điện." It is the ornate building near my house, where the clerks are rude, where I bump into colleagues, students, and street children, and where my voice echoes from behind the doors of glass phone booths.

"Ma?!"

In a hundred phone calls home, in a hundred different tongues, this sound rings out . . . "Ma?!"

After the shower I walked over to the fan and stood under it to cool the back of my neck. To settle myself I did some yoga. The breeze felt cool as I stretched and I relaxed as it flowed over me. I stood with my head and shoulders hanging, so I could stretch my neck. Standing there in the quiet, I caught a glimpse of myself in the mirror. My form was half-lit by the bathroom light, and for a moment I was shocked by the ghostly whiteness of my skin. I stretched again, turning to work my lower back. I looked at myself again as I turned back. I stretched. I looked. I stretched. I looked. It was hard to see at first, but as I turned, and the light caught me, it became more obvious. My skin was glittering. There were rainbow lights sprinkled all over me. They ran down my arms, spread like drying water across my thigh, they ran in a thin rivulet of water down my breastbone. I wiped the water away, and the sparkle stuck to the center of my palm. I ran a comb through my hair again, and water dribbled down my back. The holiday glitter had worked its way through my hair all the way down my body. I went to bed relaxed and smiling; I was touched into color by Viet Nam.

Chapter Twelve

"I've got to learn to play golf," he said.

"Why?" I asked.

"Because all the deals today are made out on the golf course," he replied.

"Oh," I answered. "Well, I suppose that's reason enough."

Try to imagine international businessmen wandering along the banks of the Red River, talking about chip shots, bogeys, and joint ventures.

I was having lunch at the Metropole, in Hanoi, with a young Korean corporate climber. I had very little in common with anyone there; there were journalists sitting at the bar, and corporate types sitting in the lounge. Our seats looked out over a small garden, neatly arranged, like a picture in a magazine. It was an environment that left me feeling schizophrenic, like all fancy hotels in developing cities.

Earlier in the week Sanh, who was buying me lunch, had taken me out to West Lake on his motorcycle. The bike was a large Czechoslovakian model I saw a lot in Hanoi; it looked shaky, and was very loud. In the new order of things in Viet Nam I knew this product would soon be relegated to the fringes of consumer society. It was ugly to look at and uncomfortable to ride. It spat out plumes of black exhaust, and made a deafening clatter. It impressed me that Sanh bought one of these instead of a flashy, high-priced Honda. We rode out past the new houses at West Lake, and through a neighborhood of restaurants; Sanh pointed to the wooden signs that lined the dirt road.

"Thịt chó. Do you know what that means?" he asked.

"No, what is it?"

"Dog meat restaurants," he said.

I thought he was trying to be provocative, and replied, "Well, a dog's an animal just like a cow."

There was always exaggerated talk among Western foreigners about the Vietnamese habit of eating dogs. Like Westerners I met in China, visitors here equated it with a kind of barbarity. In the United States we think dogs are clever, loyal, and cute, but otherwise dirty, and not to be eaten. In Viet Nam, dogs symbolize male virility and strength. As a meal they are not exactly a delicacy, rather a way to enhance male sexuality. A lot of Vietnamese dismissed it as silly superstition, but all the dog meat restaurants I saw were doing quite well.

"I mean, just so you know," Sanh continued, patiently. "You probably don't want to order it."

"Oh, OK," I replied, sheepishly.

We passed a fancy looking restaurant with a sign in both Vietnamese and Korean. The doors were closed. Sanh pointed to it and said, over his shoulder, "He's getting shut out."

"What?" I shouted.

"The Vietnamese owner," he said. "I guess he cheated his Korean investment partner, and the word went out to not go to the restaurant."

"So now Koreans don't go there?" I asked.

"Yeah."

"Hmmh." I thought about it for a minute. That was really a significant blow. In a city where the people with the most loose change were Asian, and a large portion of the Asians were Korean, to be blacklisted, however informally, is a serious loss. The business probably folded soon after.

The economic muscle of South Korean firms was hard not to notice in Viet Nam. Samsung and Daewoo consumer products were ubiquitous all over the country. I found it rather odd, given the Vietnamese government's support of the North Korean regime. Except for Sanh, and his roommate Kwon, most Korean businessmen I met frequented discos, karaoke bars, and whorehouses and, according to Vietnamese scuttlebutt, they were terrible factory bosses. In Saigon, recently, there had been a worker's strike at a Korean-owned factory. A lot of young students I knew said they didn't want to work for Korean firms, even though all business was conducted in English. The restaurant incident in Hanoi was hardly the start of a trade war, but for me the tale had the strange feel of a schoolyard squabble. I could see the men glaring at each other from across their cultural and linguistic divide and I wondered, like a teacher pulling boys apart at recess, "Who started it?"

It was the two-week Tet holiday. The week before, in Ho Chi Minh City, Thư drove me to Ben Thanh market, and we wandered through the holiday booths. The spread was significantly larger than the Christmas sales (and less familiar). We pulled up to the parking lot; I hopped off the motorbike and waited for her on the corner.

"Cô mua đi" (Miss, come buy something), a young girl called from behind a booth. I walked over. The girl reached into a basket of dried fruit and came up with a handful for me to try. Thư came up behind me as I bit into the sample.

"Mmh!" I said. "What's this?" I held up the fruit.

"We call it *nhãn*," Thư said. "In English it is longan."

"Oh, and that?" I gestured with my hand to a basket of dried papaya. The woman gave me some pieces.

"Papaya," Thư said.

"Yeah," I said. I wandered over to the next booth, and pointed to a basket of pink dried coconut.

"Là gì?" (What's that?), I said to the girl behind the counter.

"Dừa," she replied sweetly, and then placed a fingerful in my palm. I shoveled the morsels into my mouth, and they crackled softly as I chewed.

"Coconut," I said, definitively, to Thư.

"Cocona," the girl behind the counter whispered.

"Oh, terrific, I get to try stuff!" I said, excitedly. I continued on my way, moving curiously from stand to stand. At each successive booth I tried something new like a kid in a candy store. I made a fuss over the candies before smiling softly and then walking away.

"You are reminding me of a classmate," Thư said. From behind her glasses her eyes twinkled in preparation for a story.

"Yeah?" I replied. She pursed her lips and suppressed her amusement.

"When we were at university, he would go for a visit to the market during Tet, and he went from booth to booth asking what things were, et cetera. The sellers would always give him samples, and so he said he could enjoy Tet without spending any money!"

"Mmh, hmmh," I said. "Cheap?" I added, in jest.

Thư blushed at my joke, then nodded yes.

"I mean him!" she added quickly. I winked to end the awkwardness. Thư was extraordinarily generous to me with her time and money, and she spoke with disdain of people who weren't. "Cheap," was a word she used with some trepidation, since it is impolite, but she had little patience for anything that looked "poor." Poverty and hunger were shameful. The Tet market, now that was lovely. Generosity, that had dignity.

In Ho Chi Minh City it's hard to imagine Viet Nam as "horribly poor" as the Vietnamese often described it to me. The markets are now full. Comparatively, Viet Nam's economic problems seem fixable. But as late as 1989 the problem of hunger seemed insurmountable—Kim Thư, like her classmate, hungered through university and struggled with starvation.

We stood at the end of the market. "Cô mua đi, mua đi madame," the nearby vendors sang softly. The booths, like a small town carnival, continued on for the length of the market building. At Le Than Ton Street they turned into flower stands, where the bittersweet orange peel became marigold, the pale-colored longans, orchids, and the shreds of coconut were the pastel buds on gladiolas. *Mua đi.*

"Oh," I said, suddenly noticing the time, "I have to return to the house. I'm tutoring Thúy this afternoon."

Thư went to get the motorbike. I stood in the sunlight staring at the market scene. The holiday elements made Viet Nam look so rich.

"Madame!" a voice called. "Ttss!"

I looked over at a booth, where a round-faced young woman was gesturing me to come over. "No, no." I said out loud, shaking my hand to show that I didn't want any more candy.

"Ttss!" she said again, then pointed to the sun. I looked up at the sky.

"Maybe it's bad luck or something if I don't buy anything," I said to myself.

"Madame! Ttss!" her friend behind the counter said, with the same waving gesture.

I walked over to the booth. "*Nhan,*" I said. They smiled and began fingering the flesh on their arms and shaking their heads in disapproval.

"The longan," I continued, "*nhan.*" They smiled at me again and pointed to the sun. I smiled back and pointed to the basket of pale-colored candies. They looked at each other and started laughing. I bought a small bag and smiled as they kept pinching their flesh and telling me something I didn't understand.

Thư pulled up on the motorbike, and gave me the cap I had left in the front basket. The girls gestured with their hands. "Được."

"The sun will make you sick," Thư said, referring with a nod to the two girls. I put the cap on, and smiled; the girls nodded approval. I climbed on the back of the motorbike and we rode home.

*　　*　　*

Thúy was a young businesswoman I met through Bình. She ran a construction company in the city. In addition to her newly acquired Mandarin language skills, she wanted to learn English. She had very good Chinese, but her English was poor, and study seemed to torture her. The lessons were often just dull exercises and recitations designed to correct her pronunciation and bad grammar. She never seemed to have time to do homework, and was nearly always too exhausted to pay close attention. I wanted to make the lesson informal, since Tet was approaching, so I asked her what she liked about the holiday.

"Oh," she said, "I very don't like Tet." She shook her head in emphasis. "I must make much *bánh chưng*, and maybe my mother make it too, and then we visit friends, and must eat so much too." I laughed at her openness. It was refreshing to meet someone who felt as I often do: Holidays are a drag.

"Thúy," I said, "tell me the tale of *bánh chưng*."

There is very little in Viet Nam's rich array of traditional foods that does not have cultural or historical significance. The Tet celebration entails one of Viet Nam's most famous folk tales—the story of the rice cake *bánh chưng*:

"King Hùng-Vương grew old and was to die," she began.

"Which Hùng-Vương?" I asked.

"Six. He had to give his kingdom to a son, so he could not be king, so he could go to rest."

"He was going to retire," I broke in. She paused and looked at me.

"Right?" I said in English. "Retire?" I said, in Chinese.

"Retire!" she said, in Chinese. "He needed a son to be king. A prince to be king. So he asked all his sons come to meet with him one night."

The king was father of twenty-two princes from among whom he had to choose an heir and successor.

"He had to choose?" I asked.

"He had to choose," she repeated. "But he can *not* choose. He could not know." Thúy leaned across the table to emphasize the king's confusion. Her hands were pressed into the wood, and the pink manicured fingernails glittered slightly. King Hùng-Vương was not certain how to determine kingly qualities, so he thought about it for a long time and finally arrived at a very creative solution. Since there is much to be learned from travel, he decided to send his sons on a journey.

"What did he do?" I asked.

"He make a contest to find and cook a meal. To go everywhere in the world and find the best meal. The son who finds the meal make the king most happy—*that* son will become king."

"That's clever," I said.

"Vietnamese are very clever," she told me.

"What happened?"

"OK, the one son, Lang Liên, he can't cook. He knows nothing."

"Is he the eldest?" I asked.

"Lang Liên? No—he is very far son—he never be king. His mother, too, his mother is dead."

"The underdog," I said.

"A dog?" she asked.

"No—underdog—it's slang. Lang Liên is an underdog, he cannot win."

What should happen, but this: the underdog, Lang Liên, the sixteenth in line for the throne, the unloved motherless son, stayed in the castle in despair; he hadn't the slightest notion what to do. "And he was very sad," Thúy continued. "All the other sons traveled over world to find a meal for the king. Lang Liên stayed in the castle."

"What happened?" I pressed.

"He go to sleep and *bánh chưng* comes to his mind."

"He dreamed *bánh chưng*?" I asked.

"No, . . . um . . . *nàng tiên la gì? Tiếng tau . . . shénhùa.*"

"Fairy? Fairy tale?" I translated.

"Fairy told him how to make *bánh chưng.*"

That very evening he fell asleep, and in a dream a genie rose and told him: "Do not despair. It is a law of nature that man cannot live without rice, it is man's chief food." She gave him a recipe and disappeared.

By combining simple ingredients—glutinous rice, beans, pork, and spices—the prince created a dish that won him the kingdom. It is a large cake with a mixture of textures and tastes. It is both dry and sticky, the meat flavor is not strong, but the onion and seasoning do not overwhelm you either. *Bánh chưng* is eaten with a small, gluey rice cake, *bánh đấy*. "It is round," said the genie, "like heaven." *Bánh chưng* is wrapped in banana leaves and tied with string from bamboo, because all these things symbolize the earth's riches. It is a heavy cake; it fills your belly and makes you feel warm.

"And he made it!" I finished the session.

"He became king!" Thúy said.

"And you have to make it too," I added.

"Oh, I very don't like Tet."

The next day in the English department office I mentioned to my colleague Hòa that I was going to Hanoi for a week. She was from Hanoi, so I thought she would have some sightseeing advice for me.

"Oh, you are so fortunate to be going to Hanoi for the holiday," she said dramatically, "Hanoi at Tet is the true center of Vietnamese culture."

Mỹ Ngọc, who was sitting nearby, stood up and began to shuffle through things on her desk. Like Bình, Hòa spoke English with an East European accent, but it was more refined, and that lent the conversation a rather elitist air. I was taken aback by the snobbishness of her comment, and I replied with a dull, "Oh."

"When I am in Saigon," she continued, "I do not feel I am truly celebrating Tet." Her voice was thick with disdain. I found it too much to bear.

"Oh yeah?" I replied.

I despise snobbery, and nothing seemed to arouse country club style discussions in Viet Nam so much as the Saigon-Hanoi character debate. Whether I was talking with Westerners or Vietnamese, it took on a seriousness I found irritating. Which city is the most Vietnamese? Which city is more cultured? I'm from Boston. It's not Chicago, and it's not New York, but it's home and I like it, and I don't put up with disparaging comments from Manhattanites, or those living on the Gold Coast. Likewise, in the short time I had lived there, I had grown to love Saigon, and I was offended by comments from others that it was "unrefined."

"What do you think," Hòa continued, "about the changes in Viet Nam as a result of the open door policy?"

That week news was being spread that President Clinton would lift the U.S. economic embargo against Viet Nam before Tet. I was enthusiastic about the two governments establishing relations, but I'm cynical about the nature of "development," when big nations, and big business, come to the aid of small ones.

"Well," I said slowly, "I'm not sure it will have the effect people think it will. International business and capitalism bring a lot of undesirable things to poor countries."

"Yes," she agreed. "I am not so sure it is a good thing, or relations with the United States." Then she paused for a moment, before saying forcefully, "Vietnamese culture must be preserved."

It was a statement and a challenge at once. Viet Nam is a beautiful and ancient culture—this I have learned—but I knew that she had not traveled through Eastern Europe as a factory worker, like so many of the people I knew. She was married to a high-level official, and they owned a nice piece of property not very far from the university. It was significantly easier for her to say, "slow down" from inside her big house. Bình, her sister Thúy, the young faculty I knew who were only just now gaining work opportunities, they were all damn tired. Who was she to tell them to rethink things in the name of culture? Who are any of us?

"Well, I'm certainly looking forward to my trip to Hanoi," I said to Hòa, then left. Mỹ Ngọc, who came from an old Southern family, had wandered awkwardly over to the door during our conversation. She looked at me nervously as I left. With my back to Hòa I made a mocking face as I passed by, and said, "Whoa!"

As the exact date of the New Year approached I began to feel a giant national party was under way. Viet Nam's Spring Festival holiday is made up of hundreds of different tales, traditions, and superstitions. In both Hanoi and Saigon there were mountains of food being prepared with the repeated banging of knives dicing onions, parsley, ginger, and garlic. In both the markets and alleys, it was all so crazy and colorful. Shops were full of new clothes, beauty salons were crowded, houses were being painted. The moon was getting fat, and people were telling stories.

"You know," my colleague Kiều told me, as I waited in the airport for my flight to Hanoi, "one Tet I had a terrible accident and broke my finger." She held up her right hand to show a bent middle finger. "It was terrible, and I had to go to the hospital. That was a very bad year." What happens at Tet, it seems, determines your fortune for the year.

I was going to Hanoi to visit my friend Nina. I tried to call before I left Ho Chi Minh City, but couldn't reach her. All I knew was that she had arrived in-country at the start of the month, and was living in a dorm at the poly-technic, which was located at the edge of town. I thought it would be difficult to find, but the cyclo driver I flagged just nodded and said he'd take me. I showed him the map in my Lonely Planet guidebook. The city looked like a crossword puzzle, with a big puddle in the middle. We moved the book this way and that, he ran his finger over the page, I ran my finger over the listings on the side. *Bách khoa*, where Nina was living, wasn't there; I blushed when we discovered this, then put the book back in my bag. We drove a half kilometer, up and down some side streets, and I felt a bit lost. There was a lot of dust in the air and it bothered my eyes. I was dehydrated from the plane trip, and my hands had a film of dirt on them. I thought maybe I should help the driver out, so I gave him a possible address, written on a scrap of paper. He turned his bicycle around and started over again. I looked over my shoulder at him, and the words of my students came back to me.

"*Miss! Everyone is leaving the countryside to go to the city!*" I smiled at the man's green cap and jacket, and recognized the tired look of poverty in his eyes. We slowed outside a beauty salon and he yelled in to the owner. I leaned forward in the carriage to look around.

"Edie!" Nina's voice called out, "Edie!" She was sitting on a small stool in the back of a coffee shop, smoking a cigarette. Her close-cropped black hair, and her wire-rimmed glasses made her look male. Like me, she seemed oversized in Viet Nam. "Oh, Jesus!" she said, with her loud New York voice. I turned to the cyclo driver and tapped the back of the carriage.

"Here she is, here she is!" I said, "*bạn tôi*," I added awkwardly, "my friend."

He laughed at me as I paid him, and repeated, "Bạn chị."

"I tried to call," I said as I hopped out of the carriage. Nina came forward from the sidewalk.

"Ơi gọi ơi," she said.

"Trời ơi!" I replied in Saigon slang, dropping my bags on the ground as we embraced.

Nina was researching the work patterns of moving populations, looking at how the lives of people, very much like the cyclo driver I had just hired affected the economy. The dorm she lived in was populated by foreign university students and low-level foreign business employees, all in Hanoi to study language. Sanh, who was my city guide for a day while Nina attended class, shared a room with another man from Seoul—Kwon. They had earned a reputation in the dorm as particularly gracious hosts.

"Hi Kwon!" Nina said, as we went up to her corner room.

"Nina," he replied, and then stood awkwardly for a moment. He had a thin frame, and short, neatly combed hair.

"Kwon, this is Edie," she said gesturing to me, "Edie, Kwon."

"Hi!" I said.

"Hello!" he said, then looked at Nina. "Have tea?" he asked.

"Tea?" she answered, then looked at me. I nodded. "OK," she said to Kwon. He gestured for us to go to his room.

"In a minute," Nina said.

"In a minute," Kwon repeated.

Kwon was kind, but awkward. He spoke no Vietnamese, which he was supposed to be learning, and his English was terrible. Our conversations consisted primarily of "oohs" and "mmhs," with a lot of pointing. Sometimes when he was thinking he rested his front teeth on his lower lip. Shortly after we met, he decided that I should relocate to Korea and become a Seoul supermodel. He was very taken with the idea and talked about it dramatically in Korean. I wasn't keen.

"Sorry, Kwon, not interested," I told him with a shake of my head.

"Oh," he said, crestfallen.

"Kwon," I asked, "do you like Hanoi?"

"Do you like Hanoi?" he parroted.

"No, no," I replied, "You," I pointed at him and spoke very slowly, "Do . . . you . . . like . . . Hanoi?" He saw my hand and understood.

"No," he said, "I don't like Hanoi, Edie."

Kwon and Sanh were in Viet Nam because they worked for a Korean cement company. It was part of their work to live in Hanoi and learn Vietnamese so they could participate in the increasing number of business deals taking place in the city.

"Do you like Hanoi?" Kwon said, with the lilting tone of someone trying a question out.

"I like Hanoi," I said with a smile.

It was hard not to like Hanoi. After the crowds of Saigon, Hanoi's narrow streets and central lake, Hoan Kiem, seemed old-fashioned and charming. I borrowed Nina's bicycle one morning, and rode around the center of town. It didn't take long for me to realize that the city is changing quickly. There was a hotel being built nearby, and the sound of hammers continually broke up conversations. The day before I had noticed that the paint on West Lake houses was still glistening with wetness; at Kiem Lake scaffolding rattled around words and courtesies.

"Hello, Miss," a young man said, as I wandered around the lake. I politely ignored him; I knew it would be the start of an English lesson.

"Madame," a peasant girl said to me, tapping my elbow and gesturing to her basket of fruit. I smiled and shook my head a gentle "No."

"Hellooo!" two little girls giggled. I smiled. Just as I was about to say "hello" in Vietnamese a truck drove by, releasing steam from its turbine engine, and the driver leaned on the horn. The girls ran away.

"Liên Xo!" (Russian!), a boy in rags said softly. "Người Mỹ," I tried to say, but a car passed, and the driver tooted bicycles out of his way. The Tortoise Pagoda sat serenely in the middle of the lake. I stopped to take a picture.

"Madame!" a breadseller said loudly, waving a loaf of French bread. I put my camera down and shook my head "No." I reached the west side of the lake and sat on a bench under a tree.

"Hello, madame," a voice said. It was the young man whom I ignored earlier.

"Hello," I said, my voice muffled by some motorbikes passing.

"Hanoi is very noisy," he said.

"Yes," I answered curtly, hoping he would go away. I got up and began to walk a bit. He stayed beside me. He was college age, and I knew that acting as impromptu tour guides is a very popular way for young people to make money.

"Do you enjoy Hanoi?" the student continued. By now I knew he was eager to speak. "Have you seen many of" (here he stopped because another truck passed, and the engine drowned him out) "of the tourist attractions?" he finished.

"Oh, yes," I lied. I nodded to confirm what he may not have heard. Some young boys lit a string of firecrackers at the corner, and then jumped around playfully.

"And at Tet," the student continued, "there are many" (here a saw whined loudly).

"I can't," I shouted, "I can't hear."

There was a jackhammer working further down the street, and I decided it was best to try to exit the conversation. I made a gesture to say I was leaving. He smiled awkwardly, his face betraying disappointment and frustration.

"Good luck to you," I tried to say, *"Chuc mung Nam Muoi,"* but a Czech motorbike, like Sanh's, was stopped at the light next to us, and its shrill, reviving engine swallowed my words. I turned away and left.

"I can't stand these young tour guides," I said to Nina later in pique. "I can find my way around, and their friendliness is so childlike and irritating."

She nodded, smiling. Freed from her desk, she fixed us coffee, and took out some sandwiches she had bought for lunch. "How else are they going to make money?" she asked rhetorically.

"Yeah," I said, in tired agreement, "yeah."

The bread crackled as I bit into the sandwich, and the crumbs fell across the table and floor. Inside, the meat was rubbery and I chewed on it awkwardly. I took a sip of coffee.

"Oh, God!" I complained, "this is awful! What is this?" I pointed to my glass.

"It's coffee!" Nina said, losing her patience. "What's wrong with it?"

"Well," I stuttered, tired, ". . . Jesus, this place is irritating!" She stared at me. "I'm sorry," I continued. "I'm whining. This place has me out of sorts. I was tugged at all morning. And it's a sad place—this—I mean, Hanoi."

"What do you mean?"

"Well, when I arrived in Ho Chi Minh I sort of hit the ground running, the energy of the city is great. But I felt like I had to hustle to keep up—I mean, I felt like I was *late* for something, they're so on the ball. Hanoi is so . . ."

"Traditional," Nina said.

"No, no," I answered. "I feel like I'm watching something fade."

After lunch I napped, woken an hour later by a hammer pounding a steel anvil. I looked out the window. Out in the alley behind the dorm a man was breaking up the cement steps to his house, so he could repave it with a ramp for his motorbike. A small boy wandered out from another entryway, and began watching the construction. There were two men breaking up the left portion of the stairs. Their shirts were tucked in tight, but came loose as they swung. Nina rolled over and muttered, "Don't these people ever rest?"

"Nap's over!" I said cheerily. "Let's go see the Old District." I hopped into the bathroom to wash up. We climbed onto our bikes a while later and rode down Hai Ba Trung Street, past Hoan Kiem again, and into The Thirty-Six Streets.

The Hanoi Old District has straight, narrow streets that all begin with the word *Hang* (for shop). To complicate things, the names change every few blocks, and you are on a new street entirely. Each street was originally named according to its primary business, but the old names of the Old Quarter only half fit these days. Pho Hang Dau, the canopied entranceway on the south end of the district should have been cooking oil street. Instead, travelers are greeted with the warm, musty smell of leather and plastic, on what should be renamed, "Shoe Street." We rode on and went to Hang Be, but found little wood for sale. We took a left on to Hang Bac Street (silver), which switches to Hang Bo (bamboo baskets). We took a right onto Hang Thien (metal), and Hang Thuoc Bac, where some shops still sell herbal medicine in large red-lidded jars. We rode from Hang Luoc (Comb Street) to Hang Giay (paper), and then found ourselves on another Hang Dau, but there was no tone mark over the "a" on the *Dau*, so we were lost on Bean Street. We were stopped briefly by a traffic tie-up caused by a cyclo moving like a parade float, as it transported a 6′ × 5′ metal window frame down the alley-sized street. The driver bounced his hips from side to side, guided in the front by a young man on a bicycle.

"I was in an expat bar in Ho Chi Minh," I said to Nina, "and there was one of those strange pauses, do you know what I mean, when everyone stops talking, and one person's voice rises?"

"Yeah," she replied.

"And I heard this man's voice say, 'They're damn hard workers, the Vietnamese!'—and I agreed with him, but you know, I just didn't know what to make of the statement. I thought it was so colonialist."

"And then you see things like this . . .," Nina said, letting her voice trail, "and you find yourself repeating it," we both finished together.

On Hang Dong Street tinsmiths made gongs and bells, on Hang May, Buddhist flags. On Pho Hang Dao you could buy new holiday clothes from vendors who reached up to the ceiling with long hooks to grab hold of dresses and sweaters. We stumbled onto Hang Ma May and discovered paper decorations and wrapping paper. Paper pagodas hung over packages of Buddhist burning papers like multicolored flags, and elaborate party favors. They glittered in the light cast between the trees.

We tried again to get closer to the lake and ended up in another traffic jam. We sat at the intersection of Hang Bo and Hang Cau waiting for the motorbikes to move. A young boy rode straight toward me on a mountain bike, and we swerved simultaneously to avoid crashing. An old man in a khaki suit and black beret pulled up beside me on a green Honda Cub and began blaring his horn to urge traffic forward. The New Year holiday meant that everyone was buying peach blossoms and kumquat plants, so all the bicycles and Hondas appeared to have trees growing from the back. The narrow branches of the peach blossoms reached upward in the traffic, and the pink buds broke slowly out of the gray-brown branches.

The old man in the black beret blared his horn again. His face was round and wide, his eye-brows were grayed, and behind his tortoise-shell glasses, he had dark eyes. His forehead was smooth and a shock of white hair peeked out of his hat just above his ear; the traffic irritated him and he whined a bit between hits on the horn. A woman on a blue Cub tried to sneak up on his left. She had on dangling gold earrings and a flowered shirt. Her narrow face and her curled hair, pulled tightly back into a peach ribbon barrette, lent her a serious look. She had thin, pale lips, and wore only a touch of make-up. A woman in red forced her way forward. Her face was square, with thin eye-brows and a flat nose. Her hair was thick and pulled back in a black satin barrette. She had prominent cheekbones and a strong jaw, and her penciled eye-brows were thin and rounded. There was a young boy with short hair riding a bike that was too big for him. His hair was cut close to his head, and his ears small. He had thin eye-brows and a narrow forehead. He wore plastic sandals, and his feet were brown with dirt. He rode the bike by sitting on the crossbar. He had stuck a pinwheel on the handlebars and on occasion he lifted his hand to make it spin. His face was dark, but his lips were round-shaped and the skin on his cheeks looked delicate. On a sidewalk in front of a shop a peasant woman took the basket of bread down from atop her head and stopped to rest. She wore a dark-colored shirt, and underneath it her shoulders and breasts sagged in fatigue. Her face wrinkled in irritation at the crowd. Pressing my feet against the ground to go forward, I glided past the crowd and we rolled down the incline toward the lake.

*   *   *

We made it back to the dormitory in time for drinks at Kwon and Sanh's.

"Edie! Supermodel Edie!" Kwon said from across the room. I laughed at him and shook my head.

"I'll go when you learn English!" I said.

"Sorry?" he replied.

"I've had enough," I said to Nina.

"What?"

"The dancing bear thing. I'm sick of being a showpiece among Asians."

"Ttt," she said, "privileged white woman like you?"

"Don't even start," I cut her off. "This is no rural peasant curious over my skin color." She broke into laughter. It is a strange experience to see things Western exoticized in Asia. I talked to Kwon during the cocktail party, wearing Yin Yang earrings. He wore an Izod shirt. Another Korean man had a long gold chain with a cross on it underneath a blue button-down oxford. There was so much of the surface of Eastern and Western cultures we were all acquiring, but none of the beauty. We mingled around. "Have you heard about the Society for the Preservation of the Architecture of Hanoi?" a woman's voice said. I rolled my eyes in irritation as I passed. Nina had explained this new group to me at lunch.

"It's mostly expats," she said, "who think the architecture is so picturesque they want to convince the government to preserve it."

"And many of them own it?" I asked, "or would like to?"

"Well, yeah," she said. "NZ Bank owns a nice building over by the lake, some other foreign bank owns one behind the Metropole."

"Who owns the Metropole?" I asked.

"I think the group that runs it," she said.

"What's the worry?" I continued sarcastically. "Foreigners will probably own all the nicest colonial buildings soon anyway."

Hanoi is a wealth of beautiful, old buildings built during the French colonial period. The jalousied windows and the tile roofs are now worn and broken, but that only enhances their romantic appeal when you are riding a bicycle down the narrow streets. Laundry usually hangs on balconies, and there are pink crepe flower bushes growing everywhere that accent the yellow and gray of the buildings. At the end of Trang Tien Street, a well-traveled street filled with bookstores and cafes, is the City Opera House. It is a majestic looking theater that has faded beneath a gray-black soot, and looks like an aging Grande Dame watching the city change. It was the one building the Vietnamese seemed proud of, and wanted to preserve.

"The Westerners just think the buildings are picturesque, that's all," Nina continued.

"Well," I growled, "shoulder poles and cyclos are picturesque too, but I don't see anyone standing in line to use those." I was still itching for a fight from the conversation in Saigon with my colleague Hòa. Hanoi was hardly on its way to the overdevelopment that Bangkok suffers from, even Saigon wasn't close. Who were outsiders to dictate to the Vietnamese what architecture they could build?

When I admired the buildings of the Old District, or told my Vietnamese friends how pretty I thought buildings were in Viet Nam they frowned in disagreement. "They are old," people said, pointing to the moldy yellow walls, and the broken tiled roofs.

"Most Vietnamese want to rebuild," Kim Thư told me one day, "to have modern homes—they are more convenient." The modern homes were another step away from poverty for the Vietnamese, and to see alleys change from smoky confines to modern streets, with latticework gates and tiled balconies, was a source of pride and a symbol of success for working people.

"Let them tear the old buildings down," I said to Nina, "they own them. Most of them are just symbols of a colonial period they'd rather forget." The room was getting crowded. Nina and her neighbor Charles wandered outside to the balcony.

"We're going downtown for a party?" I asked.

"I guess so," Nina said.

Charles was smoking a cigarette, sitting on the balcony wall. "Downtown," he said, distracted. "Let's go sit on the stoop," I said, and the three of us moved downstairs.

Like my friend Dave, Charles was a young American in Viet Nam looking for business prospects. Consummately American looking, with blond hair and wire-rimmed glasses, he was a free agent roaming around town. He was active in the business community, and had earned an early reputation as a smart investor. When Charles talked his voice—as Daisy Buchanan described Jay Gatsby—"his voice sounds like money."

But his personality was more akin to Holden Caulfield. He had an Ivy League look, but disdained elitism, and—this intrigued me—he memorized a passage from Ranier Maria Rilke's *The Notebooks of Malte Laure Bridges*. ("For the sake of a single poem," it said, "you must be able to think back to streets in unknown neighborhoods, to unexpected encounters, and to partings you had long seen coming." I smiled at the tenderness underneath his cynicism.) He was a radio DJ in college and loved classic jazz. The Rilke quote, and a little Miles Davis, were the only things that really made sense to him. I laughed in recognition when I saw him trying to bring that knowledge into the world everyday.

During a visit to Nina's that afternoon he complained with equal bitterness about both the foreigners and the Vietnamese. The Westerners whined too much, and the Vietnamese just couldn't seem to adapt themselves to the realities of the twentieth century. Hanoi seemed a frustrating mix. At twenty-five, Charles probably tried to view the city's development with hope and enthusiasm, but was soured by the reality of both Eastern and Western culture.

We sat on the stoop outside the dorm manager's office. On a television set inside was a broadcast of Charlie Chaplin's *The Gold Rush*. A young Vietnamese woman sat watching and giggling. At first laughter bubbled across her lips, and she covered her mouth with her hand.

"Look," I said to Charles and Nina, continuing our afternoon conversation about development in Viet Nam, "I just don't think anybody visiting this city for business is really very well intended."

"Well," Charles responded, "the Vietnamese are the ones who made this mess. Their system is fucked up and *they* did it."

"And capitalism is going to fix it?" Nina asked.

On the television Chaplin was trying to read a map to go prospecting. In his black topcoat and hat he set off up a mountainside; a storm rose and he tried to find shelter. He came upon a cabin occupied by two large men. The Vietnamese woman began laughing loudly as the three men, trapped by the blizzard, were buffeted about the cabin. Chaplin was blown from one side of the room to the other, in one door and then out the back. I suppressed my own laughter at the images. Everyone looked so comic and pathetic. The woman pointed at the television and looked at her uncle, inviting him to join in.

"The way *they* do things sure isn't going to fix it," Charles said.

He was referring to all the sudden and strange decisions the Vietnamese government made in response to business developments. It looked like, to address pockets of difficulty, they clamped down on all of business, putting obstacles in the way of action, and making new rules that achieved the effect of slowing down progress.

"The occasional wave of paranoia," Charles called it.

"That sounds familiar," I said to Nina. When we worked together in China we often encountered business people complaining about paranoia-based regulation. "To them it's not paranoia," she said.

In the office, the film had reached the famous scene where the prospectors have gone for days without food, and they consider eating Chaplin. His image changes to that of a chicken and the prospectors chase him around in circles. Finally, he comes up with the ingenious idea of eating one of his shoes. Charles, Nina, and I continued arguing about what constituted government paranoia. The Vietnamese woman, old enough to remember real hunger, shrieked with laughter.

"So," I challenged Charles, "the Vietnamese government has nothing to fear from outsiders?"

Chaplin lifted his shoe from a pot on the stove and placed it on the table to share with the other prospector. The man lifted the body of the shoe from the plate and left Chaplin with the nail-filled sole. Chaplin shrugged. The woman's laughter echoed around the neighboring alley.

The Vietnamese government did appear hostile to foreign business, despite all its welcoming gestures. It slowed contracts through regulation; it was famous for having little or no laws determining land ownership; it enforced most laws, new and old, with a heavy hand. And—this disturbed me most—it seemed to be turning a blind eye to the increase in drug traffic, and the proliferation of whorehouses sucking young women into dead-end and abusive lives.

"Look," Charles said, "I mean, I'd *like* it if the government closed the whorehouses down, but that's not what they do when they clamp down!"

"Well," I snapped, "capitalism again. Whoever has the money makes the rules. The Asian sex industry is an important part of deal-making in business culture." If the Vietnamese government was going to compromise its principles, I reasoned, it might choose to do what the rest of the world did, and talk a lot about improving the lives of women and girls, but ignore the elements that trapped and destroyed them.

On the television Chaplin was watching the prospector try to eat the tongue of the shoe. The young woman shook her head in laughter.

"I mean it doesn't make any sense," Charles said loudly, "to kick up a fuss about *where* companies sign contracts," he waved his hand in irritation. "Do they have to sign here, or in Hong Kong? or Bangkok, if the company is Thai—what does it matter?!"

Chaplin took the nails from the sole of the shoe and sucked the rubber off, then licked his lips.

"They're just plain stupid!" Charles finished.

It certainly seemed that the Vietnamese government was hostile to international business, and it sometimes responded to developments in juvenile ways. But there was power involved. What government in the world wants to have its economy overrun by outsiders? Viet Nam really had nowhere to turn, but it was already sending out signals that it was stubborn and proud. Who wouldn't do the same?

"Well," I said, as we got up to leave for another party, "maybe they just don't know how to do business."

"Yeah," said Charles, still irritated, "it's a mess."

We pulled away on our bikes as the one-shoed Chaplin was being chased in circles by the still hungry prospector.

Outside the gate a Vietnamese man with gold-rimmed sunglasses pulled up to a house on a 200-cc motorbike. He looked silly wearing the sunglasses. His hair was in a neat crew cut, a little thick on top, in mod fashion. He had on a beige blazer, and matching beige shoes. It was all very "seventies," and I laughed because he was supposed to be out of fashion, but even now, all over Europe people are being paid obscene amounts of money to get us to think these clothes look good. The man's girlfriend came out wearing black platforms and bell-bottomed jeans. She climbed on the back of the motorbike and they were off.

Economic prosperity in Hanoi brought with it what the western expats called "Vietpunks." They were young people, mostly male, very similar to punks in the United States and Europe. I had encountered them already in Ho Chi Minh City, and now, in Hanoi, they seemed irritating, but harmless. They owned Hondas, or Taiwanese motorcycles, drove fast, chainsmoked foreign cigarettes, drank beer, and were loud, bordering on violent, when they taunted Westerners. Most seemed like male teens in the United States who demanded that you take notice of them by getting in your face. They started off, like my eighth grade student, shouting words at you in the street, and then egging each other on to strange acts of daring. A young man once stole my cap from my head. I often saw Western women getting pinched or harassed with lewd noises. And teenagers had this strange ritual of circling around you on their motorbikes.

Vietpunks weren't the same as street children, who aroused in me a bittersweet pity. They had money, work, and consumer items, and they seemed excited by the city's new openness. But—and here I felt bad for them—they knew foreigners had much more. They knew that with half as much work we made twice as much money, and they knew we could have doors opened for us just by asking. When we made demands there was little doubt they would be granted, and when we got tired of the difficult life of Viet Nam, we could simply leave. Vietpunks wanted to flex their muscle in response to our freedom and confidence. This was the flip side of the Vietnamese who adored the helpful and wealthy foreigner.

I thought each perspective was skewed, but the wilder, weirder response of the Vietpunks was more understandable. I saw it as the result of such greedy and power-hungry action by the international community. The presence of privileged capitalists, wherever they were from, shook up the hierarchy, and the Vietnamese would no longer be able to identify who had authority or

where they themselves—regular people—were located in the power structure. They were angry at the failures of their own government, but some part
of them had to be offended by the clean sweep approach made by foreign
business. It was out with the old and in with the new, sure, but where did
they fit in? No one knew yet.

This multilayered love-hate scenario was familiar and interesting. At a
dinner party in Saigon a month earlier a friend of Thảo's told me about his
plans to begin a shipping company.

"We are only waiting for the U.S. embargo to be lifted," he said.

"Why don't you just go ahead without them?" I asked.

"No, no," he dismissed my suggestion, "it's useless to go ahead without the
support of Americans."

I didn't know what kind of support he was referring to, and I didn't know
anything about the shipping business, so I let the topic drop. We were quiet
for a moment, and then he turned to me and said: "Tell me, are you proud of
your country?"

The question shook with its serious tenor. He looked me in the eye as he
spoke, and I knew it was a challenge. I knew he was well educated, and held
a comfortable job with the government, but he had the same disappointed
attitude I had encountered time and again in Vietnamese men; there
seemed to be this horrible sense of failure and wasted effort. But I also knew
he was going to stand up again. I knew he was going to start this shipping
company, and probably succeed.

Was he a Northerner? A Southerner? I don't recall. But his question was
not the fodder for argument that European and Australian leftists enjoy
baiting me with the half-mocking accusation I have encountered so often.
The look in his eyes, and the question—*Are you proud of your country?*—
demanded a "Yes." What else can a citizen answer? To see the Vietnamese
today, deeply ashamed of poverty, but fierce in their pride and dramatic in
their loyalty, is to understand the strange drama that is patriotism and iden-
tity. My footfall was welcome in Hanoi, and the citizens of the entire country
greeted me warmly. But a month after Tet, when Coca-Cola launched its
Viet Nam marketing campaign by placing two giant inflated Coke bottles on
the steps of the Hanoi Opera House, the Vietnamese scowled at the vulgarity
of the capitalist gesture, and I cringed in embarrassment.

*   *   *

The crowd from Kwon and Sanh's had come downstairs and we all began to
move across town.

"Look, Charles," I continued our conversation, out in the street, "did you ever watch someone handling something and feel absolutely certain they were doing it wrong?"

We braked at Bac Mai Street and waited for traffic to ease. Kwon and Sanh zipped past on a motorcycle. While Sanh drove Kwon sat backwards, he pulled his camera up to take a picture. "Supermodel Edie!" he cried.

"Yeah?" Charles said, in response to my question.

"What do you want to do when that happens?" I asked.

He looked at me, waiting for the answer.

"You wanna take it from 'em," I said, "and say, 'Give it to me, I'll do it!' Right?"

He started laughing and we rode on. He liked my analogy, but it didn't hold water for him. In the end Charles's politics were hopelessly conservative. We argued again over economics and development. He threw numbers at me, as U.S. conservatives like to do, I came back with a liberal's contextualization, and we rode down Hai Ba Trung Street, two Americans bickering over Viet Nam.

Nina was a half block ahead of us when Charles stopped at a red light. I rolled past him through the intersection. "Saigon driver!" he yelled. I rode up near Nina.

"Whose party is this again?" I asked.

"Some guy Charles and Sanh know." Nina said.

"Where is it?" I yelled over the traffic.

Nina answered, but I only saw her lips moving. A boy had walked to the edge of the sidewalk with a string of lit firecrackers. The bite of sulfur hit and, after the sparks finished flying, the smoke followed us down the street.

"Edie!" Kwon yelled again from the motorcycle as we approached another light.

"Don't fall off!" I yelled back, as some firecrackers went off again. We turned right and arrived at Nguyen Cao Street.

The new architecture of Viet Nam is townhouse style, with long narrow rooms piled one atop another, leading to balcony roofs. The Vietnamese most often converted the street level floor to shops, but the younger foreigners (those who lived without the large gates and walls of the colonialist houses) simply left it empty. In the darkened first floor room we took off our shoes, wet from early evening rain, and formed a line to go up the narrow staircase.

"Everyone put your hand on the shoulder of the person in front of you," I said jokingly. We trudged upstairs. The apartment was the size of a Tokyo studio, and it was holding about twenty-five people. There were six men up on the roof lighting fireworks. The sentence, "That's not what I heard," floated past my ear. "Who's his interpreter?" someone said. "Did they get approval from the ministry?" The U.S. embargo had been lifted only days before. Hands lay on hips, heads tilted a little in doubt, and voices slowly drew long, unsure answers. It was an exciting time to be in Hanoi, and everyone, it seemed, was living large.

I remembered the boorish attitude of Bình's director so many months ago when he tried to convince me to teach him English, and the absurd opportunism of my noodle king student, Phương. At these expat parties in Hanoi those faces were replaced with young people who read too much into the Western business press, and the arrogant look of finance industry gamblers speculating on Viet Nam's future. It all blurred to become both distasteful and laughable. The capitalists were more slick than the ham-fisted Vietnamese entrepreneurs I had met, but in my eyes they all looked like caricatures, self-important and unaware.

Nina made a beeline for a red cooler against the back wall, then came back and handed me a beer. I squeezed past a potted palm to try to reach the small balcony at the front of the room.

"From the States?" a young looking man asked. He had long, shaggy, brown hair, and was wearing an orange T-shirt.

"Yeah," I answered, "where you from?"

"Santa Cruz."

"Oh!" I smiled, "I like Santa Cruz."

"How long you been in Viet Nam?"

"Since August," I replied, "I teach English in Saigon."

"Yeah, that's how I got my start," he said.

"Sorry?" I answered.

"I taught for a while, too," he said, a bit condescending.

"Oh," I answered, dully.

"But now I'm consulting on a construction project."

"Yeah?" I said.

"I remember one teaching job I got when I first arrived. It was at Viet Nam Airlines."

"Oh!" I said lightly, "I just gave a set of lectures to them about a month ago."

The airline students were young, enthusiastic, and eager to learn. I enjoyed teaching them.

"I found," he said—and suddenly he was looking right in my eyes—"I found that in general they were terrible, but if you talked to them about gambling and sex they paid close attention."

He had the straight look of a passive aggressive on his face. I tried not to laugh at him. What kind of bullshit is this? I thought. My laugh turned into a mocking face and I leaned toward him and said, "Ya found that did ya?"

I walked away and searched desperately for an empty spot to stand. I found a corner and looked around. Kwon was listening politely to an Australian man, his head turned, his face composed. I laughed at the scene; Kwon had the worst English comprehension skills I had ever encountered, but he was so damn polite and enthusiastic it was impossible to tell he didn't know what was going on. The Australian talked, and talked, and talked.

I stood in the corner while the party sank into conversations full of juvenile bravado. We made our way to Hoan Kiem before twelve and stood near the intersection of Dinh Tien Hoang and Trang Tien streets. There was a red shadow being cast by a neon sign that hung at the corner, *Chức Mừng năm mới*, Happy New Year. The city government planted young peach trees along the shore of the lake, and Vietnamese were breaking off bud-covered branches in celebration. I stood in the crowd between Charles and Nina as the fireworks started. Over on our left a family of three stood watching, too. The mother teased her baby with a peach blossom branch and then the father picked him up and placed him on his shoulder. There was roaring and snapping and cracking and booming for about ten minutes, and the air filled with smoke. Nina walked around kissing people and saying "Happy New Year." I stared at the family, wanting to hold the baby.

It was easy to slip in Hanoi. In the romance of it all, in the architecture, alleys and the Thirty-Six Streets, in the eager energy of Vietnamese capitalists, and the new conversation and debate. In the media images and the news articles, it was easy to slip into the idea that Hanoi, in 1994, was all about us; as if it was all brand-new and ours to shape, as if it hadn't been there for four thousand years.

We wandered, en masse, back down Trang Tien Street into an empty bar. The waitress, who had, only a moment before, been sitting bored at the end of the bar, stood up and began to back away from the stampede.

The conversation was more of the same, and it moved me from irritation to boredom. I ordered a glass of red wine and began to stare into the mirror behind the bar.

"Where you from?" a man asked.

I turned to my left to find the Australian man Kwon had been talking to earlier. He was wearing a pale-colored sport shirt and khaki trousers.

"The States," I replied.

"Just arroived?" he continued.

"No, I've been living in Saigon for about five months."

"Lots of Americans coming now," he said.

"Yup," I said, in a low voice.

"Nice to be on the winning side this time, in'it?" he said with a silly grin. I didn't answer.

He stared at my reflection in the mirror. I was thinking of the family by the lake, and I wondered what street they lived on. I took a sip of my wine. The Australian man's face grew bigger. I thought of my student, Thúy, making *bánh chưng*, and imagined Kim Thư at midnight, with her hands full of candy. I hoped Kiều had good luck. The man's reflection expanded again. He was still talking. He looked like a balloon in a holiday parade.

I wanted to walk out of the bar and into some house nearby, where I could eat cakes, and listen to stories and pray for good luck. I wanted to go back to the half-light of paper street, and watch fire-cracker smoke dance around favors.

I turned to look at the balloon man. "You know something, mister," I said. "I just realized . . . I'm at the wrong party."

Chapter 13

It is always those who live on little who invite you to dinner.
—William Least Heat Moon

Khoa took a large bowl and two green papayas from the kitchen, and we went out front to the stoop. He peeled the papayas and began to shred them for the dinner salad.

"Edie ở Mỹ nhớ Cátđẳng, không?" he said. (Will you miss Catdang in America?)

"Nhớ lắm" (Very much), I replied.

"Viết thơ gởi, không?" he continued.

"Gởi?" I repeated.

"Gởi thơ, hiểu, không?" (Do you understand?), he said, smiling.

I clung to the word "gởi."

"Gởi?"

"Không hiểu" (You don't understand), Khoa said, laughing.

"Viết thơ, hiểu" (Write a letter, I understand), I said, then I broke into English, "Oh! *mail*. Write a letter and mail it!" I translated. "Nhiều lắm! Viết thơ nhiều lắm!" (I'll send a lot of letters). Khoa smiled. He had a wide gummy smile that I loved, and his brown eyes seemed to sparkle.

"Edie nói tiếng Việt tốt lắm" (Edie speaks Vietnamese very well), he said.

"I do not," I said, waving him away with my hand.

I had taken three weeks off teaching in Ho Chi Minh City to work as a visiting English teacher for grades six, seven, and eight in a small village south of Hanoi. My stay was coming to an end and the faculty were having a farewell dinner for me. While Khoa was shredding the papayas for salad, the women in the kitchen were preparing the rest of my going-away dinner. Khoa scraped more flesh off the papaya, then lifted the strands. "Nhiều lắm" (A lot), I said, referring to the fruit and practicing my tones like a child.

"Nhiều lắm" he repeated. "Tiếng Anh lá gì?" (What is it in English?)

"A lot," I said.

"A lot," Khoa repeated.

Khoa often stood at the back of my classroom during lessons. Sometimes he crossed his arms and stared at the letters and words I wrote on the board; other times he and the headmaster, Mr. Ngô, wandered in like sleepwalkers during the lesson, and stood with their hands at their sides staring at the class like it was a dream, and I was an apparition. My presence in the village was a puzzle to most of the people there. It didn't seem to make sense for an American to choose to live in a poor village. I replied by saying I was an English teacher, and I was there to teach their children. When the stay was placed in a working context, it made sense; they smiled and told me I was very nice.

In Vietnamese literature the celebration of the village is an honored tradition; in dinner party conversation, the native village reminiscence is broad brush strokes of pride and sentiment. But when I told city dwellers I would live and work in a rural northern village, I only aroused astonishment and concern. Among teaching professionals my efforts were almost dismissed.

"What country people learn in school they leave in school," a colleague commented. "They only need to know how to work."

My initial shock at this snobbery gave way to anger. "Well, I don't think it is a waste of time," I said, referring to my work with the village students.

"It's very hard to live there," she said, with continued discomfort. "They're poor." The last word rolled out, like it was dirty and contagious.

"I know," I said, "I know they're poor."

She wasn't convinced I understood what I was doing. Realizing I ruffled her social sensibilities, I assured her my trip would not be long.

Though it isn't far from Hanoi, Nam Ha Province is a stark contrast to the growing capital city. Highway Ten, going from Hanoi south, is paved with an uncomfortable combination of rock and tar. It is lined with modest houses in some areas, but in most there is a blanket of fields that are bordered by a chain of dome-shaped mountains. For much of the trip we followed the train tracks that lay parallel to the road and I watched the faces that stared out the open windows of passing trains. There was a harvest on, but from the comfort of a new Toyota the countryside looked stark, not bountiful.

For reasons of both geography and history, the landscape around Hanoi is spartan and bleak. During the American War it sustained a ceaseless amount of bombing and, now, during what is called "the opening" of Viet

Nam, the mountains were blasted for rock and minerals. In addition, villages and hamlets are marked by the haunting presence of perfectly round ponds—some in the middle of a field, some by the side of the road. Only after I began trying to reason why a pond would be placed in such odd locations did it strike me that they were made from bomb craters.

I was introduced to the school in Catdang by an American importer and a Hanoi art export firm. For hundreds of years the people of the village specialized in handcrafted baskets that were decorated with an intricate lacquer design. The baskets were a popular item in tourist ships, and the local factory was hoping to create manufacturing jobs through export. During our trip from Hanoi to Catdang, Mr. Pham—the company manager—explained that his daughter Liên would stay with me during my month long visit to "take care" of me. It isn't an uncommon practice in Asia, to create companionship for the lone traveler, particularly in northern Viet Nam where foreign visitors are a strange novelty for the younger generation. This cultural sense of obligation can feel burdensome to an independent-minded Westerner, but by now I had come to expect it as part of the travel package. I sat in the front room of the apartment as Liên and my other caretakers, Phương and Nữ, prepared our dinner. These two women, with families of their own, had taken on the burden of caring for me out of what I had come to recognize as a consummately Vietnamese sense of obligation and concern for visitors. They seemed to feel that my presence was a generous act that had to be matched with care and concern for my being. I felt humbled each time a Vietnamese person prepared a meal for me, but my awareness was heightened in the village as I remembered the words of another traveler—"It's always those who live on little who invite you to dinner."

Mr. Khoa moved from the stoop through the living room to the kitchen, the papaya falling in strands from the edge of the bowl.

"Nữ is an excellent cook," he said, as he passed through to the kitchen.

The kitchen was really nothing more than a tiled five-by-five foot space with a refrigerator, a hot plate, and a tap. It was located between the bathroom and the drain room. Phương brought in a gas cooker, to supplement the hot plate, which was slow cooking because of the unstable electrical current. The water tap was drawn from a well, so it was located low on the wall. This and the lack of counter space meant that everything was prepared on a chopping block on the floor. I squatted in the doorway to watch. I knew there was nothing I could do to help. The women had not allowed me to cook since my arrival, and my culinary skills had become the topic of an amusing story Phương told over and over again to everyone's amusement.

On my third day in town Liên had gone out early, and I got up and prepared a porridge with the rice left over from the previous evening. The milk I used was sweet and warm, and I ate it sitting in the front room, looking out my door at the schoolyard. Across the dirt yard was a white cement building with five classrooms. Each door had stairs, at the foot of which were flocks of children hunkering in the morning light. The school had 800 students in grades one through eight, so that meant their conversation and play was a virtual cacophony from six in the morning until the lunch break at eleven, then again from one until four. Eventually it became a white noise that was penetrated by the occasional shout of "Hello" from underneath my window.

Across the yard a young boy pulled open the shutter to the classroom, and climbed in the window. I pulled my foot up on to the chair and ate some of the porridge. Phương, who was also one of my teaching colleagues, walked through the doorway with her daughter Lan Anh.

"Good morning," I said, then took a spoonful of rice.

"Eh? Cái gì?" (What is that?!), she said.

"Mmmh?" I replied.

She looked in my bowl and then made a dramatic face.

"Không!" she said, "No!" and she took the bowl away. She put it in the kitchen next to the pot of rice, pointed and said, "Không!" then explained by pointing to her stomach.

"Bad," she said.

"Well," I replied, "it wasn't the best rice I've ever had," I agreed, "but with the milk it was OK."

Phương shook her head. Lan Anh was standing behind me. "EEED-DIIEE," she said, then put her hand over her mouth and laughed.

The problem wasn't the rice. It was that the rice was a day old. Leftover food is bad, the villagers told me, it makes you sick. Phương handed me a bánh chưng and threw my porridge in the trash. I went to the front stoop and sat down to eat the cake. I untied the string that held it together and began peeling the banana leaves that were wrapped around it; the large pieces slipped easily away. I pulled at the inner layers, which had a sticky film. The rice peeked out from a corner. The big leaves lay on my lap as I peeled. One leaf split; I picked at the remaining side like it was a roll of tape; it split again. I started to tear in frustration as Phương walked up behind me.

"Ơi," she said softly, then lifted the cake from my knee. She held it by a corner, so it rose as a diamond shape from her left hand. With her right she peeled the leaves away quickly, wrapping them around the body of the cake, then handing it back to me so half the cake stuck out neatly.

"Oh yeah," I said, "like that."

I guessed that Phương was about my age. She had two children, Lan Anh, who was ten, and a little boy named Đức, who was seven. She had a plot of land that she worked in addition to teaching algebra to the seventh graders. Every evening she came by with her daughter, hoping that Lan Anh would somehow absorb English by being around me.

Lan Anh strutted around the apartment in a pair of pink plastic Cinderella shoes, looked in the mirror, and asked Liên questions about her make-up. She had long hair that she tossed when she thought we weren't looking, and a dimply smile that accentuated a scar she had below her left eye. She smiled and giggled often, and while other students were bound by courtesy to keep their curiosity in check and stay away from my apartment, Lan Anh strolled freely in and out of the front room between classes. I went to school with a lot of small town girls like Lan Anh, and the teachers called them "spitfires." Often Phương insisted she behave politely during our evenings together, and so I invited her to sit with me at my desk. We sang the alphabet song, I let her color and write with some pens I kept on my desk, and we sat for hours each night curled up in a chair trying to talk to one another.

✳   ✳   ✳

The lacquer factory and hamlet were separated from the school compound by a half kilometer of rice fields. The next morning I stood in the corner of the showroom during the business meeting with the factory director. Liên was sitting outside the front door talking with Bình, our driver. I walked out to the stoop and sat on my heels. As Liên bemoaned her fate, Bình mumbled softly in agreement. Her voice rattled and whined, Wasn't it terrible to have to stay here?! Who knew it would be so poor out here? Shouldn't she be back in the city with her boyfriend running their computer store?

"Yeah," Bình said, sympathetically, "yeah."

Liên had walked over to the factory that morning from our apartment. She wore a flowered skirt with a blue shirt, silk stockings, and a matching beige blazer. In a pair of high-heeled pumps with small bows, she walked out the school gate and tried to make her way down the unpaved road to the factory. A small group of schoolchildren in the road pointed at her and yelled "*đài*" (foreigner). The rain from the previous evening made the road soft and the resulting mud coated her shoes. As she sat talking to Bình, she reached into her purse, a small evening bag with a gold snap closure, took out some tissues and began wiping the mud from her heels. On the other side of the stoop a peasant woman in a red jersey and conical hat was staring at her. I caught her eye. She gestured to Liên's purse with her head and made a face to ask, "What is that?"

I didn't know how to say "purse," so I made a face back and mouthed the words for "I don't know." She looked at me a moment longer. I was wearing a pair of jeans, a blue shirt, and some worn-out black sneakers. My hair was cut short, like a boy's, and since the sun was out, I wore a baseball cap. From opposite ends of the stoop we puzzled out the purse situation. I had a small leather satchel strapped across my chest, so I grabbed hold of that, and held it up to show "it's one of these." Her face lit up, and she nodded to say she understood. I walked over to stand next to her. We looked a moment longer at Liên.

"Is she Chinese?" the woman asked.

"No, she's from Hanoi," I explained.

"Oh," she said, again nodding in understanding.

Liên was wearing pink lipstick, blusher, and mascara, and her hair was neatly styled. The peasant woman elbowed me, then nodded toward her and said, "Đêp" (beautiful). I nodded agreement and repeated, "Đêp."

"Where do you work?" I asked.

She gestured to the stone buildings at the back of the compound. I made a motion with my hand to ask the woman if she would show me the buildings; she agreed.

"Liên," I said, "let's go see the workshops."

She stared in shock for a moment to make sure she understood, then followed us. As she crossed the courtyard her heels clicked loudly against the cement.

"What's your name?" I asked the peasant woman as we walked.

"Lôc," she replied.

"Cô Lôc," I said, using the honorific for older women.

"Lôc," she said, brushing away my formality. She took my arm and pulled me close to her as we walked. From over my shoulder I saw the male supervisors watching us move away from the showroom. One of the men yelled something to Lôc; she gave a short answer and continued walking. After we went another fifty yards she looked over her shoulder again, then pulled me toward her, made a dramatic face and said, "Vietnamese men are very small."

I laughed out loud. Liên blushed and looked away. Lôc smiled at my laughter. As she smiled she lifted her mouth on the right side, so it turned into a cross between a smirk and a wink.

The women who worked in the factory had all returned home for lunch so the workshop was closed. There was a single light bulb hanging from a wire in the middle of the room, and the air was full of the dizzying smell of varnish. Lộc began to open the shutters to let in more light.

The baskets the women lacquered were of handwoven bamboo that the factory bought from residents of a neighboring hamlet. In the factory the baskets were edged with paint and varnish, then topped with an intricate design that the workers painted on by hand. The back wall of the workshop was lined with drying shelves and they were covered with half-done baskets, sitting neatly in rows. On the right wall was a set of shelves full of bowls of paint and varnish. The small bowls were covered with pieces of wax paper. Most of them had black paint in them, but since the company was trying to sell the baskets to the Western market they began experimenting with different colors, so the floor was covered with open paint cans.

The workers began to straggle back in after lunch. Each of the workshops had five to ten women.

"A Chinese lady?" one mumbled as she passed Liên standing timidly in the doorway.

"Hanoi," Lộc replied quickly.

I was standing at the back of the room staring at the drying baskets. When the workers entered I lifted my arm, smiled and said hello.

"Who's the foreign guy?" a woman said, surprised.

"*She's* an American," Lộc said.

I walked over to a young woman who was working on a basket and sat on my heels next to her. She looked down at her work shyly.

"Chào chị" I said.

Before beginning her work one woman picked up the wire hanging from the light bulb and walked with it over to an outlet by the door. She separated two strands and placed the lines into the connection. A spark flew, the bulb flickered, and the light was on.

Another young woman approached me with her chair and gestured for me to sit.

"It's OK," I said, with a wave of my hand. She insisted, and I awkwardly accepted. Both young women continued with their work, dipping their index fingers into bowls of black paint, then running them around the lip of the basket. At a table by the window a woman was staring at the edge of a basket cover and painting a design in silver paint, over the black lacquer. She held the lid close to her eyes and ran the small brush over her first coat of curls and loops.

"Khó" (Difficult), I said to Lộc, as I watched the tediousness of the process.

"Khó lắm" (Very difficult), she replied.

"Doesn't it bother you?" I asked, in reference to the paint odor.

"We're used to it," Lộc said.

Over by the door at the back of the room an older woman was sandpapering a layer of varnish in preparation for a top coat of black or red paint before the design was put on. Her face was lined with wrinkles, and her eyes looked dull and sad.

"Chào Cô," I said as I sat down next to her.

"Chị," she replied softly.

"This will be sanded, then painted again?" I said to Liên. The woman explained that the bottom layers of the lacquer were sanded by hand until they were smooth enough for the top coat of paint, then the design was put on and finally, another coat of varnish was added to protect the colors.

"It's very slow," she said, "very difficult."

"I know," I said, "But the baskets are so beautiful." I looked at her and smiled. She didn't smile back. The baskets did come out beautifully. The black paint was accented by red and gold flowers and covered over with a red-hued varnish. The sets were placed neatly one inside the other in descending order of size.

During the ride from Hanoi, Liên said to me that the villagers were happy to have jobs in the factory, since it meant that they could earn more money than just growing rice. But the work looked terribly difficult, and the environment was full of hazards.

"Do you like Viet Nam?" a young woman asked from across the room.

"I like Viet Nam very much," I said.

"It's very poor here, and the life is sad," she answered.

"Are you married?" someone else asked.

"No," I said.

"She's going to be the English teacher for the school," Lộc explained.

"How old are you?" another woman asked.

"I'm thirty-two," I said. "Are you married?" I asked, wanting to switch the focus of attention.

"Yes, I have three children."

"How old are you?" I asked.

"Twenty-four," she answered. "How come you aren't married?"

"Too many headaches," I said.

Lộc laughed out loud.

"Do the women have to farm in addition to working here?" I asked Liên.

"Some of them do," she said.

"How many hours a day do they work here?"

"Eight," she said.

I admired the baskets drying on the shelves. "The baskets look really pretty," I said. "Could you ask them if they like their work?"

Liên looked at me quizzically. "I mean," I continued, "do they like this kind of work, do they like their jobs?" Liên shook her head to tell me she wouldn't translate, and gave me a look that said even *she* knew not to ask that question. These women were poor, and if you are poor work is not something you have the luxury of liking or disliking. They worked—it was simply what they did. *This* work yielded more than *that* work, so they took it. But it meant working in poorly lit rooms, dipping their fingers into paint that eventually seeped in under their fingernails, breathing in fumes that were probably toxic, and doing the same intricate thing over and over again for hours at a time. I looked out the door at the rice fields that extended toward the horizon; there were four or five figures stooped over cutting grains. The work the harvesters were doing at that moment was the only other choice the women had. The village, with its traditional houses and cozy atmosphere, looked beautiful, but it was difficult to see the work without aching in sympathy for the workers.

*   *   *

With little by way of entertainment for the evenings I picked up the habit of walking a loop around the rice fields, the nearby hamlet and the river. One afternoon, at dusk, I walked outside the schoolyard gate, then heard anxious footsteps behind me.

"Where are you going?" Liên asked from the road. She had followed me out of nervousness, "You shouldn't walk alone in the village," she said. "You maybe are hurt."

I smiled at the polite but strange reasoning.

"Well, why don't you join me?" I said.

Some students were returning home by crossing the fields, I snapped a picture of them.

"Goodbye!" they yelled, giggling.

"I'm going for a walk," I told her. Liên was a beautiful young woman who wanted to spend time with me so she could improve her English. But she was also a city girl cast into the countryside for the first time. Initially, Liên was shocked by the spartan living quarters we were provided. On our first evening walk she whined for a minute about the length of our stay, and then turned to me and said, dramatically.

"I very regret my suggest."

"Oh," I replied, realizing that she had requested to stay with me, not been asked. "Well, it is very quiet here," I said. "Do you think the village will be too boring for you?"

"Yes," she said, on the verge of tears, "but it was my own suggest, and I cannot take it back!"

"Well . . .," I said softly, then tried to think of a diplomatic way to get her back to Hanoi.

"I think it is, the life is, too difficult here, and you return to Hanoi early, OK?" she said.

"Maybe," I replied.

Catdang village is made up of three hamlets, all built around a water source. Never far from any home was a stream or pond, and they were all crossed by either stone or bamboo bridges. The ponds had an assortment of greens growing in them, flowering Japanese water hyacinth or lotus, and though they appeared unpolluted they were often covered with a scummy film. The banks were damp and sometimes mossy. Since there was a harvest on during my visit they were often covered over with hay.

The hamlets are laid out in blocks made up of houses with Chinese-style courtyards, so each cobblestoned or dirt alley was a series of low and high walls, and small gates that allowed you to peek into the courtyard of the two families. Homes were made of whitewashed stone and tropical fruit trees grew easily, shading the stone courtyards. The tile roofs were often supplemented at the end of the harvest with hay to make thatch roofing. In the courtyards were hulling machines and rice grains laid out to dry. Nearly every yard had chickens, and now and again a rooster would roam the bushes and pathways. Chicks ran like cartoon birds, cheeping and speeding along as if they hadn't figured out they couldn't take flight. A mangy dog nearly always slept near a tree, or tucked into a pile of hay. Grapefruit, lime, and banana grew in family compounds, occasionally sugarcane. The homes were—in their traditional architecture—quaint. Tile roofs and wide wooden doors that stayed open meant families shared all the intimate moments of daily life. They washed in a courtyard tap drawn from a nearby well or pond; they prepared meals in a small cookhouse and ate in the front room, in full view of passersby.

To me it felt romantic, but the smoke from the cookhouse often grayed the whitewashed walls, and the Vietnamese told me they were tired of the troublesome tile roofs. We passed a rice storage building, then turned a corner and came upon a house under construction. I recognized it as the style of home found in larger towns and cities. There would be two floors, a balcony, and a flat roof. In the front on the first floor would be a large high-ceilinged room that could be used as a shop or restaurant, in the back a new-style kitchen and bathroom, and on the second floor two or three rooms for sleeping. The bamboo scaffolding was empty, but inside the mud and brick room on the second floor some men were smoking cigarettes and drinking beer. Bags of cement were piled on the first floor, and two women standing in the road were looking at the construction, talking. I smiled and remembered the clusters of people that gathered in my hometown to watch the yachts of summer residents being launched into the harbor each spring.

When the village's communal elements were transferred to the neighborhoods of larger cities in Viet Nam (and the Vietnamese often referred to Hanoi as their largest village), they were transformed to an openness that I found amusing. Everyone hunkered down on doorsteps or perched onto tiny wooden stools outside their open doors. Babies grow up wandering around crowds; the young and old do business from their household shops. Occasionally in Saigon and Hanoi I come across a boy brushing his teeth at a sidewalk tap, or an old man washing his face, and suddenly everyone is a villager once again.

But in Catdang I knew that the numbers politicians and business people were throwing around in Hanoi, all the talk about change, wouldn't be felt here by most people for a long time. All my teaching colleagues in Catdang still lived a life they referred to as "Khổ lắm. Có buồn." One with great difficulty and sadness. Things grew old and broke down, and, what I admired most about the houses, their intimacy and quaintness, held no appeal for the Vietnamese owners. They preferred the new cement architecture with flat roofs, where they could spread the harvest to dry.

We circled around the other side of the village to head back to the school. In another courtyard there was a rice machine clanging and picking grain off stalks. There were large strands of straw flying over the wall onto the pathway. A schoolboy walked unblinking over the growing pile of straw as the spent stalks rained down on him. The rice stalks, after they were hulled, lay in damp mounds on the side of the road. Dry strands scattered under our feet, cracking like whispering voices, as we walked. We turned around at the river and returned home.

After a few minutes on the road I heard the warm lowing of a cow, and turned to see three boys walking slowly behind me. I continued on toward the school, listening to the footsteps of the cow.

"Miss Edie Sillue!" one of the cowherds called. I turned to look at him.

"Hello," I said.

The sky was fading to a pale gray-blue.

"I've always loved this time in Viet Nam," I said. I turned to Liên and said slowly, "Do you like this time of day?"

She shook her head and said, "Buồn. sah."

"Sad?" I asked.

"Sad," she said.

People began to burn wood and gas for cooking and the smell of smoke got stronger.

"Miss Edie!!" the same boy called again. I turned to look again. He was small and thin, with bare feet and a dark shirt. He carried a switch in one hand, so he could prod the cow when it stopped, and in the other he carried a small cloth bundle.

"What's in the bundle, do you think?" I asked Liên.

She looked, then answered, "Potato, or turnip, something to eat."

We continued walking. One of the boys ran up close behind us, then stopped, turned and ran back to his friends, tripping on a stone as he went. This set off the giggles among the boys. The cow continued walking and slapped locusts off her flanks with her tail. The boy with the switch tried to walk, talk, and balance the turnips on his head. This incited full-blown laughter and one boy laughed so hard he had to cross the road to a nearby tree so he could pee.

"Eee-lee," he said, trying to repeat my name.

On the right, a calf ran toward the road from the field and banged head-long into the cow. The giddiness of it all caused the boy balancing the turnips to fall to the ground and roll toward the rice stalks. He stopped himself and, from the ground, pointed in hysteria at his friend. The second boy doubled up in laughter, facing the tree, with one hand on his penis, and the other on his ribs, he lifted an accusatory hand and gestured toward his friend on the ground. The end result was that he dribbled on his pants, which was another reason for laughter. The third boy, stopping in the middle of the road, was laughing at them both, which folded his face into wrinkles of silliness. Then his hand also went up in gesture, and they formed a triangle of arms in the smoky evening light.

We went over a bridge and walked home. In the twilight an old woman climbed up the stream bank. She was finishing bathing, and pulled her clothes up to cover her breasts. Her hair was unbound and hung like a thick strand of gray yarn over her hunched back. As she stepped slowly over the gravel path, she left a trail of water in her wake. Something about the quiet descending reassured me, and we went inside to eat.

Phương put the rice pot on the table, and sat down across from us as we ate. She would not join us, but often stayed until after we were done, so she could clean the dishes. Seeing the calluses on her palms, I remembered the words of my colleague Kiều, who said, "In Viet Nam children are told that to leave rice on the plate is an insult to the farmer."

Until then Vietnamese farmers had simply been misty figures on the horizon. Now Phương wandered around my house and I was keenly aware of where my meal came from, of who, exactly "the farmer" referred to. She sometimes sat across the table from me, wearing a yellow flowered shirt, on which she had made a lace collar by cutting out a pattern in the fabric. She wore her hair pulled back, and tied it at the bottom of the ponytail, so it lay thick and soft at the back of her neck, and strands fell forward over her forehead. Her eyes were a deep brown and her eye-brows thick. Under her nose there was a small beauty mark, and her teeth were straight and white.

"Ăn nhiếu" (Eat more), she said.

"Ăn rồi" (I'm full), I replied, referring to my unclean plate.

Phương was very polite, and seemed genuinely undisturbed by the fact that I couldn't finish a meal, but I thought that it must be different with the older people. There must be some part of the elders that was repulsed by the dregs of food I left in my bowl. They could partly reason—"She is thin, perhaps she is sick." They must have partly wondered: "In what place can you leave food uneaten?" And then they responded with courtesy. It poured out like running water—"Is the food all right? Does she want more meat? Give her some fat, she looks unhealthy, give her more rice. Does she need Coca-Cola? Give her more. Give her more."

After dinner we sat out on the stoop. Liên sighed dramatically and rested her chin in her hands as she stared at the empty night. I pushed mosquitos and moths away with quick, nervous jerks. Lan Anh looked at my discomfort and giggled. Phương sat down next to me, took my hand and murmured something.

"Đi vei, ha?" (Going home?) I asked.

She nodded and began rubbing the top of my hand, then cracked one of my knuckles.

"Ouch!" I yelped.

We looked down together; my hand sat, bony and pale, in her palm. The difference struck us, and we started laughing.

"Đi vei," she said, then walked down the stairs to her bike.

"Lan Anh," she called behind her, "you be polite."

In the field across from the school some boys were finishing a soccer game. Phương went through the gate.

"See," said Liên, pointing to the sky, "*Sao hôm.* Evening star."

I smiled at her and said, "Starlight Starbright."

In the road Phương's bicycle creaked, and a stone shot out from underneath her tire. The heavy wheels of nearby hulling machines slowed, pulled the last grains from the day. Crickets began to sing, and a frog climbed out of the well near my stoop. The sky paled further as the hour wore on, and the stringy outline of trees stood still against the sky. Children sang, then let their voices fade. An old woman in the house across the stream called out, "Ăn đi!" ("Come, eat!").

And it was night.

*   *   *

Mr. Khoa, who made the papaya salad at my going-away dinner, was a math teacher. Like most of the faculty, he had befriended me by stopping by to visit my small apartment on the school campus. He had the same comical physique and gesturing as Mr. Lam in Ho Chi Minh City, but here, in the quieter, village context, it appeared less anxious. He stopped by one evening when the apartment was full of seventh graders. He slipped off his sandals, and parted the bead curtain.

"Ăn cơm, chưa?" (Have you eaten yet?) he asked.

"Ăn rồi" (All done), I replied.

"Lemons," he said, holding up a small bag, then giving it to Liên to take to the kitchen.

"Great, thanks," I answered.

A group of young girls was huddled around me, looking at their English textbooks and playing with one another's hair. Occasionally someone would whisper something to a friend, trying to work out English words to ask me a question, but often shyness overtook them, and when I prodded them they retreated into panic-stricken silence. Lan Anh laughed at them. "Nói gì?" (What'd you say?), she teased. Liên walked up behind her and pinched her ear and growled, "What do you think you're doing?"

"Edie biêt nói tiếng Việt" (Edie knows Vietnamese), Khoa told the girls.

"Không biêt nói" (I don't know how to speak!), I said. "Anh muốn học tiếng Anh" (He wants to study English!).

Khoa began laughing. "English is very difficult," he said.

"Vietnamese is very difficult," I said.

"Vietnamese is very easy!" he joked.

"Look, *they* can speak English!" I said, pointing to the girls. "Watch." I began to sing the ABC song, which they had recently learned.

"ABCD . . .," they joined in sweetly.

Khoa turned to Liên and repeated the letters in Franco-Viet pronunciation, "Bay, say, day, I understand."

"EFG,"

"E is eh, what's G?" he asked.

"HIJK," the girls sang slowly. Khoa looked around, as if the song was getting away from him.

"H is ash?" he asked Liên. "Difficult," he added, shaking his head in admiration at the children. "LMNOP," the girls sang quickly.

Khoa's eyes widened. "This really is a difficult language," he said with certainty. "It's very difficult." He crossed his arms and looked at me across the room, then said loudly, "I'm not going to study English. Edie, come live here and study Vietnamese, OK?"

"Edie đến ơ đây," one of the girls cried out, "Edie come live here."

"No, không," I said, "Edie đi vei Mỹ" (I'm going to return home).

The girls looked disappointed.

"Do you miss your mother?" Khoa asked. The intimate nature of the question cut me, and I paused before I answered.

"Yes," I said, "I miss my family."

The girls understood the question and the answer perfectly. There was no shame in talking about yourself in such an emotional way in Viet Nam; they were all very familiar with feelings of longing, and when I appeared vulnerable like that they responded with understanding.

"It's eight," Liên said, after a minute. "Miss Edie is tired."

The girls all made sounds of resignation, and then said good night.

*   *   *

Like my classes in Ho Chi Minh City, the village school was crowded. The lesson was the students' first after the lunch break, and they often came in from playing at home, or running through the fields. There were forty students in each class and a little conversation, comment, or instruction between themselves was the beginning of a tidal wave of talk that resulted in complete chaos. The Vietnamese teachers rapped on their desks with rulers when the class got out of hand, but I just let the kids talk. They were often trying to understand how English sentences worked, or what specific words meant, and what the Vietnamese equivalent was. I appreciated the creativity of the talk, and the way it fed imagination and humor, so I let them run with it. The lesson was supposed to be divided up into two forty-five minute sessions, but I didn't like the broken feel of that, so I worked with the students for a full hour and a half without a break. We began after lunch and finished by 3:30, doing a variety of tasks, sometimes playing games, and sometimes simply listening and repeating.

We began each class by writing out the English alphabet. Vietnamese students are exposed to the Roman alphabet only as it was applied to their language by the French missionary Alexander de Rhodes in the eighteenth century. There are As, Bs, and Cs, but as many as three different kinds of each. There is no F, no J, they have three Os, two Us, and series of consonant clusters that boggled my mind. There is the famous Ng that foreigners never seem to master, Kh which comes out like a throaty h, and a Tr that mimics Ch, or rather would mimic it if they didn't also have the Ch—which sounds eerily like a J to me.

The writing session at the beginning of each period was originally my attempt to deter onlookers. Students from other grades crowded around the windows of my classroom when I taught. Hanging on the wooden bars and huddling around the doorway, they created a strange and bothersome distraction. I wrote on the board and did "listen and repeat" in an attempt to bore the uninvited audience away.

One day, after the students finished writing, we recited the alphabet and then set out to copy vocabulary from the textbook. As the students settled into their work I wandered up and down the rows. In the back of the class some boys began to talk. I stopped to talk with a girl who was having trouble writing the word "eraser."

"Miss, may I go out?" a voice called from behind.

"Yes," I replied, automatically. A murmur ran through the class. In the back of my mind I noted the clarity of the boy's pronunciation.

"Miss, may I go out?" another voice called.

I turned back, there was a boy standing up at his desk, shoulders back, like he was a tin soldier, head up, his arms straight and stiff by his sides.

"Yes," I replied again, smiling at him.

The murmur that my response brought grew louder. Outside on the steps the first boy stood waiting for his friend. They greeted each other with giggles, then clustered together to talk once more. I grew suspicious. The phrase rose again. I said yes, again, with one eye on the boys outside.

"May I go out?" a young boy wearing a large white baseball cap asked.

Girls began to ask and before I realized what was happening the question popped up again and again, like bubbles breaking the surface of water. I watched for another moment and then realized what was happening.

"May I go out?" a timid girl in the back row said softly.

"Yes!" I said, with eagerness to each student.

The students were using phrases they had never been taught.

These English words grabbed hold of the entire classroom. "May" never appeared in their textbook, nor did "go," "come," "in" or "out." They had uncovered their need for these requests, figured out the English translation on their own, and used my class as a language laboratory. They were infinitely more interesting than the words and phrases in the textbook. In the units in the book students wrestled with phrases like, "This is an eraser" and "These are trousers." In the textbook none of the words they needed appeared. There was no "May," only "what" and "who." There was no "go," only "is." "Is" is an important but oblique word in English and it has no counterpart in many languages of the world. For my students it had none of the appeal of "go," none of the magical effect.

"May I go out?" yielded instantaneous results. They stood outside the classroom window for a moment marveling at the effect of the words and, in giddy excitement circled around again and continued on with the experiment. Even better than the first question, was its equally effective partner, "May I come in!?"

"Yes," I replied from the front of the class.

The tin soldier reappeared and asked, "Miss, may I come in?!"

The other students had their eyes glued on their classmates. They put their pencils down and watched.

"May I come in?!" a girl asked quietly.

The boy with the white baseball cap stood in the doorway and stared at the classroom wall, "Miss," he said nervously, "may I go in?"

"May I come in," a classmate corrected in a whisper.

"Yes, you may come in," I said.

"Yes, you may come in," he replied.

May I go out. May I come in. The students turned to each other and started murmuring in awe. They began repeating the phrase and teaching each other. "Go," one girl said, pointing out the window, "Come," she finished, gesturing with her thumb back inside. For a few minutes English was pure magic. These phrases had the same mysterious power as the light switch in my apartment. *Click*—you're out. *Click*—you're in. As they say in the sixth grade: It was excellent.

That night the children peopled my dreams. As I began to fall asleep their faces floated toward me, and occasionally I would be jerked awake by the sound of their voices. In one dream they appeared in a distant rice field, just as they had on my first evening walk. I walked toward them. One of the pathways turned into a conveyor belt, and the children stopped talking for a moment, and then stood in line to approach me. There was a young boy who came forward and winked at me, then a girl with a white shirt that had grayed from dirt. A round-faced girl with a dirty forehead and ink on her fingertips laughed loudly, then tripped and fell into my arms. The boy in the white baseball cap stood proudly and said, "May I go out? May I come in?" One boy looked like a straw doll, with hay and rice seeds falling from his hair. Lan Anh, came forward, pushing her younger brother Đức along, then giving up as he turned and ran in shyness. She wore bright pink Cinderella shoes, and they glittered in the sun. She reached up to take the ribbon barrette from her hair. "Edie, ơi!" she called from the distance.

The beltway moved her closer. As her hair fell down I looked again, and saw she was my university student, Subtlety.

*   *   *

The next afternoon, I wandered in to the teacher's room after class. It was the end of the day and Nữ and Phương were sitting eating fruit and talking with some of the other female teachers. I walked in and said hello.

"Chào Cô!" I said, dramatically.

"Edie!" Nữ said, "biêt nói tiếng Viet" (Edie speaks Vietnamese), she said to the others. They agreed politely. The gym teacher, Bích Hạnh, was sitting on a bench by the door.

"Edie," she asked, "how many bowls of rice did you eat today?"

I blushed as I answered, "Two."

She shook her head in disapproval, "You should be eating three at each meal."

Most of the teachers were also farmers, and their bodies were fueled, in the classroom and in the field, by rice. Phương brushed some chalk dust from the calluses on her hand. She took my hand when I sat down next to her, and held it in hers. Then she began gently rubbing the skin on the top and massaging my fingers. Nữ placed an orange in front of me.

"No, thanks," I said.

"Eat," she encouraged.

I smiled and refused again. Kiều Thu, a math teacher, sat across from me and spit orange seeds into her hand.

The Vietnamese refer to country women as *béo* (fat), but to me their bodies have an unsculpted athleticism. In Catdang their broad shoulder and breast area brought to mind competition swimmers, and when I saw a woman climbing and crossing streams, or stooped over harvesting rice in the fields, I admired the wide swath of her hips and thighs.

Nữ swung into my house early every evening to help Phương prepare my meals. The door to the apartment was always open, and we could see each other through the curtain as she arrived. With an unfailing air of expectancy, she hurried up the stairs, slipped off her sandals, parted the bead curtain, and said, "Đói chưa?" (Are you hungry yet?). I blushed and replied, "Chưa" (Not yet). My appetite, or lack thereof, was a deep mystery to her and all the other women, but it was understandable to me: My days passed without my doing one-third the physical labor they did.

After class one day I wandered out the school gate to take some pictures of the harvest. It was early evening, and I thought the light would make interesting photos. Liên came running up behind me a few minutes later.

"Hi," I said with a smile, then held up my camera to tell her what I was doing.

We crossed a small stream and moved onto a pathway. Rice fields are made up of square and rectangular blocks of land that are surrounded by small waterways. The small channels are fed by larger streams that circle the larger land expanse. Each pathway is a high embankment, rather like a small dike, the larger, wider ones leading to small ones cutting up blocks of land. The irrigation was unstable, and often the rice had to be watered by hand in a tedious process that entailed lifting buckets of water from the small stream and swinging them upward so the water flew across the pathways and landed in the field. Between the rain, the streams and the repeated foot traffic many of the paths had become soft and muddy. The earthiness of this life has never escaped the attention of poets, like the nineteenth-century female poet Hồ Xuân Hương:

> Not a drop of rain for this dry heat!
> Come, girls, let's go bail water.
> Let's drag our delta-shaped buttocks to that huge square field
> where our bodies can pulse to the water's lapping.
> Crouched, straining to catch each trickle from the rockheads,
> our buttocks tighten with such labor.
> Indeed, we work so hard we forget the effort
> and, taking a final stance to bend and lift—
> you part your legs a second, and it's filled.

I walked further out in the field and a woman stood up straight amid the grains to stare for a moment. Mosquitos rose from the water and began bouncing around my ankles. Another called out to Liên as I walked by.

"Người gì?" (What country?)

"Mỹ" (America), Liên said.

I stared down at the pathway. Locusts scattered with each step I took and dove into the rice, plinking, like strange hail, against the ripe stalks. Farther out, an older man cut the rice with a sickle, and the sound of the blade against the bundled stalks reminded me of tearing stitches out of fabric. The woman who had stared at me moments earlier stood upright again as she reached the end of her row. She took the sickle and looped it, blade down, through the fabric tied around her waist, so the hook of the blade hung down across her hip, and the thick wooden handle stood straight against her ribs. When they harvested, women and men bent, grabbed a handful of rice, pulled the base taut, then took the sharp side of the blade and cut. The previous day I was watching in an iron works as two men hammered out new sickles. One man held the hook against an iron base using a pair of tongs and swung a hammer up with his right arm, the second swung during the impact, and hit during the other man's up-swing. Initially there was a vibration, but as the iron got thinner the hammers hit the base harder and the sound became stone on stone. There was no artistry involved; it didn't appear the least romantic. Even as the man sharpened the blade to a proper cutting edge, it all seemed so pragmatic. This work was done in order to make a cutting blade, something that, combined with the muscle of the human arm, cut the stalk so it could then be threshed.

I stepped off the path at the approach of a young woman pushing a bicycle loaded with rice. It was a larger amount of rice than could be carried on her shoulder and I wondered how she would do it without the bike falling over. She steered by working a bamboo pole attached to the handlebar, and the bike wobbled a bit as she tried to balance the bundle on the seat. Straddling the back wheel were two other bundles tied on with black rubber bands. The woman dug in with her bare feet as she tried to push the bike tires on the soft earth, without veering off the bank. She pushed and grunted softly as the front tire turned toward the field.

"Chị được, không?" (Are you OK?), I asked.

"Được, được," she said quickly.

I offered to help her work the bike toward the road. Liên looked at me nervously, but the precarious wobbling of the bike was driving me crazy. I moved to the right side, and began pushing. My shoes slipped in the mud. The young woman pulled the bike toward herself, so she bore all the weight, and it veered left. She began walking and pushing from the muddy left bank.

"Is she OK?" I asked Liên.

Liên jumped behind and began to push from the back. They talked among themselves. I couldn't see the other woman, but I saw her feet pushing through the muck on the left bank.

"Is she OK?" I wondered out loud, from behind the mound of rice.

"Được," Liên reassured me.

My hands were only lightly pushing the bicycle, as the woman pulled the bike toward herself to insure I wouldn't bear too much weight. It became clear very quickly that my presence disturbed her, and instead of distributing the weight evenly, as I had hoped, I was simply shifting the burden on to her. I looked for an opportunity to let her go ahead alone. Fortunately, we reached a small cement bridge.

"Được, không?" I said again.

Liên and she talked quickly.

"Ya được, cam ơn Chị" (I'm fine, thanks), the woman said, as the bicycle rolled across the bridge. "Cam ơn, nha," she repeated. She continued walking down the road, the mud now spread thick down the back of her ankle, her calves flexing as she pushed forward.

I remembered the young woman's politeness and strength as Bích continued to lecture me about eating more rice. Ngọc, another teacher, walked into the room with a small bundle of clippings in her hand.

"Planting?" Nữ asked.

"Yeah," Ngọc replied, then went out to a plot of land near the building. Because the school district did not have enough money to pay teachers, they were often paid partially in clippings and planting space. Any vegetables they could raise on the land were theirs to sell.

"Do you have a boyfriend?" she asked.

"Yes," I lied, "he's a businessman in America."

"I thought he was a lawyer?" Nữ said. I had lied to Nữ before about a boyfriend. I often did this with older women in Viet Nam because I didn't want to endure the nagging advice and encouragement to get married and have children.

"How come you didn't bring his picture?" Bích asked, curiously.

"Because he gives me a headache," I said, trying to drop the subject.

Nữ began peeling a grapefruit. Kiều Thu nodded in understanding, "Husbands are a headache," she said.

"Boyfriends aren't!" Nữ said. She dug her thumb into the grapefruit's thick skin, and I admired the strength I saw in her hand.

"So your boyfriend's a businessman?" Kiều Thu continued.

"Yeah, I guess," I mumbled.

Phương took my hand again, and placed a grapefruit section in it.

"Oh, no," I said politely.

"They're from Cô Nữ's grove," she said. "Eat."

I put the section down on the table. Carrying on the conversation, Kiều

Thu held a piece of chalk up in front of my face and said, "Vietnamese men."

Working completely in tandem Bích leaned forward with a banana and said, with a loud laugh, "American men!"

My mouth fell open in shock, as Thu and Bích sat back elbowing each other and nodding in agreement.

I began eating the grapefruit as the women talked quickly among themselves. Nữ lowered her voice and leaned across the table to Phương. Bích joined in from the other side of the room with a steady stream of "I know"s and "mmh, hmm"s. Clearly they were talking about married life.

The grapefruit was thick skinned, but sweet. It had a fleshy pink middle that went down sugary, with no biting aftertaste. Phương continued lifting my hand as she talked, placing section after section in it.

Ngọc came in from outside.

"Finished?" Nữ asked.

"Some," Ngọc replied, then sat to listen to the other women talk.

I finished another section of the fruit, then gestured that I didn't want any more. Nữ turned to Ngọc.

"Anh ay vei nha, chưa?" (Husband home yet?), she asked.

Ngọc snorted her contempt before she answered, "Đi an cơm phơ, roi."

She was complaining of her husband having an affair. The women shook their heads in disapproval.

"Would you like my boyfriend?" I offered.

Phương giggled, and everyone else smiled, except for Ngọc.

"Do you miss him?" Kiều Thu asked me.

"No," I answered with a smile.

"Do you miss America?" Nữ asked.

"Sometimes," I replied.

I finished the last section of grapefruit, then put the skins in a neat pile on the center of the desk. Bích sighed, then got up and walked to the door. It was late in the day.

"Đi vei" (Gotta go), she said.

"Had enough?" Nữ asked me. "Was it good?"

Kiều Thu stood to say good-bye, then paused so I could answer Nữ. I could reply with the word "good" alone, but I wanted to practice the word for grapefruit, since it was difficult for me. I thought for a moment, then formed a sentence, and said loudly.

"Bưởi có Cô Nữ ngon lắm!" (The grapefruits of Cô Nữ are delicious!)

We sat in the innuendo for about ten seconds. Then, like the source of a river, Nữ's bawdiness rolled forward until it flooded the room, and we all laughed until we had to hold on to each other for support.

*   *   *

In addition to salad made from green papayas our farewell dinner menu included a variety of fried meats, sauteed vegetables, fried spring rolls, boiled shrimp, a cooked chicken, and plenty of beer and Coca-cola. When the electricity faded, as it did every evening around eight, Nữ pulled three small candles from her bag and placed them down the center of the table. For rice we had cốm—pounded young rice, sweetened with sugar, it is served with sticky rice, that has been seasoned with squash pulp. Eaten together, by hand, the two combined deliciously, and I reached out to the bowl like it was popcorn, irresistible and addictive.

"We've never met a foreigner," Phương said during the meal.

"Oh, well," I said, not knowing how to reply, "here I am!" I smiled.

"We all thought foreigners were unkind," she said, referring to the village.

I paused. "Well, not all of us," I answered, not quite sure what response would be the right one. Their perspective is understandable, and would probably be reinforced in the future. They would, no doubt, have "troublesome" guests eventually or somehow be "invaded" by commerce and capitalism. The new houses being built told me all that.

As we ate Liên quietly told me about Phương's family life. "She was raised by her mother. She's the only child," she said.

"Oh?" I said.

"Her father died in the war."

I asked, "Her father was killed in the war?"

I stared at Liên.

"Yes," she said, matter-of-factly, "in 1965."

My citizenship hit me in the head like a rock. Phương waited on me hand and foot. She sat with me on the stoop like an old friend. She thanked me profusely for what she called "kindness for my children." She told me I was beautiful and intelligent and loved to rub the top of my hands with her palm. I was the first foreigner she'd ever met, and I was American.

I had again wandered onto the doorstep of history via culture. The void I found a year earlier, in American library stacks and conversations, was suddenly filled. It was not a story, a folk tale, or a poem; it was a comment made during a dinner party, but it shattered the silence I had encountered in the United States. The Vietnamese told tales, held celebrations, wrote poems, grew rice, and made it into beautiful food; I could feel it in my hands. The bombs books talked about became unnumbered and real. The "facts" and "reports" that veiled this country for years were ripped away through the death of a father. What joy, then, for citizens to sit over dinner loving one another.

That evening rice filled my belly and sugar stayed on my tongue. I knew then the answer to the question people badgered me with before (and during) my trip to Viet Nam. "Why?" everyone asked. "Why Viet Nam?" Because in 1994 the American War is not what Viet Nam offers the traveler, and unkindness is not what I brought to them. Viet Nam gave stories where there was pain, graciousness where bitterness and cynicism had visited, food where famine struck, lightheartedness after sorrow, and beauty rising up from darkness.

During the meal everyone laughed at my "May I go out?" story, and commented on the success I had teaching the students to write the English alphabet. Mr. Khoa drank wine until his cheeks were flush, then told me how much he would miss me. Every few moments Phương lifted handfuls of sticky rice and put them on my plate. And for a moment everything was far away. The bombs that killed Phương's father, the work that tried to break the villagers' backs, the poverty that tried to humiliate them, the strange languages we spoke to one another, and the awkward cross-cultural interactions all faded. In the candlelight the meat, fruit, and vegetables covered the tables like a holiday banquet. In a timed exchange of motion, people reached forward, balled the orange sticky rice, picked up the sweet green pieces of pounded rice, and ate. Nữ's face looked beautiful in the shadows, Mr. Ngô's face softened, and Liên sighed contentedly. It was a very good harvest.

After everyone left I found Liên sitting on the stoop staring out at the darkness. "It's as dark as ink!" I said, a teasing reminder of her initial culture shock. She smiled and blushed. Liên's lipstick had melted away quickly in the dirt and sweat of country living. She quickly converted her wardrobe to a sensible T-shirt and sandals, and wore her long hair unstyled. But her face, with its thick lips and high nose, maintained its fashionable pout, and her eyelashes, long and delicate, continued to look made up even without the aid of mascara.

"Can you tist?" she asked.

"Can I what?"

"The dance, tist?" she repeated.

"Twist," I said. "Yeah, I love to dance."

"Can you show me?" she asked, eagerly.

"Sure, I'll teach you."

I put Paul Simon's "Graceland" in the tape player and we began to twist. She put her left foot out delicately, as if she were testing water, and slowly moved her hips to the African music.

"Yeah, that's it," I encouraged. "Now, relax your knees." I bent my knees. She began to giggle. Lan Anh, who stayed with us in the evening, laughed out loud as she joined.

These are the days of miracle and wonder.

"You can swing your hips too!" I said cheerfully, and I broke into a side step and swing. Liên followed timidly.

"Now try your shoulders!" I added, excited by the music.

This is the long distance call.

Lan Anh stood behind us, smiling widely and moving her shoulders back and forth in imitation. "C'mon Liên!" I said, then I shook my shoulders provocatively and began to move around the room.

"Oooh!" she said, shocked.

I began to sing along with the music and dance in a circle.

"You can lift your arms!" I said loudly, "Look! An African man I met once taught me this!" I swung my arms up, alternating each, and then began to stomp my way forward. Lan Anh squealed with delight and ran around the room, then through the front door.

The way we look to a distant constellation, that's dying in a corner of the sky.

"Or without the arms," I said, placing my hands on my hips and moving my shoulders and hips. Liên's eyes widened. Carried away, I passed by her and began to dance in a circle again.

These are the days of miracle and wonder, so don't cry baby don't cry . . .

The music faded a little and I stopped turning to find Liên standing timidly in her starting pose, left foot out, hands delicately splayed in front.

"I just like to twist," she said, and she began her gentle motion once again.

Meanwhile, Lan Anh had danced her way out onto our porch, and as I passed through the doorway she turned and landed. Facing the darkness, she growled softly and struck a karate fighting pose.

Chapter Fourteen

Yet Kiều possessed a keener, deeper charm—
She excelled Van in talent and in looks.
Her eyes were autumn streams, her brows spring hills.
The flowers and willows envied her fresh hue.
A glance or two from her, and cities rocked!
                    —Nguyễn Du, *The Tale of Kiều*

One evening after I returned to Saigon I walked into the house and slipped off my shoes. Nục stood alert in the kitchen doorway.

"Anh, ơi" I called.

He ran toward me clipping his toenails, wagging his tail, and whining hello.

"*Anh ơơơiii!*" I sang loudly.

"Anh ơi" is how women refer to their husbands and sweethearts. If it's used in the wrong social circumstance, it's flirtatious. Thảo laughed at me and nodded his head.

"Yes," he said, "you sound just like Vietnamese woman."

I smiled proudly, pleased that I could accurately mimic Vietnamese women. *Ơi!*, they call to loved ones and children. *Anh ơi, Con, ơi!* It is a high-pitched call, coy, flirting and comforting all at once. When I heard it from women the call was loud, but it was soft at the same time. I liked saying *ơi!* and being soft in a place where I felt like a stick figure—all length and edge, all lines and limbs.

Em, ơi!

Later, during dinner, we all laughed when Thảo told me about a Vietnamese proverb: "In Viet Nam we say, 'First, you fear God. Second, you fear your wife." He paused for a moment then waved the saying away, "but I am not like that."

"Really?" I asked.

He smiled slyly, "I know God is very far away."

"Smart husband!" Bình and I said together, and we all laughed.

Later, I told the family that my weekend student Minh Ngọc had given me a Vietnamese name. It was interesting to be given a new name. In China my students were always asking for Western names. They turned themselves into Daisys and Daves and Martins. Some simply translated the meaning of their names, so they were called "Lotus" or "Jasmine." In the United States all my Asian students did it; they considered Western names "more practical." I never understood this ability to deface yourself to such an extent, so I attributed it to cultural upbringing and a fascination with things Western. I was grateful when my Vietnamese students expressed no interest in acquiring Western names, but this was the first time an Asian friend suggested I change my own name. "Edie" cannot be gracefully transliterated into Vietnamese, so Minh Ngọc, an actress and playwright whom I tutored on weekends called me "Bạch Yến"—White Swallow. When I mentioned the name to Bình, she furrowed her brow and pursed her lips as if she had bitten into something distasteful.

"Oh! I don't like women named after birds!"

She shook her head and informed me that White Swallow was a bad name because women named after birds "are always sad." When I asked other Vietnamese female friends they agreed. I couldn't actually say the name correctly in the first place, so this negative response gave me another reason not to use it, but I like the name Bạch Yến and its suggestion of grace. Thư, who knew me a bit better than Minh Ngọc, later named me "Thanh Ngọc"—Blue Pearl. She said it was because "pearls come from oysters—they are hard and rough on the outside, but delicate inside. Like you."

The administrative office Thư worked in was next to the English Resource Center. It was large and dusty, with two desks and a Ricoh copier that was frequently broken. A set of bookshelves on one wall, gathering dirt and soot, housed only a few neglected copies of English and American novels. There were two sitting chairs and a coffee table. Since the room was only used for a portion of the day, it had an air of abandonment. But it provided cool relief for me on hot afternoons and became somewhat of a meeting place for me and my Vietnamese colleagues.

"Be careful, she understands more than you think," Thư said one afternoon to the university librarian. They were standing by the copier sorting papers and talking. I laughed softly from across the room. I was, in fact, listening; they were talking about whether I could speak Vietnamese. This was during one of the many informal study schedules I started and abandoned. After Quí and I parted ways, Thúy Kiều became my tutor. During each lesson she would read from the university textbook pattern exercises, and I would repeat the sentences. Thư had seen me look up from my lesson book and try to interject some comment in their conversation.

"Does she really?" the librarian responded.

"Tôi không biêt nói tiếng Việt Nam." I said over my shoulder, smiling at her. She and Thư started laughing. She came over, patted me on the shoulder and said "Very good! Your Vietnamese is very good!"

"Yes, it is," Kiều agreed.

It's not true, but they were kind to say so. Like my lessons with Quí these informal meetings were more an extension of my curiosity about Vietnamese than lessons. I was never prepared. What I wanted to do was listen to Kiều's accent and learn to imitate her.

Thư and Kiều were part of another of my weekend trips down the Mekong Delta. We were invited to present a "teaching methods" workshop to teachers at an evening school in Soc Trang on Saturday, and then on Sunday to examine local students for the A, B, and C Certificates. The trip was arranged by Bích Ngọc, an older faculty member who was the head of the University Learning Center, and we were joined by our colleague Tô Minh Thạnh.

Minh Thạnh was part-time faculty at the university. She had short hair, and often dressed in fashionable silk slacks. Because of her large stride, and professional demeanor, our university colleagues referred to her as "aggressive" and "immodest." I loved talking to her. Like so many of my friends in Ho Chi Minh City, she was a marvelous contradiction. She was raised with traditional beliefs and family practices, but was intensely strong and ambitious. I thought it was Thạnh who started the "notorious" trend that week. On Monday evening she turned to me in the teacher's room and said,

"You know, I'm notorious among the students for being a witch in the classroom. I'm very serious and I always assign lots of homework."

I patted her hand, empathetic to the experience of being thought "not nice." "In my classroom in the United States I'm notorious for that too."

"Notorious" turned up all that week. Thư told me the "saucy girls" were notorious among the teachers. A male colleague said he was notorious for heavy smoking. Mỹ Ngọc, the giggly, timid secretary of the department, was notorious for driving fast. Linda's class was notoriously difficult.

"I think they must all own Word-a-Day calendars," I reasoned in my journal.

*   *   *

Most of my colleagues at the university were women, and most of the students who sought me out were female. I taught young, shy first years, awkward, bookish fourth years, saucy and savvy third years. In the night school I met factory workers and housewives eager and loud in my classroom. In private lessons, I taught a doctor who had lived for two years in the jungles of Cambodia aiding the Viet Cong. They were all a far cry from the "frail" women I had been taught to expect in the United States. Minh Ngọc was one of nine children born in nine different provinces because her mother was on the run with the Viet Minh. I have a hard time imagining my mother, safe and settled in a Boston suburb, handling eight children for a day at the beach. When Minh Ngọc told me her mother moved from province to province aiding Ho Chi Minh and his revolutionaries with nine children in tow—I *couldn't* imagine it.

On Wednesday I told Minh Ngọc that I would be unable to tutor her over the weekend since I had to attend the workshop in Soc Trang.

"Oh!" she smiled, "I go to Soc Trang before. With my boyfriend I ride motorcycles down. Very nice."

"I love the countryside," I added.

She paused, thinking before she replied. "Next week?" she asked awkwardly.

"Next week we'll have lessons," I reassured her.

"No, my play . . ." she corrected, "see my play I am in."

"Oh yes!" I said, "yes, what night?"

"Tuesday."

"Great," I said.

She was performing in a play that was very popular in Saigon, *The House without Men*. A third-year student had offered to take me a number of times, but I never got around to accepting. It would be wonderful to go and see Minh Ngọc on stage. Like many others, she was a far cry from the stereotyped image I saw plastered in magazines and movies, where a woman with almond-shaped eyes looks out timidly from behind a hand-held fan.

There are those who will tell you that the "secret" in Vietnamese women's social strategies is their endurance, their ability to take the hits of misfortune and humiliation. Thúy Kiều, the central character in *The Tale of Kiều*, a narrative poem written by Nguyễn Du in the eighteenth century, is a classical model of endurance in the face of bad karma. For Vietnamese women she is a portrait of their "fate" and that of all women. Born beautiful ("Supreme in loveliness"), Kiều spends her life enduring a never-ending series of misfortune—lost family, lost love, betrayal, and accusation—with admirable humility.

When her family is unjustly accused of crimes and persecuted by police, her whirlpool of bad karma begins. She forfeits the opportunity to be with her new love Kim and sells herself:

Kiều had to save her kin, her flesh and blood.
When evil strikes, one bows to circumstance.
When one must weigh and choose between one's love
and filial duty, which will turn the scale?
Kiều brushed aside her solemn vows to Kim
she'd pay a daughter's debt before all else.

Oh pity her, so young and innocent. The happy ending is a long way from there. Kiều is cursed because of her talents and loveliness, Nguyễn Du writes: *"In talent take no overweening pride—great talent and misfortune make a pair."* Kiều endures all of it with acceptance and patience. These are not aspects of character that we hold in high esteem in the West. In the United States we love independence and confidence, we admire women with moxie; in Viet Nam it is endurance.

"I don't like Kiều," Thư said during the drive to Soc Trang.

"The tale of Kiều is a beautiful portrait of the perfect Vietnamese woman," Thúy Kiều said, then reminded us she had been named after the heroine. "It is a pity young women today are not like her."

"She always gave in to misfortune," grumbled Thư.

"It is an old-fashioned book," said Minh Thạnh, dismissively.

Like my saucy student "Subtlety" and her friends, Minh Thạnh is part of a new generation of Vietnamese women. They wear their ambition and pride on the outside, only with a little less certainty. As we rode to Soc Trang, I told them all the story about my confrontation with Lotus and Subtlety when we were studying U.S. westward expansion.

"They didn't do what you told them?" Minh Thạnh said, shocked.

"Well," I started to apologize for the girls, "it was a pretty complex topic, even for a native speaker, and I was asking them to present their ideas to me in English!"

"That doesn't matter," Thư said.

"Yes," said Bích Ngọc quietly, "they are very impolite."

The contrast between the names of the "saucy girls"—Lotus and Subtlety—and their behavior still makes me laugh. They are strong and bold in both new and old ways. I snapped at them in class, but overall I can tolerate their behavior because they are both alien and painfully familiar at the same time. At home there are at least a dozen photographs of me making a dramatic gesture or face like Lotus and Subtlety; they are the spoiled girls of the middle class I grew up in. "Get me outta here," we mumbled in ignorance and frustration. "Take me where the action is."

In family pictures my hand throws an imaginary scarf over my shoulder, my teenage face turns toward the sky in a mock gesture of burden, as I imitate Nora Desmond in *Sunset Boulevard*: "Oh, Max." When my students leaned forward on their desks and sighed over their burdens, I remembered boring summer afternoons and dreams of faraway places, imagined while I rested my chin in the heel of my hand. On the way to Soc Trang, everyone "tsked" in disapproval over my leniency toward the students; they found the girls terribly disrespectful.

We arrived at the Soc Trang Hotel at sunset. It was located on the riverfront, by the market, and looked over a small park. The end of the work day brought families out and an increase in sampan traffic. There was a restaurant on the river decorated with multicolored lights; as they blinked, they cast a small rainbow on the water. Bích Ngọc, showing Thúy Kiều and me our room, pointed to the air conditioner and said "Ooh, how nice. A.C." It was a gesture casual enough to go unnoticed by most. My ear perked because in saying "A.C." Bích Ngọc was using "real English," like a native speaker; I smiled at her, knowing the pleasure of choosing contracted words in Chinese and remembering how excited my village students were with the discovery of new words. As she was leaving, she told me my workshop topic was "Techniques for Teaching English Composition," and that I would present third, just after Kiều, who was talking about test preparation, and before Thư, who was presenting techniques for conversation class.

Around ten o'clock, after much lying around and talking out loud, I pulled a large scarf from my bag and decided it would be the center of my presentation. I would hand it to a student and say, "Let's begin a story. Where did this scarf come from?" Then, we would create a chalkboard narrative.

Kiều watched me from the bed. She had two textbooks in front of her and was writing extensive notes in Vietnamese and English. I wrapped the scarf around me and spun dramatically. Then, imagining the blank look on students' faces, I fell back on to my bed and sighed.

"They'll hate it," I said.

"Noooo," she said soothingly, "it's very cweative."

Late the next day we began the workshop. The teachers were a combination of recent university grads and graying former ARVN, who all spoke with broad American accents. My talk—opening with a large flourish of the scarf—was stared at rather than listened to, and soft laughter greeted my answers to questions; they were answers that were not answers.

"How do we teach writing the introduction?" a man asked.

"You wait until the essay is finished," I replied.

"How can we teach them to write for the TWE test?" a woman inquired.

"You can't. Or at least I can't! I teach students how to rewrite," I told her. They laughed and nodded, familiar with my failure. When Thư finished her presentation—full of ideas for vocabulary building games and conversation starters—the Test of English as a Foreign Language (TOEFL) test reared its ugly head.

"If we don't teach them grammar first, how can they be prepared for the test?"

"Many students have already memorized grammar rules," I explained, "but they can't use the language in conversation or writing."

"But they must pass TOEFL," someone said.

We released a collective groan. There's no answer for this dilemma. Students all over the world must pass this arcane test, which comprises some one hundred or so questions about the intricacies of English grammar, in order to be considered "English speakers." They could easily be categorized as fluent without uttering a word.

"This is giving me a headache," I mumbled to Minh Thạnh, who was beginning to fidget.

Thạnh was a city woman in the peasant-filled countryside. Many of the housemaids for the expanding middle class in Saigon may have migrated from this town in the Mekong in search of better economic resources for their families. The women of Soc Trang paddle sampans, carry baskets to market, and speak proudly among themselves of their children attending university on scholarship.

"She can speak English!" they brag. "She can take care of me when I'm old."

They moved around the streets wearing simple black trousers, colored tops, and conical hats. Thạnh moved swiftly past them on her motorbike, like a corporate employee pushing upward to break the glass ceiling. In Soc Trang she leaned toward me, complicit in whining complaint.

"I just want to leave," she said, seriously.

"Let's go eat!" I said anxiously. After further questions, an interminable amount of time posing for pictures and saying polite goodbyes, we left for dinner. There was a popular restaurant at the center of town and, we were told by the owner's cousin, they served a delicious seafood hot pot.

After we arrived, Bích Ngọc said she would sit across from me at the round table, Thư was to sit to my right, Minh Thạnh on my left, and Kiều next to Bích Ngọc. Though we were all friends, the proper seating arrangements were relevant, and the women negotiated among themselves as I sat down and began to fiddle with the chopsticks. "I'm hungry!" I announced, like an American kid at Thanksgiving. The waiter arrived some moments later, with a steaming silver pot and flame. He put both in the center of the table and surrounded them with plates of greens, cucumbers, and bean sprouts, as well as two bowls of sauce.

Minh Thạnh picked up her chopsticks and began stirring the soup, turning the fish over and over to make sure it cooked properly. Thư moved the bowl of fish sauce, to the other side of the table. Bích Ngọc picked up some greens and pressed them into the soup.

"Let's gossip about our students!" I said.

Everyone blushed.

"OK, OK," I said, trying to keep a bad joke rolling. "How many of you hate giving oral interviews?"

They all laughed.

"I get so irritable!" I said, gesturing with my chopsticks.

"There are so many students," Bích Ngọc said diplomatically.

Minh Thạnh deboned a piece of fish and placed it on the bowl of rice in front of me.

"Thank you," I said to her, softly. "And they all say the same thing!" I said across the table.

Thư dipped a piece of lettuce in soy sauce and placed it on my plate.

"Thank you."

Minh Thạnh gave me a slice of cucumber.

"Th . . ." I started, then stopped.

"I think they are very nervous because you are a native speaker," Kiều added. She picked up some bean sprouts and tried to lean across the table to put them on my plate, but fell back when she realized it was too far away. The sprouts fell into the pot. Filling in for her, Minh Thạnh lifted the bean sprouts from the soup and placed them on my plate.

"Em, thanks . . .," I said. I lifted my bowl and ate some of the fish, and a little rice, then I had a sip of my Coca-cola. Thư ladled some more soup on my rice while my bowl was down. I put my glass down. "I make people nervous?" I asked.

I turned to Thư. "Thư, what do you think?" I asked. We spent a lot of time together and I felt comfortable enough to tease her by putting her on the spot. I leaned close and asked loudly, *"Do I make people nervous?"* She turned away in laughter. I sipped my cola. Another piece of fish had somehow appeared in my bowl; I stared at it. Kiều stood up, leaned across the table, picked up my Coke can and refilled my glass. I watched the bubbles, then looked at my plate full of food. Minh Thạnh gave me some more; with each gesture my friends made the table seem smaller.

"Anyone feeling cramped?" I asked.

"Sorry?" Minh Thạnh said.

"Nothing," I said, smiling.

It all seemed to be natural reflex for my friends to treat me this way, pouring attention on me, and finding just the right moment to assist me. I marveled at their timing.

✳   ✳   ✳

On Sunday afternoon I had to return to the hotel from the school because I was overcome with a migraine headache. Thúy Kiều returned with me and offered to provide some relief by giving me a massage with menthol oil.

"Does the A.C. bother you?" I asked when we were back at the room.

"Not tat tall," she said.

As I lay on the bed her fingers worked ever so slowly and gently around my forehead and brow—allowing the heat of the camphor to loosen up my temples and jaw. The air conditioner rattled.

"I feel bad I'm not helping much with exams," I said.

"It's OK," she reassured me.

"There are a lot of students."

"Oh, come on. Don't worry," she said.

"Well," I sighed, "OK."

When I am alone with my Vietnamese friends, they often become confessional. Bình broke down into tears one day as we were drinking orange juice, telling me that she worked so hard because no one else in the family had any money to help support her sister and her kids. There was a young student in the third year who spent our lunch together telling me why she was marrying her boyfriend before she graduated college. She said it was because her parents wanted her to. They were leaving to go to the United States, and they felt she needed to maintain her morality while they were away, and she could only do it if she married. Minh Ngọc once confessed that she was told by fortune tellers she would never marry. She had tried four times only to suffer some last minute disaster—a death, a departure, madness. "I am loved by too many ghosts," she explained, with a sad laugh.

On this Sunday afternoon I knew Thúy Kiều was going to talk about visiting her father in prison.

"I remember," she said, "visiting my father one afternoon," then she paused.

"The prisoners were all forced to stay in certain areas, and even if their families arrived they could not leave unless the guards gave them permission. I saw an old man who came running forward to see his family—he is so eager to see them he forgets the rule. There was a young guard who stopped him and humiliated him in front of everyone. He spoke to the man with a raised voice and then punished him by making him stand in the midday sun for one hour." She was quiet for a moment, then continued, "It's not right. For a young man to treat an older man that way."

"He couldn't visit with his family?" I asked.

"No."

"How often could people visit family?"

"Once each month for one hour only."

"The bastard," I mumbled.

"Hmmm?" Kiều said.

Bastard can be such an appropriate word, but I couldn't teach the timing of its placement, or its degrees of meaning.

"Nothing," I said. I was getting sleepy, and a shiver ran through me.

"Does the A.C. bother you?" Kiều asked.

"No," I said. "I'll just put on the blanket."

"I can turn the A.C. off," she offered.

"No, no. I'll just get hot," I said, then I yawned.

"The A.C. can often cause colds," she said, trying the word again.

The camphor floated around my nose and made my eyes water. Kiều worked her fingers around my ears. It was the end of the day and the sun was setting, changing the light in the room. I could hear activity on the river increasing. I opened my eyes.

"Kiều, are we correcting exams tonight?"

"Never mind," she said.

"There's a lot," I said.

"Don't worry, *my pwincess*," she teased me.

I closed my eyes again. While she massaged around my temples, my eyes opened again briefly, and fell softly shut. I relaxed, but something in me strained to identify the ground rhythm of the evening. I could hear river traffic steadily increasing; restaurants turned on their colored lights and karaoke bars began playing music. A young woman's voice sang out in syrupy tones. My eyelids fluttered. I felt guilty about the extra work Thư and Minh Thạnh would be forced to do. I sighed. "Listen to the boats," I murmured, "listen to the people."

I opened my eyes and Kiều seized the opportunity. Moving her face directly into my line of vision, her button nose bearing down on me, her eyes widening, she said boldly, "The women on the watewfwont are notowious."

I remember laughing as I fell asleep.

Almost with the wave of a hand Vietnamese women had a way of making me feel comfortable in any situation. But they did it in hundreds of intuitive and intimate ways. It was as if they had raised the personal gesture to an art form. Vietnamese theater owes a great deal to this graciousness of gesture. Whether it is the campiness of celebrity shows, where they wear dresses with ruffles and sing songs in syrupy English, the tradition and grace of Cái Lương or Chêo, where women's hands move like ghosts from under long pieces of silk and their voices rise dramatically, or the playfulness of Hanoi water puppets where they hide behind screens coordinating the action of multiple puppets balanced at the end of bamboo poles, women seemed to do it all with spare, gentle motions noticed only in reverberation. They are like rudders that steer ships with only the smallest movement.

When I returned to Saigon, I saw Minh Ngọc in *The House without Men* and watched her move with an exaggerated version of that classic grace. She was portraying the unmarried aunt in a family of women—a mother abandoned by her husband and left with three daughters to raise. The mother is angry over her burden and hurt by the humiliation of abandonment so common in a postwar country. The oldest daughter is intellectual and cold, the middle one loose, flirtatious and money-hungry, and the youngest naive. The drama of the play lies in their arguments among themselves, and their romances and breakups with men. The oldest daughter pushes away a nice guy for no particular reason, the middle one is interested only in men who bring her gifts, and the youngest falls in love with, and marries, a poor man. But Minh Ngọc's character, the eccentric, middle-aged aunt, has the most painful struggle of all: She is—quite literally—waiting for Prince Charming.

Though much of the play was whispered to me in translation, I found it enjoyable. And in my memory there is one moment that is still crystal clear and beautiful. Minh Ngọc stands alone on stage at the end of Act 2, lit only by a single spot. She is wearing an *áo dài* with a white silk scarf. She lifts the scarf and places it over her shoulder and announces to the darkness that she is not marrying because she is "saving herself," not simply for a man, but "for tradition."

"What tradition?" her niece asks, from the surrounding darkness.

Originally I interpreted the story as a criticism of "modern women," but I came to see it as more a portrait of the clash of traditional culture and the desires and demands of modern society. Vietnamese women grow up on ancient soil and bear contemporary burdens, are exposed to modern opportunities and are forced to struggle with these under the weight of traditional expectations. The play meant a great deal to my female friends. For them it captured the silent drama of the decisions they make every day about their lives.

The end of Act 2 is a powerful scene, both for the dialogue and for Minh Ngọc's grace. This grace on stage came from a woman I considered beautiful and beautifully clumsy. It was interesting for me to watch her in class and in her community. She had a voice rich with Southern dialect, and enunciated as if she were always on stage. She spoke English haltingly during lessons but, like Bình, gave me tough answers to modern dilemmas. In response to an Ann Landers letter about a troubled marriage, she swept the problem away by saying "the woman should get a new husband." She was "old" in a circle that valued youth, thoughtful in a society that likes women to be shrinking violets (at least on the outside). She had none of the features valued by traditional Asian culture—her hands are thick, her shoulders large; she has big feet and hips. And she was a bit clumsy; she carried a big cloth bag, and this often hung open by her side, or fell out of the basket of her Honda. It was full of papers, books, theater tickets. On payday she sometimes took me out for lunch. Like all the artists and writers I met throughout the country, she was paid by the government and her salary was doled out in copious amounts of 2,000 đong notes. She blushed as she counted out the money for the thirty or fifty thousand đong lunch. I smiled softly as she counted, remembering when I was a waitress and often paid my grocery bill in quarters.

Minh Ngọc smiled and laughed readily (with her mouth open and uncovered), showing a sincerity that I felt was lacking in the more polite giggles young Vietnamese women are taught. Each time she came to see me, she pulled up on her Honda, smiled, and called hello with a casualness I found to be a great relief in a place where I was constantly being "handled." She often wore baseball caps, but regardless of the type the hat was frequently askew—as if she had more important things on her mind. This is the same reason her lipstick often faded and her stockings fell down around her ankles. She was a breath of fresh air in the affected environment that is theater circles.

Perhaps I noticed all this movement because I studied dance from early childhood. As a kid I treasured every hour in the dance studio as the single most important time of my day. I studied ballet—lifted my arms, tucked in my buttocks, straightened and bent my knees. I learned how to stand on my toes and hold my hand in that indefinable gesture of the ballerina—whether they are holding a flower, a teacup, or a wine glass I still cannot say. I loved it all, but it wasn't me. From the start I was a tap dancer—snappy, loud, and foot stomping. I wanted the flash and challenge of the eight-count step in double time. I loved trying to make sounds so complicated people stared at my feet to see if they were really moving. But with all those years of practice behind me, I know I will never have the form of the Vietnamese women and girls I saw on soundstages and streets who also threw white silk over their shoulders and then moved forward with ease and grace, fabric billowing softly behind them.

Of all the studies that I made of Vietnamese culture—the observing, interacting, and watching—nothing proved so rich, contradictory, and complex as the women that I met. It is not an intellectual thing I'm talking about—it is physical and spiritual. It is the way they handle things and people, the way they walk, talk, and teach. It is so many burdens they bear and calculations they make. They told me they loved my "openness" and confidence (I was "so bold," they said). But at the same time Vietnamese women were wise. They knew that underneath the hard edge and forthright demeanor of Western women lies something more fragile. I adored their physical grace and the sound of their voices. I could watch them move and listen to their conversation for hours. But they were the converse of me, with something steely and determined inside them. As more time passed, I realized my students and friends were made of contradictory traditions. They were raised to be as beautiful and yielding as Kiều and, at the same time, as tough as their national heroines the Trung sisters. "A woman proudly led a young nation," the textbooks teach; "even the Han emperor heard of it and was terrified."

I lived one block away from Hai Ba Trung Street (Trung Sisters Street). It is a long straight avenue, crowded with food shops, clothing stores, new hotels, and bakeries. There are bars and ice cream shops, cafes and offices made from old French schoolhouses and hospitals. One of the anchors of the city map, it is named after the two sisters because they repelled the Chinese from the Red River Delta in northern Viet Nam in the fifth century. In modern Viet Nam the women are genuine historical figures turned to myth.

Trưng Trắc was the passionate wife and daughter of a political family; her father was the Lac Lord of Me-Linh, her husband the Lac Lord of Chu-dien. A conflict between her husband and the Chinese governor Su Ting moved Trưng Trắc to action and she became the central figure in a successful uprising against the Chinese imperialists. In the spring of A.D. 40 Su Ting fled and Trưng Trắc established a royal court in Me-Linh, her family home. She was recognized as queen by sixty-five strongholds and, along with her sister and constant companion Trưng Nhị led a renaissance of traditional culture, yielding a temporary return to matriarchal leadership.

In A.D. 41 Chinese leaders decided to push south, again. They appointed General Ma Yuan ("The Wave Calming General") to recapture the lost territory of the Vietnamese Lac Lords. By the spring of the next year he and 12,000 militiamen had advanced by foot along Viet Nam's eastern coast, followed by a fleet of 2,000 ships working their way inland through a maze of rivers.

But Ma Yuan is trying to reach the Imperial Court of Trưng Trắc; it sits on the Red River, located at the base of three mountains. He has to move inland, across deltas and up rivers. He has to contend, first, with Trưng Trắc's greatest strategic asset: Viet Nam's landscape. In the spring, his ships sitting in Lake Lang-bac, his troops waiting in a base camp in the heights he wavers:

> When I was between Lang-bac and Tay-vu and the rebels were not yet subdued, rain fell, vapors rose, there were pestilential emanations, and the heat was unbearable; I even saw a sparrow hawk fall into the water and drown.

It was a difficult place, with unbearable humidity and an atmosphere powerful enough to frighten the world's greatest army. But the mere presence of that army was enough to unnerve Trưng Trắc's followers. Though she gave fight as the Chinese advanced, her soldiers dispersed out of fear and pursuit of their own interests; the year-long battle that followed ended in defeat. Ma Yuan captured Trưng Trắc and Trưng Nhị and executed them.

The Trưng sister's story has been handed down through literature, historical records, and tales. The fifth-century heroines were cult objects throughout northern Viet Nam as late as the twelfth century, and their actions prompted scholarly comment into the eighteenth century:

> At that time the country of one hundred sons was the country of the women of Lord To. The ladies used the female arts against their irreconcilable foe; skirts and hairpins sang of patriotic righteousness, uttered a solemn oath at the inner door of the ladies quarters, expelled the governor, and seized the capital—the territories from Cuu-chan to Ho-p'u again saw the light of day. Were they not grand heroines?

Popular legend and historical record merge over time. The Trưng sisters are now lacquer ladies—inlaid mother-of-pearl in mahogany. They are ubiquitous in shops selling tourist memorabilia. There are plain, small wood panels, large, intricate wall hangings, and kitschy, colorful portraits of women riding elephants and wielding their "female arts against the irreconcilable foe." They look beautiful—as if characters in a fairy tale. They wield weapons deftly against overpowering foes; schoolchildren call them heroines, saying they killed themselves rather than serve the Chinese, saying they are Viet Nam's first women warriors. They were hardly the last.

After I had left Soc Trang and the Mekong Delta behind, after I had already visited northern Viet Nam and wandered among the highlands, I agreed to visit what sat in my own backyard. Thư and I traveled twenty-five kilometers outside the city to the tunnels of Cu Chi, a tourist site that was a strategic fighting post for the Viet Cong during the American War.

We arrived in the early afternoon and were escorted by a military guide through a set of foliage-thick pathways, over hidden doors and past tunnel exits. Then, climbing underground and looking into the darkness, I imagined the determination it took to fight from underground. I mumbled in awe over the geography, while Thư followed behind me whispering: "These are not the real tunnels. They are just for tourists, really, these are not the real ones." I didn't really care about politics. I was interested in the logistics of it all—how a command center was run ("a single desk and a two-way radio"), a surgery ("performed without anesthetic, behind a cloth curtain, with only oil lamps for light"), a kitchen ("the smoke was blown out through distant pipes in order to throw off search dogs"). During the war entry holes were no larger than thirty-two inches across, and though the walls have been widened, and the dirt patted flat, the dust makes breathing difficult. The time we spent crawling along a ten-yard tunnel between an office and a surgery felt like an eternity. I moved forward, my knees hitting rocks, dust sticking in my throat, and thought the tunnel walls might be closing in on me. Each room felt smaller than the last. I climbed out, using the ladders and stairs now provided for tourists, and wandered through the foliage until we lost our guide—who had turned to help another group of people negotiate their way—and arrived at the mess tent. As part of the tour Thư and I sat with the woman who was the cook and ate cassava, the staple food of the Viet Cong, and drank a brown, dull tea. Like our guide, she was a veteran of the war.

"Geez," I said, referring to the cassava, "this is good." I dipped a piece into a bowl of ground peanut and sesame.

"There were times when the soldiers had to go months with nothing but this to eat," Thư said.

"Really?" I said, popping another small piece into my mouth with one hand, and rolling another piece with the other. Cassava is dull, but filling. It is a bit like a potato, with a milkier flavor. The ground nuts gave it a bit of snap. "I didn't have lunch today," I said. "This is good." Thư smiled, but refrained from eating. I continued, one cassava following another like they were potato chips. "Really," I said with the food in my mouth, "good." I swallowed, then took another in hand as if I were hypnotized. I thought Thư was simply being polite by not eating, then I stopped suddenly when I considered wartime Viet Nam for a moment.

"Did you eat a lot of these when you were a kid?" I asked.

She laughed softly, "Yes."

My hands slowed as I thought about things. I couldn't imagine myself moving through the wartime tunnels of Cu Chi. Even with their enlarged size I got cornered and jammed. My back ached, my shoulders stiffened, and I groaned with pain. I thought of women who ran generators and operations rooms, who cooked and doctored for years from underground. I imagined digging tunnels by hand and crawling through them. I continued eating the cassava and began asking the cook all the questions that ran through my mind. She was older, her hair completely grayed, her face leathery. Thư told me she had lost all her children in the American War. She was dressed entirely in black and answered patiently, even kindly, as I pestered Thư to translate my questions.

"Ask her what she did . . . ask her how often she came out . . . ask her what the villagers nearby did . . . ask her how many hours she worked each week . . ." She worked. I ate. Thư translated. A group of middle school students wandered by, tripping and laughing their way through a school field trip.

"Should we go?" I asked Thư, realizing the time.

"No, it's OK," she said.

I rolled a piece of cassava in the ground nuts. The beige color spread like a gritty paint across the white. I put it in my mouth; it felt warm going down, but hit my stomach with a thud. By this time I was aware of something very important—I turned to Thư with a disappointed look on my face. "This stuff is actually quite dull," I said, referring to the food. She started laughing loudly.

"You know, in Viet Nam we say 'The French have their wines, the Vietnamese have their sauces.' Imagine the poor soldiers fighting for all those years with only such flavorless food to nourish them!"

The older woman moved from the stove to the table, she lifted the plates, replaced the cassava, answered my questions and looked over her shoulder at her boss as if it were all choreography. I thought perhaps my lingering made her nervous, but I wanted to keep watching her. So much of Viet Nam went from the unreal to the real for me, except for this fluidity of female motion;

with all that dirt under their nails, all that sacrifice and endurance, Vietnamese women have a grace that mystifies me. The woman sat down across from me again. We looked at each other. I wondered if, ever in her life, she thought she would one day be sitting across the table from an American tourist, serving her a snack and explaining how people worked in the tunnels of Cu Chi.

My mind moved from food and logistics to politics. She was the first woman I met on the tour and she was in the kitchen; this irritated me. I began to formulate a feminist theory on women in warfare. It raced through my mind like a fast-moving train. I imagined researching and collecting data, talking and talking for hours to women all over Viet Nam. At the end of my theorizing, I created a title for my study: "The Marginalization of Women's Roles and Contributions during the American War." I danced around the topic with my new friend, the woman I was still referring to as "the cook," asking vague questions, trying to hear her say that women were pushed aside, ignored, or confined to nonleadership positions. I waited and then asked the question I hoped would be the mother lode: "Yeah, but what was it that women did? What was their main job during the war?" As I overlooked the obvious, her patience wore out. She crinkled her brow, and looked me in the eye: "We were guerrillas."

*　　　*　　　*

Like many of my female friends in Viet Nam, I have a love/hate relationship with their legendary Thúy Kiều of poetic history. She suffers so gracefully. Kiều's endurance is admirable, but I am moved more by the drive to protect and fight for that which is your own. This drive has none of the violation that imperialism has brought with it through history—it has only a well of force. So in Cu Chi this force challenges all who encounter Viet Nam's female myths. If you pause for a moment—pause while you are crawling along the ground, pause as you wipe the dirt from your face and hands, pause, as I did, when you are thirsty—then you can see the misimpression that has coupled femininity and frailty. The Trưng sisters and their ancestors are not like the lacquer ladies of myth. Again and again Vietnamese women have reached into the violent face of history and refused its terrible plan. When a traveler embraces the idea that women, too, dug and worked the tunnels of Cu Chi, that they rebuilt bridges and buildings all over the country—that in blunt terms, "We were guerrillas"—the tourist memorabilia, with its elaborate, frilly images is smashed to bits, the shards raining down in mahogany and mother-of-pearl.

Chapter Fifteen

This endless multitude of beings swarms
from the Creator's hands, not from shoots or symptoms.
We are no different, though we have brains
we thoughtlessly forget to use,
and thus are born again from the unborn,
our noses enslaved to fragrance, our tongues to flavors,
our eyes lusting for color, our ears for pitches.
So we become the world's guests, wandering unhomed forever,
the day far off, home endless miles away.
                    —Tran Nhan-tong, "The Four Hills of Existence"

The woman got on the bus slowly. I saw her from where I was sitting, near the back; her arms were full of grocery bags and I thought someone should help. I picked up my bag, hat, and gloves and stood up.

"Cô được không?" (Are you OK?), I said.

She looked at me, surprised. I smiled. A young man behind me stood up and gestured for her to take his seat.

"Chị biêt nói tiếng Việt" (You speak Vietnamese), the woman said.

"Chưa" (Not yet), I said, with a smile.

It was winter, and I couldn't accustom myself to the cold winds in Boston. As I sat down again I wondered where the woman was from, then remembered the map my friend Trish found in Saigon. I wondered if her village was on it, or if she was from a city.

Trish found the map in July, a month before I was to leave.

"Wow!" I said as she slowly, and dramatically, unrolled it. We were sitting in the front room of the house. Out in the alley Nục was barking.

"Don't ya love it?" she said.

"Where did you get it?"

"I found a bookstore!" she said with a sparkle in her eye. "It's down behind Dong Khoi Street." The dog barked again.

"Nục, ơơii!" I called, "Nục Nịch." He continued barking. The old woman stormed out onto her balcony and threw a bucket of water at him. "Sss!" she hissed, as Nục barked once more, then scurried back behind our gate.

"I love it!" I said, referring to the map.

"I was just wandering around, when I stumbled on to the shop," Trish said.

I can see her still; she is walking down Dong Khoi Street, it is full of souvenir shops, art galleries, and clothing stores. In the afternoon sunlight she squints into the shops, adjusting her eyes to the darkness created by the long, narrow buildings. Women mumble softly to tourists on Dong Khoi Street; trying to guess at nationality, they blend French and English.

"Madame. Very beautiful."

Trish's blonde hair and pale skin contrast with the hundreds of colorful needlework displays for sale in the shops. In the blue wall hanging just above her head, village scenes are carefully stitched in bright colors. Women in conical hats bounce over bamboo bridges crossing rivers of white thread. From behind the counter a young woman holds up a bolt of silk chemise, but Trish is not interested and moves on, past the newsstand, past the coffee shop, past the statue of Ho Chi Minh.

She comes across an antique shop, stops, places her hand on one of the glass cases in the front, and looks down at the junk and jewels on display. On the second shelf there are Chinese compasses, small and large, in round wooden cases; a manicured hand reaches in to showcase them, tilting one forward. The red needle bounces back and forth on rusty springs, *wind* . . . *water* . . . *earth* . . . *fire*. Coolies walk across the lids of gold pocket watches from the 1920s. Blue glass pushes up out of the inscribed mounting of high school rings from the 1980s ("West Springfield High, Class of '81"). She picks up junk that has passed through the hands of hundreds of dealers all over Asia. But she also handles the silver butane lighters that speak Viet Nam's history in carved block letters: DANANG 1968, . . . JBT, USMC 1970, . . . I FUCKING LOVE THE ARMY AND THE ARMY LOVES FUCKING ME. On the bottom shelf of the case are sandalwood chopsticks sold in bundles of ten, laughing jade Buddhas laid next to tortoise-shell necklaces, and, invariably, a dead moth in a corner of the worn shelf lining.

In the alley between these shops and Nguyen Hue Street is a used bookstore. Its cramped quarters provide cool shade. Trish goes in; there is a fat woman dozing in the corner, she sits up straight in her chair when Trish crosses the threshold.

"Chào Chị" (Hello, Miss).

"Chào Cô."

She sorts through the mildewed French paperbacks and looks at the French-Vietnamese dictionaries and the books on the great art collections of Russia. Her foot brushes against a box on the floor. It's waterstained and worn, but inside is a thick, plastic bag stuffed full of old maps. There are maps made by the French colonial government outlining the landscape of Viet Nam, Cambodia, and Laos, maps made by the U.S. government measuring the depth and scale of Vietnamese harbors, maps isolating small towns, maps of the beaches, mountains, and plains that are Indochina. Trish buys a 1939 "Cartes d'Indo-Chine" in a black frame. The whites have paled to gray; the folds have turned into seams; and the French names, printed in an old black type, seem like places in a story, a myth of exotic lands. *Annam, CoChin Chine, Tonkin.* I want to reach inside the image and touch the landscape; I want to iron out the wrinkles that make up all the highlands and mountain ranges of Cambodia, Laos, and Viet Nam.

You too may want to place your hands on the geography of this region. In your atlas it is the knot, looking like tangled yarn, hanging under the Middle Kingdom. Run your fingers down the coast, touch the green underbelly that is the Mekong Delta. Close your eyes and imagine the warm winds of the southern coast and feel the heavy heat of a northern summer.

I see a map and I can feel myself crossing the bridge that spans the Red River in Hanoi. Underneath me is a vibration that takes me aback; the river rushes with greater force than I could imagine. I see a map and I remember standing on the windy shore of China Beach, watching a child fish from the unsteady hold of a large handwoven basket-boat. I can feel the sand and salt, see the strange bobbing figure among the waves. When I follow the green and brown lines, I try to see the Purple City of Hue, home to the Citadel that housed the last dynasty of Viet Nam. I listen for the conversation of rice pickers working golden fields in Catdang village, or I imagine myself on a coffee plantation in the highlands. I cannot think of Viet Nam without imagining, remembering, landscape.

*   *   *

By the end of my year in Viet Nam I was running in and out of Bình and Thảo's house as if I'd lived there all my life. I loved the humidity of the rainy season, and the dry, warm winters. I was accustomed to their son Thanh's shyness and I was hopelessly attached to their dog. I loved the way he slid across the tile floor when he was excited, how he joined in business meetings by climbing on the wooden furniture, sitting down and staring. I loved the clang of the house gate and the whiny, high-pitched greeting Nục gave me when I came home. During the afternoon siesta I talked and giggled with Bình's friends, saying the same thing over and over again, making faces and laughing. I felt close to them because with no English and no Vietnamese, laughter was all we had. I made comments at the ends of conversations, though they were in Vietnamese, and when I left the house I nodded to the neighbors with the casualness of a community member.

On spring afternoons my friend Kim Thư rode me around the city on the back of her Honda. I told Thư that riding around like that made me feel part of the place. I liked to move around without destination, to stare at the crowds, look into restaurants and homes, to watch people dozing in the shade and vendors waiting for customers. I loved every inch of the place, every storefront, cafe, bakery, boutique; I loved the computer shops, the video stores, the migrant vendors, cigarette sellers, and shoeshine boys. I loved the dirt, the humidity, the soot, and the smell.

If you go to Viet Nam today, you'll see this too. You'll see the spirit of place travelers love to talk about when they return home. You may pass an alley and, in a casual glance, be taken by this everyday sight: The sun—high during the afternoon lunch hour—will cast light on only half the homes there. The robin's-egg blue on window shutters and door frames will shine like Caribbean color, and drying laundry will appear bright, as in a child's picture. Now listen . . . You can hear the sounds of the twenty or so households that live there, the plates clinking as they are washed after lunch, the snap of the newspaper that is half read before sleep falls, the call of toddlers, restless and bored during nap time. You'll hear the jangle of metal as bicycles are moved in and out of houses. You'll hear computer games, news broadcasts, the aching sound of opera music. And you'll hear the voices of women; they are calling to each other and their families, scolding husbands, urging children to eat, or whispering deep and low in voices that spread gossip. The sudden splash of water on pavement breaks a momentary pause—a communal intake of breath, the silence before deep rest; it is the rhythm that close quarters brings—everyone works, plays, and rests, in an unwritten choreography.

You may try to take a photo of this, but it will serve your memory only. It will be explained to your friends in terms of what happened before or after— the way the kids were laughing, or wrestling, the way the woman leaned out the window. Stepping by accident into the intimacy of the Vietnamese you will capture all these elements in a glimpse—the old man resting in the shade, the ten-year-olds playing, and the toddler who has lost sight of her grandmother. You'll see the alley and the sunlight, the children in the blue-gray shadows; you'll see who they are.

In the spring evenings at the end of my year I saw the family two doors down as they gathered outside their gate to enjoy the cool air. The children stopped by, with the grandchildren, and the baby waddled around the alley. The grandfather nodded to me each evening, as I passed on my way to class.

"Bonjour Madame," he said, and strolled along proudly with a carriage in front of him. Like many successful couples, the young people have their own place now and make frequent trips back home for company and conversation. This is a new practice for the Vietnamese. It is not the communal living of yesterday. It is modern. Some may approve, some may not. My sympathies lie with the children, who have told me again and again of their desire for prosperity and independence.

In the United States I have a friend who had a baby just before I left for Viet Nam. After discussion, debate, and a dose of economic reality, Michelle, her husband, and her son moved into the house her parents live in, which is the house her grandparents lived in. I remembered their decision as I wandered around Saigon and these same generations sharing households without question wandered in and out of my viewfinder.

In a Boston suburb my friend's little boy toddled and toppled on doughy legs in his grandmother's kitchen. When he was first born, Michelle suffered a sleeping schedule that kept her awake from 2 to 5 A.M. To relieve boredom, she put on her velvet robe, strapped the baby to her breast, and walked the neighborhood surrounding her home. She mumbled and gurgled to the baby in the silence. Chris's body was resting on her hips, and they carried him through the same streets his grandmother, and his great grandmother, had walked. She stopped at a street corner and said, "This is your hometown, Chris." The baby's head bobbed, and his blue eyes glowed as he "aw"ed and "ooh"ed over the houses lit by streetlamps and starlight.

Michelle jokes about living in her parents' house. Like most Americans she values a high level of independence. In Viet Nam I was taken by the custom of valuing your family home, making a pilgrimage to your hometown, and ritualizing your respect for the place where you came to life. Like the Chinese, the Vietnamese refer to themselves as being natives of the place where their ancestors were born—whether they have lived there or not. Friends born and raised in Saigon tell me they are from Hanoi—that is where their parents came from. It is as if the rituals, events, and land of the ancestors shaped the youth, actually gave them form.

In that Saigon spring I heard that my parents were planning to sell our family home. One day at lunch I told Kim Thư I hadn't lived there for many years, but the prospect made me feel cast adrift.

"I know a bit what you mean," she said. "Our first house—my family moved from our old home when I was only five, but I still feel it as a loss . . ." she paused. "I remember, every evening my mother and father would give me a shower, and I can still see the light of the bathroom, and remember the image of one of my parents pouring water over me. It is one of my favorite memories of home." She handed me a plate with sliced papaya from a tray her mother brought out.

"That's interesting," I said. "I always recall my parents' home through sound."

Thư tilted her head. "What do you mean?" she said.

"Well," I explained, "we live by the ocean, so I remember the sound of the waves from the beach at the foot of the street. And when winter storms came, the wind blew in off the water and made the house creak and groan. It's an old house, and the wooden doors often swelled from the moisture, so we'd have to push them open and closed, and they'd make a shaking sound," I paused for a minute. "I hear my mother walking down the stairs in the middle of the night, because she can't sleep, and my father listening to the radio . . .," my voice trailed off. I hear things in stories. When Thư told me about her childhood home I heard the sound of the water in the shower and her feet slapping against the tiles, just as I heard her mother working in the kitchen, running water to rinse vegetables and encouraging her family to eat.

I am an American and I was raised to believe in the power of breaking with my past and starting over. For Vietnamese the tie between generations is what makes home. For them, repetition, ritual, and place are what link the past and the future. The link is real. I met a young woman in Saigon who had a nervous breakdown at the prospect of breaking it.

The story began when she had an opportunity to go to the United States to join her father, who escaped Viet Nam by boat some fifteen years earlier. For years the man cursed the communists from Texas, or California, or wherever he lived and worked. He called and wrote to Saigon; he told her that she would join him soon. He wrestled with immigration laws and citizenship rules, he worked and saved, he struggled and hoped. After more than a decade he told her he would get her over to the United States. "Don't do anything!" he yelled into a phone one day to his sixteen-year-old daughter. "Just study English and wait." She finished school, but didn't get a job. She sat at home each day, and attended English classes in the evening. She waited. Two years later she received a postcard informing her of the date of her interview with the U.S. State Department. The day had arrived.

On the morning of the interview she refused to go. "What?!" her mother said.

"What are you doing?!" her brother screamed.

The family gathered around her. Grandparents, aunts, uncles, friends, and neighbors asked her if she was crazy, and yelled at her to attend the interview. Her behavior took on a mental and physical paralysis that with time, became a great burden to the family, upsetting her mother (who had been abandoned by her husband) and creating a painful stigma. She just went crazy.

When I met this young woman, she had been treated by traditional Vietnamese medicine and could move and interact with people. She would get better, people said, and then she would go to America. But I thought her presence was ghostly. She didn't seem to own her body; she floated along the ground and moved as if she had stiff or sore muscles, as if interaction pained her. She had a vacant look on her face, with eyes that stared but did not look.

"America is very beautiful," she often repeated to me, with the emptiness of a parrot. Her mother would shake her head and mumble over the mystery of it—"she was so beautiful and smart."

I wonder if it was the idea of America that frightened her into madness. Maybe to a young girl in a small country America is too big a concept to handle—it is too much information, too many people, and too much danger. She heard that schoolchildren carry guns. She was told that children don't live with their parents. And the space. She heard of great stretches of emptiness, and was told that Americans like to put much space between themselves and others.

America is too much space to a Vietnamese who sleeps cozy and loving with her entire family in one room, who hears the dinner conversation of her neighbor, and rides through the evening darkness with her grandfather, looking in the windows of houses and seeing people living lives she can recognize. Maybe to a young girl this crowding and enduring—the getting-by of city life, the continual work of country life—they are not too difficult. They are not sad. She is loved in Viet Nam, and each day is almost exactly the same as the last. It is lunch and dinner with her family, it is her grandparents, her mother and her brother all sharing the same house. How could families live apart in America? No. I can see some primitive part of her refusing—No. And it seemed to me that she wasn't crazy. To not want to leave this place was not crazy—the others had it wrong. Fathers are important, but a father in America—a father who has left—cannot give her this safety and intimacy. And so . . .No, she refuses to go. She slips away to where the space is not so great. Her behavior was inevitable. Everyone condemned the decision, but I thought, even when I was on my way home, that she was right. "Why go to Viet Nam?" everyone asked me. "Why not?" I could reply. "Don't you want to leave Viet Nam?!" people would ask the young woman. "Why?" she replied again and again, "why?"

*   *   *

"There is something very strange about the dream of another place coming true," I said to Kim Thư.

"What do you mean?" she asked.

"I couldn't imagine Viet Nam before I arrived here," I said.

"You know, I don't think I can imagine America," she said.

"I know what you mean. Did I tell you about the woman I met on the plane to Hong Kong?"

"What woman?"

"I didn't tell you!" I said, shocked at my failure. "Oh, Thư, she was beautiful."

I was flying to Hong Kong from Saigon to visit a friend. A Vietnamese woman sat next to me on the plane. She was middle-aged, with a short, neat haircut and no make-up. She wore a cinnamon-colored silk outfit and black strap sandals. After we boarded she would not simply sit on the seat, but instead got settled, slipped off her sandals, and brought her pink painted toenails up in front of her, knees bent in the half crossed position of country Æ!comfort. This showed her village roots, and I found myself admiring her. The plane was a new and strange experience for her. She was overly curious, looking into the aisle and leaning across me to look out the window. Beneath her silk and soft perfume, there was the unmistakable odor of garlic. As we were sitting on the runway for take-off there were announcements from the pilot, but she didn't understand them. She looked at the ceiling in confusion. I couldn't fully understand the words, but I knew the language was Vietnamese. I wondered, were the speakers muffled? An Australian man across the aisle gestured to her to put on her seat belt; she held it in her hand. I smiled and hooked the buckle for her. The Vietnamese stewardesses were ignoring her (she is a country woman, and they are city girls). She leaned forward in the aisle during the taxi and the safety instructions. She didn't understand what the stewardesses were doing, so one woman, walking by quickly, grabbed a copy of the explanation card and handed it to her. She shook her head and flicked the card with her finger as if to say, "What good is this?" and I realized she couldn't read.

After takeoff she leaned on the armrest and touched me in the way country women do, jabbing my upper arm with her index and middle fingers. She looked at me and said, "Canada?"

"No," I said, "Tôi la người Mỹ" (I'm American).

I want to stop the conversation, but we're trapped together in the plane and its progress is inevitable.

She continues talking to me, and I tell her I do not speak Vietnamese. She stops, but only for a moment; she wants to ask me questions about myself. They are the usual questions I encounter throughout the country: Are you married? Do you have children? I say no, and no, and then I point to her, "Cô?" She has children—in Canada.

"Có Anh, không?" (Do you have a husband?), I say clumsily.

She pushes away the husband question with irritation, as if to say "Who needs one?" This is a tough edge born of hard times. Her hands bear the same message; they are browned, cracked in places; the nails are painted but the palms callused. I look at how she handles things and imagine her in a country house in the Mekong Delta. . . . I can see her holding a knife, slicing fish and shrimp, or dicing green leaves. I can see her working to clean the tough skin off a pineapple, or peeling, ever so delicately, a ripe mango. I can see her lugging heavy things around and taking care of kids who will one day leave her. The young stewardesses, raised, like so many of my students, in Saigon or Hanoi, snub her. She is clumsy in the city. She has the right clothes, but not the right carriage.

She came from Bac Lieu. It is far down in the Mekong Delta. It is further south than Soc Trang. In the Mekong Delta waterways outnumber roadways and nine rivers empty into the sea. It is warm in Bac Lieu; it is always warm. She was in Viet Nam Airlines seat 15B and she was going to Canada. In the airplane, with the air conditioning on, she was already cold. She wrapped the blanket around her toes. In her lap she carried a pink purse that held all her papers. She was eager to give them away, to show people where she was going. She could not read them, but she knew they were important. She had a passport, a plane ticket, and a note from her children: "Dear Sir/Madam: Our mother is traveling to Calgary, Canada. Please be of assistance to her, as she has never been in airports before. Thank you."

"Oh, Thư," I said as I told the story, "the note was the best part. She kept giving it away! Twenty minutes into the flight, the stewardess arrived with our meal and asked her if she would like chicken or fish. She—the country woman—took out her note and showed it to the young, city girl."

"What happened?" Kim Thư asked, laughing.

"She got fish," I said.

While I was trying to eat, the country woman jabbed me again, pointed to her tray and furrowed her brow, as if to say, "plastic forks, packaged food, what is this?" She didn't understand the tray, so I had to take the foil lid off the entree for her. She laughed at herself, but examined the cover closely, then shook her head, as if she was amazed at the practicality of it. During the meal I continued watching her, she pointed to her tray and smirked—they call this food?

"Of course!" Thư piped in. "She comes from the Mekong Delta, how can we expect her to enjoy such a poor meal?!"

The woman gestured that her meal had no flavor, then leaned over and looked at mine. She pushed her tray away, snobbishly amused, leaned toward me and poked me with her elbow like some character in a comedy sketch—"Big fancy airline—gee, no flavor at all." She leaned back and started to pick her teeth.

"Now, Thư," I continued, "you know me, halfway through the flight I'm beginning to worry about her."

She needed to stay in Hong Kong overnight, and I was convinced she would never even make it out of the airport. I imagined her wandering around the seamier side of Kowloon with her suitcase and her sandals, and I decided that I would take her with me to my hotel. "Meanwhile," I said, "she's still trying to talk to me, why I do not know, it seems like she is trying to convince me to go to Canada with her."

"Tối không đi Canada" (I'm not going to Canada), I said. She made a face, as if to ask, "What do you mean you're not going to Canada?" I told her I liked her earrings. They were small diamond studs, backed by jade disks. Her face lit up.

"Yeah?" she said. She leaned back in the chair, satisfied, and began playing with one. "Bạc Liêu—200 U.S."

Another forty minutes passed and we landed in Hong Kong. She looked out the window, nodded and said, "Đẹp" (Beautiful).

"I'm still worrying, Kim Thư," I said, with drama. "So, I'm thinking of Vietnamese words and phrases during the taxi, so I can help her find her way, but she disappears before I can turn to her and say 'Come with me.'"

The woman worked through her bags, shuffled her papers, and got in line; she pushed her way past some people, but then she held everyone up. She arrived at the door, then stopped. She grabbed the stewardess by the arm and, like a woman who had already traveled far and could not imagine such distances and such places, she pointed to the Hong Kong skyline and asked: "Canada?"

Kim Thư nodded her head. She knew the end of the story before I reached it. I did not rescue the woman from Bac Lieu. She was taken in hand by a Viet Kieu couple from California, who spoke in soft voices and, in the chaos of Kai Tak Airport, motioned, with a nod and a gentle wave of the hand, for her to join them. Thư leaned on her hand, smiled at me, and said with a sigh, "Now you know my people."

We are fin-de-siècle travelers. A Vietnamese in Canada, in Calgary or Vancouver, shivers with the cold of winter and snow. Where she came from is palm trees and humidity, where seasons were determined by the color of the rice. Where she came from—the land her ancestors lived on—is heavy rain on orchids and the sweet, druggy smell of ripe pineapples. It is jasmine and camellia wafting through the soot of the city, and it is the song of bread sellers at 5 a.m. The women who passed her and hundreds of babies like her, from hand to hand had round faces and cooing voices. They held her just as my American friend held her son Chris—like he was the whole world—and this place, with its music and color, its sunlight and shadow, was the secret recipe making her person. Home must be all of these things for a Viet Kieu. In the snow of Canada the softness and green shine through in ways we cannot see, and the voices lay hidden beneath linguistic struggles and gracious manners.

One day soon my friend Michelle will move from her apartment, and with her husband and son plant her feet somewhere far from home. Chris will say he is from that place—and he will be right. His world will be what he sees around him, not knowing that when he was new, when he was warm and fresh, absorbing smells, sounds, and light, he was being carried in footsteps two generations deep, and that light, that smell, and that sound— that is where he came from.

When the Vietnamese asked, I told them I grew up in a small town on the ocean that has rocky beaches, large families, and people full of funny remarks. I told them everyone knew each other, "just like here," and that the cycle we lived in depended on the water—with more people and boats in the summer, when it was warm, and few people when the winter came. That's where I came from. If people think I have a stern demeanor, it may be the jagged coast; if they think I make witty remarks, it may be small town banter; and if they think I'm overly romantic, that I am a princess not a laborer . . . it may be the view of the ocean from the brown house at the top of the hill.

*   *   *

Some time later, in a moment of candor, my mother confessed that she felt she could never sell the house. "No, I can't do it," she said. "The thought of leaving all this intimidates the hell out of me."

I went back to Boston in the summer, but it was months before I really arrived: It is October and I am walking through the breezeway of my parents' house, commenting on the tart smell of the apples my mother likes to leave out in a straw basket; I push away dried leaves and tighten my jaw as they crinkle and fall apart. I can still see the wide boulevards of Saigon filled with the fast-moving, the ambitious; I see the wide expanse of China Beach, with waves to ride and basket-boats bobbing up and down. In Catdang it is still warm. There are tiled classical houses in narrow lanes. I reach out to touch my friend's arm and say, "Aren't these the most beautiful people you've ever seen?"

Exhaust burns my eyes in the city, wood burning dries my throat in the mountains. I can hear voices echoing, bouncing off the craggy mountains of Ha Long Bay. I can hear the fire crackers of a hundred weddings in Saigon, and Tet in Hanoi. I can see the squatting shape of the trash picker who took refuge in my alley to count her money.

There are countless rows of flowers in my memory. Bachelor buttons lay in bundles on wooden tables outside my friend's dorm in Hanoi, roses wilt in Saigon, orchids fall limp against plastic wrapping. Poinciana trees blossom a shocking orange in the spring, raining petals that students pressed into butterflies. Marigolds are carried in giant bundles down hilly roads leading to Hanoi.

Rice falls through my fingers and mango slides across my tongue. Shrimp rests on piles of shredded lotus and mint, and peanuts hide beneath green papaya. A thousand knives bang a thousand chopping blocks, building a mountain of green leaves for seasoning. I can see soot settling on my skin from the pollution in Saigon and taste the relief of fresh pineapple after an early evening traffic jam.

It is November . . . December . . . and I remember all of these things. Women's faces smile softly at me, and I can finally recognize their steel. Children laugh and play endlessly and I can still recognize their ambition. I can hear the voices of my Australian friends calling to me over the sounds of the street, and the whispered words of nervous ten-year-olds in crowded classrooms.

Back at home, my father falls asleep listening to big band jazz music, and the wind makes noises that I could not remember in Viet Nam. I curl up under heavy blankets, and listen to the windows rattle. In sleep heat and cold converge. Southeast Asia returns to my memory through dreams, and I wake up thirsty.